Psychoanalysis from the Indian Terroir

PSYCHOANALYTIC STUDIES: CLINICAL, SOCIAL, AND CULTURAL CONTEXTS

Series Editor
Michael O'Loughlin, Adelphi University

Mission Statement
Psychoanalytic Studies seeks psychoanalytically informed works addressing the implications of the location of the individual in clinical, social, cultural, historical, and ideological contexts. Innovative theoretical and clinical works within psychoanalytic theory and in fields such as anthropology, education, and history are welcome. Projects addressing conflict, migrations, difference, ideology, subjectivity, memory, psychiatric suffering, physical and symbolic violence, power, and the future of psychoanalysis itself are welcome, as are works illustrating critical and activist applications of clinical work.

Titles in the Series

A Three-Factor Model of Couples Psychotherapy: Projective Identification, Level of Couple Object Relations, and Omnipotent Control, by Robert Mendelsohn
Psychoanalysis from the Indian Terroir: Emerging Themes in Culture, Family, and Childhood in India, edited by Manasi Kumar, Anup Dhar, and Anurag Mishra

Psychoanalysis from the Indian Terroir

Emerging Themes in Culture, Family, and Childhood

Edited by
Manasi Kumar, Anup Dhar,
and Anurag Mishra

Foreword by Erica Burman

LEXINGTON BOOKS
Lanham • Boulder • New York • London

Published by Lexington Books
An imprint of The Rowman & Littlefield Publishing Group, Inc.
4501 Forbes Boulevard, Suite 200, Lanham, Maryland 20706
www.rowman.com

Unit A, Whitacre Mews, 26-34 Stannary Street, London SE11 4AB

British Library Cataloguing in Publication Information Available

Library of Congress Cataloging-in-Publication Data

Names: Kumar, Manasi, editor. | Dhar, Anup, editor. | Mishra, Anurag, editor.
Title: Psychoanalysis from the Indian terroir : emerging themes in culture, family, and childhood / edited by Manasi Kumar, Anup Dhar, and Anurag Mishra ; foreword by Erica Burman.
Description: Lanham : Lexington Books, [2017] | Series: Psychoanalytic studies: clinical, social, and cultural contexts | Includes bibliographical references and index.
Identifiers: LCCN 2017058174 (print) | LCCN 2017055696 (ebook) | ISBN 9781498559423 (Electronic) | ISBN 9781498559416 (cloth : alk. paper)
Subjects: LCSH: Psychoanalysis—India. | Psychoanalysis and culture—India.
Classification: LCC BF173 (print) | LCC BF173 .P77536 2017 (ebook) | DDC 150.19/50954—dc23
LC record available at https://lccn.loc.gov/2017058174

™ The paper used in this publication meets the minimum requirements of American National Standard for Information Sciences—Permanence of Paper for Printed Library Materials, ANSI/NISO Z39.48-1992.

Printed in the United States of America

Contents

PART II: FAITH, RELIGION, AND VIOLENCE

PART III: CULTURAL IDENTITY AND INDIAN IMAGINATION

Foreword

Erica Burman

This extraordinary collection highlights the emergence of a new strand of critical psychoanalytic theory and practice that is debating how culture and psychoanalysis mix and make each other. Each term in this cryptic title, *Psychoanalysis from the Indian Terroir,* poses rather than answers questions. It sets in play a terrain of inquiry that it refrains from fixing or stabilizing. *Terroir*, a suitably technical name for the combination of climate, soil and texture that allows for cultivation (of wine or other specialist food crop), topicalizes the question of setting and outcome without presuming what its constitutive elements are, or what it is they produce. Such technical obscurity of terminology perhaps befits a practice that is typically seen as being as elitist or inaccessible as psychoanalysis. This is notwithstanding the commitment to free psychoanalytic provision that characterized the early institutionalization of psychoanalysis in inter-war Germany from the 1920s until the Nazis closed down (and repressed) the public psychoanalytic clinics, as well as driving the psychoanalysts into—at best—exile. Further, the French allure of *terroir*—that, to a British reader like me, conveys sophistication as well as the requirement for delicate appreciation—speaks to the necessary specificity of readings of psychoanalysis that are ever at play. But even if we encounter British or German psychoanalytic authors in this text, as well as Green, Deleuze, and Lacan, their reading or "application" does not presume a mere transposition from one geopolitical space to another, in the course of which such spaces acquire a spurious reification. Rather, we are invited to explore the how, the making and re-making of "psychoanalysis" in a particular, rich, biopolitical environment, where psychoanalysis is as much what is grown as what is imported.

Indeed the botanical metaphor is extended: the editors discuss the question of planting as well as what is planted, and play with whether this process is an implanting or something that becomes "home-grown." Discussion of hybrids could incite a previous or prior authenticity. But this would essentialize that which might be understood to be contingent, if not arbitrary. How significant is it that psychoanalysis was developed in Judeo-Christian societies as, perhaps, an effect of the alienation produced by industrialization in the late nineteenth century? Can, or should, we disaggregate capitalism and modernity from what is sometimes called "westernization," albeit that this was resourced by as well as warranting colonial exploitation? How are we to understand the forms of experience, including the distress and social suffering wrought by dispossession and social exclusion that were the underside of the story of European "development"? How should we address shifts in family dynamics, the (re)invention of the bourgeois nuclear family, the forms of forced or elective migrations to cities, the intensifications and reformulations of class/caste and gender divisions and relations enabled, produced, allowed by such seismic shifts?

Clearly, the sun-lit hillsides of proliferating vines envisaged through the trope of *terroir* are neither stable, nor are their limits enclosed. Indeed the focus on (im)plantation seems also to evoke—albeit implicitly—questions of violence, cultural appropriation, and perhaps even sexual/reproductive manipulation; of surrogacy rather than conception, commerce or exploitation rather than (only) intimacy. In his *History of Sexuality: an introduction,* Michel Foucault writes of the implantation into bodies of forms of power/knowledge relations around sexuality that owe their current forms to a secularization and scientization of the practice of religious confession. Indeed it is this incitement to self-knowledge and giving an account of one's true, innermost thoughts and feelings that form the conditions of possibility for psychoanalysis. The "perversion" of this "implantation," Foucault writes, is not that aberrant impulses or fantasies should be silenced or erased, but rather that the demand to speak of them in fact constitutes, stabilizes, and naturalizes them. Thus the cultural-political terrain of and for the development of psychoanalysis as a "talking cure" or at least a talking method, comes to be situated in specific socio-historical and material conditions such that its emergence or incursion into India calls for reflection and interrogation. Questions of power are foregrounded, not only through topicalizing cultural imperialism and class/caste privilege in what counts as "culture," but also in pursuing a psychoanalytic inquiry to explore why and how these power relations come to structure embodied histories that are inhabited, lived, and lived out in particular geopolitical conditions.

Such themes anticipate much of the content of the chapters that follow, with the focus on gender and women much discussed—whether in the social imaginary, in dreams, in the cultural-religious appeal of female deities or even the quasi-religious figure of the mother. All these structure gendered patterns of relationships, including as they appear in the consulting room. They are also embodied in the wandering, homeless women who sleep in the New Delhi train station or the women pilgrims seeking healing and solace at a Sufi shrine. Indeed women and children do not merely haunt this text, they inhabit it. The only place where the question of masculinity forms the overt, primary topic is in the (only jointly written) chapter exploring juxtapositions between gender, trauma, and political violence across two different catastrophic contexts.

This volume is, then, a response to as well as development of, the monumental initiation of this field of debate of Indian Psychoanalysis/Psychoanalysis in India (a half century after Girindrasekhar Bose tried to engage Freud) via Sudhir Kakar's 1970s study of the psychic development and life of the Hindu boy child. Kakar's field of inquiry has continued to expand, as his contribution here indicates, moving from that earlier quasi-developmental and gender and caste-specific account to a wide-ranging analysis of the ways cultural-political nuances enter and configure individual psychic lives. His presence in this book reflects a continuing project that has now been taken up widely and in manifold directions, as these diverse chapters indicate. Perhaps the most visible twenty-first century reconsideration of the earlier formulations is evident not only in the primary focus on women's gendered experiences but also in the chapter on how Hindu-Muslim relations come into the consulting room, as forms of transferentially invested, relationally produced but socio-politically overdetermined forms of otherness, attention to which not only inflects analyst/analysand dynamics but also forms a vital arena for re-working these.

Here we see a different politics of psychoanalysis emerge—one that destabilises psychiatric and psychological "truths" or notions of "mental illness," to show how the symptoms so displayed are not only individual. Rather, they indicate not only the individual struggle with obstacles and constraints in particular lives but, via the psychoanalytic dialogue which slows down and focuses on processes of relational engagement (including defenses against, or repudiations of engagement), a recovery of the "other" as always produced by and as a disavowed part of the "self" is made possible that addresses political, as well as personal, transformation.

As the editors note, a key ambiguity or debate traverses the book's thirteen chapters: is its object an exploration of Indian psychoanalysis or a document of Indian engagement with, and reflection on, psychoanalysis? Does psychoanalysis require indigenization (to render it "Indian"?) or rather is "Indianness" itself, what it is to be Indian and the relationship with the contemporary nation state named as India that is rather under psychoanalytic scrutiny here.

Such questions are, of course, not only those addressed by this book, or in relation to the status of psychoanalytic theory and practice in India, but also those which exemplify the wider challenges posed by attending to the ways culture, history, and biopolitical conditions write themselves onto bodies, into minds, and are lived out as both singular and collective biographies.

The trope of *terroir* names land (*terre)* or turf without presuming its ownership or territorialization. This mobilizes an attention to placed-ness or specificity without falling foul of the kind of methodological nationalism that characterizes so many transnational research encounters. What "India" or "Indian-ness" is posed here as a question, a topic, rather than a foundational assumption. As such, the book as much diagnoses the contemporary (clinical) state of the national entity called India as its citizen-subjects. This relationship between one's own mental state and the cultural-political entity end territory within which chronological, biographical lives are lived out is, as the editors note, a troubled and troubling interface, articulating "cultural questions in clinical contexts" with "clinical questions in cultural contexts." Its treatment here is beautifully composed, and illustrated.

Acknowledgments

To think is to thank. To thank is to think. To think along Sudhir Kakar's path is to thank him. To think along Ashok Nagpal, Rachana Johri, and Honey Oberoi's works—who are the founders of the School of Human Studies and the Centre for psychanalytic psychotherapy and long-term clinical work—is to thank them. One also needs to thank the Indian Psychoanalytic Society and the members of the Delhi Chapter. The editors would also like to thank the Fortis Psychoanalytic Unit for their support during the 2013 conference on Psychoanlysis in/from India. Urvashi Pawar needs to be thanked specially for her assistance in the early days of bringing the papers together and giving shape to the initial manuscript. Special thanks are due to to all the reviewers for their constructive criticisms and for helping authors rework their chapters. The process of internal review has sharpened the arguments of the chapters. The editors would like to acknowledge the support of Michael Loughlin, Kasey Beduhn, Becca Rohde, Meaghan Menzel, and Molly White at Lexington Books and Rowman & Littlefield for having dealt with the manuscript with utmost care and close reading. Special thanks are due to Ram Ashish and Manu Singh for editorial support. Finally we would like to thank Erica Burman for cheerfully supporting us by extending the analogy of "psychoanalytic wine in/from the indian terroir."

Introduction

Manasi Kumar, Anup Dhar, and Anurag Mishra

This book is a critical reflection on the question and the somewhat troubled interface of psychoanalysis *and* culture. It is a long-due reflection on the "and" that connects psychoanalysis and culture. The book is also a critical reflection on the mutually constitutive terms—"psychoanalysis" and "culture"—that are connected by the uneasy "and." Neither term—psychoanalysis and culture—is taken as given in the book; they are rediscovered, reinvented. Nor is the "and" taken as simply additive. The book is hence a reconceptualization and a rewriting of both psychoanalysis and culture through the mutual constitutivity or "overdetermination" (as Freud suggests in *Interpretation of Dreams*) of each—a process of reconceptualization and rewriting initiated in India under the proper name Sudhir Kakar decades ago. Andre Green (1999) argues in the context of the question of the relationship between psychoanalysis *and* culture:

> . . . psychoanalysts today seem to stand out more particularly in terms of their *divergences*, resulting from different conceptions about the mind, but also because of the *differences stemming from their cultural traditions*. Lacan's work could only have evolved in France, and I believe that Winnicot's work is intimately related to what he owes to his native land [and perhaps, Bose's work could only have evolved in 'India,' from the *YogaSutra*, the *Bhagavad Gita*, and the *PuranaPravesa*]. (Green in Kohon 1999: 4; italics/emphasis ours)

The book is hence premised on the research questions: what happens when psychoanalysis—born in Western Europe, having Franco-German and Anglo-American moorings, and in a largely Judeo-Christian milieu (i.e., with paradigms *stemming from its own cultural tradition*)—travels eastwards and meets a somewhat *different cultural tradition*, as early as the 1920s (Bose

1999). What happens when the psychoanalytic (im)plant grows roots in a somewhat different soil, or what we would like to call a different *terroir*, perhaps, having its own characteristic and moisture-mineral content, having its own history, and cognitive-affective archi-texture? Does the (im)plant change as a result of the interaction with another soil, or another terroir? Does the soil or the terroir fundamentally affect the (im)plant? Or does the (im)plant change the nature of the soil or the terroir, the book asks incessantly, somewhat obsessively? It also asks: how have European analysts made sense of India? How have Indian analysts—Girindrasekhar Bose (1999)—made sense of European psychoanalysis?

Put telegraphically, the book is thus an explication of *clinical questions in cultural contexts*. Or perhaps *cultural questions in clinical contexts*. The book is an exploration of what happens to the two determinate poles of clinical work—diagnosis and cure—classification of suffering and approaches to healing—when psychoanalysis finds itself immersed in another culture (in this case India which in turn is not an undivided perspective), with its own constellation of shamans, mystics, and (faith) healers (Kakar 1982; its own nosologies of mental suffering; most importantly its own exegesis of parenting, maternality, child rearing, gendering, intimacies (Kakar 1989); its own hermeneutic of love, sex, and danger (Kakar and Ross 2011); its own ideas of purity-pollution, shame-guilt, good-evil; its own "Totem and Taboo"; three or more theories of Infant(ile) Sexuality; its own *beyond* to the pleasure principle; its own structures of loss, recovery, and mourning, marked by "god of small things" in a largely non-monotheistic milieu.

Sigmund Freud never completed "An Outline of Psychoanalysis" (Freud 1940 [1938]); returning yet again to an earlier project of providing an overview of psychoanalysis, Freud began writing in Vienna in 1938 as he was waiting to leave for London; by September 1938 he had written three-quarters of the book, which was published in 1940, a year after his death.

How does one complete the unfinished project of writing *An Outline of Psychoanalysis*?

Can "The Indians" (Kakar and Kakar 2007) contribute to the completion of the manuscript? How can The Indians contribute to the completion? By providing case material, data, empirical content? Or by offering *new theories of mental life*, as Bose did (1948). How does one write *An Outline of Psychoanalysis* in India, from India?

Would it be an outline of *Indian* psychoanalysis, "Indian" not in a *nationalist* sense?

Or would it also be an *Indian* outline of psychoanalysis?

The chapters in this volume address the question of an outline of psychoanalysis in India. In the process the authors also inaugurate (clinical) thinking around an *Indian* outline of psychoanalysis. They also address the question of *difference*; how India marks *difference* with respect to Freudian psychoanalysis. Then the question: how is the Indian analysand different? How is the *Indian* analysand with a history of Partition different? How is the Indian analysand with a history of Hindu-Muslim conflict different (see Zehra Mehdi's paper in the volume); the chapters in this volume make an attempt to place psychoanalysis in a context other than the Holocaust; they also place psychoanalysis in the context of partition and the Hindu-Muslim conflict—either in the session or in psycho-social contexts. Mehdi shows how what Indian political and social scientists have described as the "precarious relationship" between Hindus and Muslims, where each carries the other's rejected and unacceptable parts, especially after Partition, and find themselves playing out once again in the analytical space between a patient's psychosis and a therapist's historical reality. The chapter attempts to comment on how a psychotic state parallels the psychosis of the embattled Hindu Muslim relations. In that sense, the analytical space becomes more than a space for recovering one's inner realities and psychic truths and could be in fact considered a space for "recovering" the Other, the *historical* Other.

Atreyee Sen and Manasi Kumar in their *disaster diaries* offer a critical interdisciplinary perspective to the narrativization of trauma among young children affected by Hindu-Muslim riots in two different communally sensitive urban areas in India. By drawing select strands from psychological and anthropological approaches and relating it to the articulation of trauma among small children, the authors attempt to review what trauma signifies among children, how attachment and trauma frameworks are useful reference points toward comprehending childhoods afflicted by brutal collective violence, and how complex memories and discourses of physical disability and social disconnection are developed and sustained by riot-affected children.

How is the Indian infant, how is the Indian mother, how is the Indian infant-mother dyad different (see Urvashi Agarwal's paper in the volume; where an attempt has been made to describe "infantile feelings" in India in terms of psychotic and borderline states; it has been further argued how infantile feelings are elusive and formless and are hard to represent in language and how they are often felt in the body in a "raw fashion" and largely "enacted out"; to listen to the body and bodily expressions becomes perhaps the only way to access and *know* them; such an experience could be fundamental to *experiencing the analysand* in the analytic setting). The volume thus asks: if Freud's experience of his analysands gave birth to his psychoanalysis, what kind of psychoanalytic logic-language-ethos would be born from our experience with *our* analysands?

If Freudian psychoanalysis is born out of a largely Judaic-Christian-Hellenic milieu, in other words, in a monotheistic milieu, what kind of psychoanalysis would be born in a largely polytheistic milieu, with a long history of non-theological non-scriptural forms of subaltern religiosity, marked at the same time by a logic of the spiritual (see Sabah Siddiqui and Bhargavi Davar's paper in this volume: "how will psychoanalysis set up relations with different forms of religiosity? What happens when psychoanalysis and religion come face to face? When and where do they come face to face?") and an equally long history of Other forms of healing of the mind: Yoga for example (see Ajeet Mathur's paper in this volume)? Mathur in his chapter titled "Two Cultures? Frontiers of faith in yoga and psychoanalysis" holds up the traditions of Yoga and Psychoanalysis against the light to examine their "correspondences, differences, convergences and divergences." He notes that both these practices arose in different cultural contexts and indeed their "communities of practice" are like "flag bearers of two distinct cultures" sometimes treating each other as "untouchables." In this paper he endeavors to bring them closer together through looking at their common values ("empathy, compassion, tolerance, human dignity") and objectives of "human well-being through increased self awareness" while at the same time being aware of their distinct "evolutionary trajectories." He looks at the importance of sound, states of consciousness, meditation, yogic postures, the guru-chela relationship, knowing and not-knowing and the Indian "bhava" and "rasa" theories, and compares them to psychoanalytical concepts like transference and Bion's "virtuous imperative of dwelling in ambiguity and uncertainty" (Grotstein 2007), reverie, alpha function, and Bionian basic assumption groups (among others). He remains aware that these are very different languages which resist simple translations. They are based in different ways of experiencing and cultures of knowledge generation and transmission and indeed having different evolutionary trajectories, but both having to be rediscovered experientially as an act of faith by each practitioner in their particular time and place. He concludes that "Attention to spirituality can help the analyst exercise more empathy and compassion whereas attention to the unconscious through psychoanalytic insights can expand the horizons of yoga to understand and use the psychic force of "prana" in many new ways."

While the focus of Freudian psychoanalysis was on the (Names of the) Father, what kind of psychoanalysis and what kind of *infant inner worlds* take shape in the "maternal-feminine nurturing continuum"? Does such maternal enthrallment paradoxically foreclose the women-feminine? Do we need to bring to dialogue clinical and critical/cultural thinking in psychoanalysis? Do we need to think the psychic and the social as overdetermining and contradicting each other? Amrita Narayanan in her chapter sees maternal enthrallment as the cultural tendency of the Hindu male to idealize women as mothers and to direct phantasy life toward the maintenance of this idealization. Narayanan examines this process of idealization and this "culturally enacted phantasy" from the absenced viewpoint of woman in the patriarchal national polis and the perspective of psychoanalytic feminism in her chapter. The perspective of maternal enthrallment is problematized through the invocation of matricidal phantasies in Nilofer Kaul's chapter "Myth, Misogyny and Matricide." Kaul uses the myths of "Putana" and a Kannada creation myth along with a patient's unsettling dream to illustrate her hypothesis that "ordered, civilized, patriarchal society must have been founded upon matricide"; Kaul argues that misogynous oral myths may be far more foundational than the classical Freudian-Greek-Sanskrit myths of Oedipus-Ganesha, thus also making a case for a more extensive examination of non-classical cultures and traditions in which one finds more primitive Kleinian matricidal defenses which have not yet been "domesticated" into repression. Narayanan's and Kaul's chapters produce a necessary dialectic between the clinical and the critical in the volume. Most of the chapters also exhibit a sensitivity toward questions of gender and culture. Shifa Haq, on the other hand, building on *The Inner World* (1981), shows how Kakar makes a case for the powerful presence of the Sita Ideal—standing as a symbol of chastity, wifely devotion, and self-urrender—in the psyche of Indian women and men. Haq shows how the internalization of the Sita Ideal makes the repudiation of desires, including the rebellion against "the constraints of impinging womanhood," possible. Haq however reflects on the Sita Ideal not as a motif emblematic of the moral order it perpetuates in the Indian psyche, but more specifically as the psychological ground for the "will to renounce" in Indian women. The paper thus approaches the Sita Ideal not from the angle of the *dharma* of a devoted wife but the *depressed* and the *renouncing* Sita, who is an *ascetic* ideal or an ideal of feminine asceticism, Haq thus explicates the journey of Indian women in psychotherapeutic settings.

The chapters redefine the concept of the analysand by bringing into discussion the phenomenon of possession, specifically Devi-possession (see Sabah Siddiqui and Bhargavi Davar, and Shalini Masih's chapters). How will psychoanalysis set up relations with different forms of religiosity? Siddiqui and Davar explore what happens when psychoanalysis and religion come face to face in India. In the process, they also explore how the secular and the scientific come to an encounter with the everyday praxis of faith and healing—praxis that does not accrue either what is conventionally understood as religion or science. They explore such interfaces in the context of the phenomenon of possession, specifically Devi-possession. The chapter thus raises a fundamental question: is the trope of Devi-possession at all a site where science and religion come to a dialogue? Or is it something else entirely; an algebraic 'x' which requires fresh thinking? Shalini Masih's chapter is an attempt to give the reader a "tiny taste of terrors" encountered by therapist-researcher thrown into an *uncanny* culture of deities and demons, an uncanny culture that is gazed at, rather precariously, from the familiar cliff of psychology. The author argues that such an experience required that "all memory, desire, expectation and understanding" (Bion 1967), attempts at making sense, be abandoned and a stance of a "faithful devotee" be assumed in order to go beyond one's disciplinary and familiar clinical limits.

The chapter by Sudhir Kakar on psychoanalysis, culture, and the cultural unconscious is an attempt at the "translation" of individual unconscious processes and their reliance on the web of cultural unconscious processes and mechanisms which is often ignored in mainstream psychoanalysis. The chapter delves into the author's therapy experience with a German analyst with a view to interrogate how cultural alienation—a kind of 'un-understoodness' and unmetabolized otherness comes in the way of cure and insight into oneself. The paper offers some critical interventions that a therapist/ analyst venturing into cross cultural practice can take into consideration to work through various elements of "unregistered otherness." The response by Sudhir Kakar in the chapter titled "As Psychoanalysis Travels" develops once again some of the arguments developed in this chapter. Kakar was responding to the questions posed by the editors of the volume; questions like: What happens when psychoanalysis travels to India? How does the Indian analyst receive psychoanalysis? How does the Indian analyst receive the Indian analysand? How does one attune one's knowledge-praxis of psychoanalysis to the needs and idioms of the Indian analysand?

Alfred Margulies makes the argument that each culture imagines reality, creating "factions" determined by its own socio-cultural history, "worlding" if you may with a Heideggerian twist. Psychoanalysis too is such a culture caught up in its *Nachtraglichkeit* as much as neuroscience, each presetting its own imagination of reality. Not only do culture and the unconscious "co-create" reality, but the "worlding" of reality is midwifed by the particularities of time, place, and person. The occurrence of the *Unheimlichkeit* (the Uncanny) opens an opportunity for empathy to apprehend the sublime in all its bestial glory, but for empathy to be so operative it needs another culture to act as its fulcrum whether the "culture" is of another part of the world (for example India), practice (like psychiatry, psychoanalysis, etc.), religion (as beautifully illustrated by "The Pieta" dream of the author), or the cultural "Russian doll" that each person is. Empathy, as uncanny as the Uncanniness it seeks to study, rooted in our internalization of other cultures from mother, to father, to other people and cultures allows us a kaleidoscopic view of our wonderfully "weird" world in all its sublime bestiality. The response by Sudhir Kakar (in the chapter "As Psychoanalysis Travels") to the questions posed by the editors also delves into some of these issues.

Anup Dhar's chapter is a *reflection* on the two possible titles to this volume: Psychoanalysis *in* Indian Terroir (which is a description of how psychoanalysis has evolved, or got transformed in practice in India) and Psychoanalysis *from* Indian Terroir (which is an audit of the theoretico-practical contributions of "India" and of Indian analysts like Girindrasekhar Bose and Sudhir Kakar to the corpus of work called "psychoanalysis"). The chapter asks: how does it matter whether it is "in" or "from"? How does it matter what the preposition is? The chapter is thus a reflection on how the preposition matters; how it matters in the context of a particular question, the question of *sexuation*; or it is in the context of the question of sexuation that this paper explores how the preposition matters.

As editors of this volume we would like to add that all our contributors have removed any patient identifiers from the case vignettes and pseudonyms have been used.

REFERENCES

Bion, W. "Notes on Memory and Desire." In *Cogitations.* London: Karnac 1992, 1967.

Bose, Girindrasekhar. "A New Theory of Mental Life." *Samiksha* 2(1948): 108–205.

Bose, Girindrasekhar. *The Beginnings of Psychoanalysis in India: Bose-Freud Correspondence*. Calcutta: Indian Psychoanalytic Society, 1999.

Freud, Sigmund. "Abriss der Psychoanalyse." *Internat. Zschr. Psychoanal. Imago* 25(1940a [1938]):7–67; G.W., XVII, 63–138; An outline of psychoanalysis. SE 23: 139–207.

Grotstein, J.S. *A Beam of Intense Darkness*. London: Karnac, 2007.

Kakar, S. *The Inner World.* New Delhi: Oxford University Press, 1981.

Kakar, Sudhir and Kakar, Katharina. *The Indians: Portrait of a People*. New Delhi: Penguin-Viking, 2007.

Kakar, Sudhir and Ross, John Munder. *Tales of Love, Sex and Danger.* New Delhi: Oxford University Press, 2011.

Kakar, Sudhir. *Shamans, Mystics and Doctors. A Psychological Inquiry into India and its Healing Traditions*. New Delhi: Oxford University Press, 1982.

Kakar, Sudhir. *Intimate Relations: Exploring Indian Sexuality.* New Delhi: Penguin India, 1989.

Kohon, Gregor. *The Dead Mother—The Work of Andre Green*. London: Routledge, ed. 1999.

Part I

MOTHERS, THERAPISTS, AND MATRICIDE

Chapter One

When the Enthralled Mother Dreams

A Clinical and Cultural Composition

Amrita Narayanan

As a woman, practicing psychoanalytic psychotherapy with women in India, I am intimately concerned with the cultural backdrop of my patients' stories. The Indian woman's canvas is dotted with pictures: of individual and groups of women in relationship to men and children; in between these images peek blank white spaces in the canvas, marking the deprivation of personhood for the Indian woman outside of relationship, a dream—or sentence—of the Indian polis, that dates back to antiquity (Marguelis and Kakar 2014). Women, in the Indian male unconscious, exist only when they are in relationship to a man: as mother, daughter, sister, or wife; Outside of these relationships, a woman is no longer a subject but an object, available for use by men (Marguelis and Kakar 2014). Given this canvas, there is a very strong possibility that gender-located disappointments—often with accompanying depressions—are normative, meaning expectable, for the majority of Indian women (Kakar 1989a, 1989b). Hyper-visible amidst these normative disappointments is the image of the powerful mother (Kakar 1978, 1989a, 1989b). The narrative of this hyper-visible Great Mother obfuscates the invisible, or barely visible, female narratives outside of motherhood and relationship that nonetheless exist in Indian mythology, and therefore in the cultural unconscious (Kakar 1978, 1989a, 1989b, 1995; Marguelis and Kakar 2014; Narayanan 2008, 2014).

Paying close attention to the cultural backdrop is typical of the Asian varietal of psychoanalysis, a varietal that has frequently been spoken of as a tale within a tale (Dettbarn 2013; Kitayama 2013). Here, the stories that arise within analytic space have their background, foil, or sometimes even their genesis, in the cultural Grand Recits, the myths and Big Dreams of the culture-as-a-whole. Psychoanalysts speak of cultural myths and stories that are repeated, and eventually worked through, in these analyses, such that an individual can place their personal story in some relationship to a cultural story (Dettbarn 2013). Other, non-Asian, geographies have also acknowledged that the cultural arises alongside the individual in the analytic situation (Mori 2013). In Europe, analysts most often cite the World Wars as an example of the social arising in the personal narrative, as war links are worked through, sometime even generations later (Faimberg 2010).

Cultural narratives thus insert themselves as metaphor into individual narrative, and the analyst-patient narrative takes on a cultural metaphor within the analytic space (Akhtar 1999, 2000; Dastur 2013; Kakar and Kakar 2007). A cultural unconscious shared by the majority of Hindu Indians[1] (Kakar and Kakar 2007), adds, for the analytical psychotherapist in the Indian terroir, a layer to the archaeological metaphor that Freud invoked in *Constructions in Analysis*. In this layer we might add that, in our geography, the construction that the analyst makes "from remains found in the rubble" (Freud 1937) connects not only to the patient's family and early life, but also to the state of the polis, the culture, in which the child (and often the analyst) was conceived and raised. Since the unconscious is also composed of cultural elements that pre-date infantile life, the analyst in the Indian terroir understands, in the words of Alfred Marguelis, that "culture and the unconsciousness are co-primordial" (Marguelis & Kakar 2014).

Part of the Indian cultural rubble is the circumscription of women's subjectivity to the relational realm. Since 2012, gradually escalating social protest relating to violence against women in public spaces has made clear that, in the Big Dream of Indian civilization, the only female subjects are mothers, sisters and wives, women who are in relationships with men. As psychoanalyst Sudhir Kakar observes, the Indian Tale involves "a deprivation of personhood for the woman who has stepped out of relational categories" (Marguelis and Kakar 2014, p.1). The Indian female narrative is characterized by invisibility and absence (Kakar 1989a, 1989b; Kakar and Kakar 2007; Kumar 2014), as well as loss and disappointment (Kakar 1989b). From Kakar's (1978, 1989 a,b, 2014) work on Indian women, can be culled a stage-wise structural model of the process by which a deprived personhood occurs: at birth where the mother experiences disappointment at delivering a girl; at puberty where the girl is distanced from her father; at marriage which is an invariable disappointment; and, at the birth of her first child, the closure of her erotic life.

How is such a trauma to the self endured by women? Three important contributions come to mind, all suggesting the use of defenses, whether primitive or higher level. First, Kakar (1989a, 1989b) who writes about how Indian women accept life in a culture that allows only a circumscribed space for them: on one hand embracing and seeking power in these spaces (in the relational realm and in the kitchen), and, on the other hand, accepting the inevitable and expectable disappointments of being a girl and a woman. Second, Kumar (2014), who writes about an absence of imaginative capabilities, verging on a discomfort with an individual fantasy life. In her study of the post-trauma narratives of Kucchi girls, Kumar (2014) noticed that, relative to the boys, the girls had a tendency toward concrete metaphors and a difficulty with the open-ended quality of fantasy life or imagination. Kumar's other findings for this cohort of girls included a narrative of absence and invisibility, mental numbness and shame about gender/gender ideals, and gendered identifications with domesticity and docility, a result of excessive exposure to household work, to the extent of obstructing other potential functions, such as knowledge seeking, education, hygiene, health, leisure activities (Kumar 2014). A third contribution concerns the efforts of young women to obfuscate the trauma toward women through an embrace of consumer culture (Johri and Sachdev 2009, Johri 2011). Johri (2011), a psychoanalytically oriented psychologist and cultural researcher, analyzed models of global womanhood offered via advertising to young women. In her work, she has located an "irrelevant mother," in the contemporary Indian imagination, an older woman and a homemaker who did not have the opportunities of the neo-liberal generation, and who is subtly presented in the consumer culture as obsolete. The implication, from an analytical perspective, is of youth manically embracing the new opportunities as a defense against an uncathected mourning of what was lost in pre-liberalization India.

The work of the above three researchers, as well as my own clinical and cultural experiences, presents a problematic regarding female autonomy outside of relationship. The problematic extends to both genders and particularly to the relations between the genders, but in this essay, I explore a way in which the problematic impacts women's autonomous capability for eros and a fantasy life.

MATERNAL ENTHRALLMENT AND THE FANTASY OF THE "PERFECT" INDIAN MOTHER

From a theoretical perspective, central to the cultural backdrop in India is a concept that Kakar (1995) calls "maternal enthrallment." The term—that Kakar describes as the dominant scene in the Indian family drama—arises, as do many concepts in the language of Indian psychoanalysis, from a scene in a myth. The myth of Ganesha has been reproduced in various places (see for example Kakar 1995) and consists of several "scenes": Parvathi's creation of Ganesha in Shiva's absence; Ganesha standing at the closed doors to Parvathi's bath (the oedipal scene); Shiva's decapitation of Ganesha (fillicide);

the now elephant-headed Ganesha who, upon being asked to circle the world, merely circles his mother and wins the prize, while his brother Skanda rushes off to circle the world.

"That Ganesha's lot is considered superior to Skanda's is perhaps an indication of Indian man's cultural preference, in the dilemma of separation-individuation," writes Kakar, "He is at one with his mother in *her wish* not to have the son separate from her; individuate out of their shared anima" (Kakar 1989a, p. 358, italics mine). Kakar explores the concept of maternal enthrallment from the perspective of the young boy, who, even as he grows into a man, endeavors to preserve this oneness with the mother, and projects the childlike wish for eternal reunion onto the mother as well. In Kakar's words, "a dominant motif in Hindu myths and other products of cultural imagination, is the centrality of the male Hindu Indian's experience of the powerful mother" (Kakar 1995, p. 2). The fantasy of a mother who could be a substitute for the world, a mother so interesting that the world pales in comparison, is a child's fantasy (Chodorow and Contratto 1982). Yet, this child's fantasy forms the fulcrum of the Indian cultural scene, and is based in the belief in a particular kind of female power that is rooted in a child's fantasy.

Taking a fresh look at the notion of maternal enthrallment invites a return to the scene of Ganesha walking around his mother, fixing and circumscribing her with his eyes, making her his world. The mother's response depends also on how the listeners to the tale in the Indian polis perceive Parvathi. If listeners watch her with the idealization of the young Indian boy, a boy who has most likely experienced his mother as unhappy in love, and whose fantasy is that he has the pressure—and power—to satisfy her, then we succumb—as have all patriarchies and most feminists—to the fantasy of the perfect mother (Chodorow and Contratto 1982).

However, Kakar derived "maternal enthrallment," not from the story of Parvati but from the stories of his patients, who were the data for the presence of the omnipotent mother. He then returned to the myth to shed light on the cultural themes in his patients' dilemma. Yet, the analytic situation provides an opportunity not only for the analyst to witness the patient's relationship to the dominant scene, but also his or her relationship to the unplayed scenes that nonetheless form part of the myth of Ganesha. What Kakar describes in the polis—the socially sanctioned erotic renunciation for women and the deprivation of their personhood—can also be "heard" in the narrative of absence in the analysis with his male patients. The focus on the enthralled mother who cannot bear to be apart from her child raises the question of whether a mother exists who can take time and space for her own eroticism, reverie, and imagination. Or, does enthrall connote the Latin origins of the word, *in-thrall*, meaning, in-the-trap?

We return then to the less dominant motifs in Indian culture, the neglected scenes in the Indian myths. What we hear, in large relief, as the myth of Ganesha invariably involves the scenes of fillicide (Shiva beheading Ganesha) and of maternal enthrallment (Ganesha circling his mother, Parvathi, his "world"). However, the creation of Ganesha is a scene that remains largely un-mentalized in the Indian unconscious with important parallels in the Indian polis. Parvathi's creation of Ganesha from the soap scum on her own body is a non-relational sexual act involving Parvati, her own body, and her fantasy inner world. The unmetabolized narrative of Parvati before Ganesha's birth is congruent with a polis that holds, as its aspirational ideal, the perfect mother, content with a circumscribed, relationally oriented world.

Prohibition and caution on women's fantasy lives has been always been an important part of Hindu culture since antiquity. The Manu Smriti, an ancient text whose discourse continues to unconsciously regulate the lives of Indian women across all income levels, associates the act of *wandering* into reverie with loose women.[2] Likewise, the sexual acts of a woman, outside of her relationship with the man to whom she is affiliated through marriage, are equated with immorality. To ensure women's chastity, the Manu Smriti suggests "keeping them busy,"[3] and encouraging and rewarding the acts of spending money and performing household tasks, in the chapter on the "good wife."

"Good" is a very critical word here. In a polis where narcissistic supplies for women are available on condition of relational behavior, there is more pressure on women to behave in a "moral" manner, that is, in accordance with the ego-ideal of the society. The injunction of the 3 C.E. Manu Smriti for women to be praised for domesticity and chastised for "wandering" is eerily congruent with the present-day findings of Kumar's (2014) cohort of girls having gendered identifications with domesticity and docility, obstructing other potential functions. As maternal enthrallment is a central dominant scene of the Hindu drama from the point of view of the Hindu boy, it hinges on the Hindu woman, his mother, repressing her imagination, her auto-eroticism, and her sexuality, such that she (the mother) can cleave to the fantasy of the child as her world, re-constructing as her world the shared fantasy of the men and children of the polis.

Maternal subjectivity, and the lack of space thereof, is not of course an Indian problem. The fantasy of the perfect mother is a phenomenon that feminists worldwide struggle with, often without resolution (Chodorow and Contratto 1982). Parvati's narrative of absence and its converse, the "dominant scene of the Indian family drama" described by Kakar, have in common the problem that Chodorow and Contratto (1982) described with feminist views of mothering: that is "the union of infantile fantasies and culturally child centered perspective with a myth of maternal omnipotence, creating a totalistic, extreme, yet fragmented view of mothering and the mother-child relation in which both mother and child are paradoxically victim yet omnipotent." (Chodorow and Contratto, 1982, p.56). At the present time in history, women fiction writers worldwide are bringing their pens to this topic of mothering and its hues (Cusk 2015; Ferrante 2008; Koshy 2009; Offil 2014) and in doing so perhaps, take a stab at the wish that Chodorow and Contratto articulated over two decades ago "To begin to transform the relations of parenting and the relations of gender, to begin to transform women's lives, we must move beyond the myths and misconceptions embodied in the fantasy of the perfect mother" (Chodorow and Contratto 1982, p. 20).

AT THE CONFLUENCE OF THE CULTURAL AND THE INDIVIDUAL: A CASE OF NARCISSISTIC DISTURBANCE

My patient, a young woman who suffers from a lack of basic narcissist supplies, is especially reliant upon the cultural self-granting apparatus to feel any sense of self-worth. Lacking a foundational sense of self, she finds her narcissistic supplies in the fantasy of the enthralled mother. Since she experiences a sense of self only when in relationship, it is very difficult for her to engage in solitude much less conceive of self-directed activity. Yet, she enjoys painting and is interested in creating art, and deeply longs to be more productive as an artist.

Agni[4] entered therapy with the stated wish of "improving myself so my husband can have a better life" and in the same breath added that she hoped very much she could "make something of myself in life."

Who this "myself" was to Agni was both an intellectual and affective mystery. Her self was experienced in large part outside of her control and even outside of her thinking. Agni felt "clear about myself" only when engaged in household activities in service of the joint family into which she had married. She felt a combination of dependence on these activities as a source of identity and "goodness," a compulsion—that she located as external to her—to perform them, and an anger about the externally located others who were "putting pressure" on her. Some of Agni's experience is resonant with the findings of Kumar (2013, 2014) and Kakar (1995), on some degree of pattern in the Indian female narrative, including a tendency to create self-worth and value based on service and on relationships. Her symptoms—self-aware hypochondria, clamors for attention both in dreams and in waking life, a sense of feeling empty and, in her words, "mechanized"—bespoke narcissistic vulnerabilities that were born out in the accounts of her history which suggests her parents had been preoccupied during the time at which her primary narcissism might have developed, leaving her with an unquenchable narcissistic fragility.[5]

At the beginning of our work together, Agni expressed a desire to begin and sustain attendance at a drawing class. Initially, she spoke for months about her sense of duty or responsibility to her mother-in-law that prevented her from drawing. Over time she slowly admitted that the problem was bigger than this and related to a "blank sense of nothingness" that she felt when she was alone, making it difficult for her to produce a drawing. On the other hand, she said that if someone—say her mother-in-law or husband—would set aside the time for her to draw, then she was able to produce.

Agni spoke incessantly about her mother-in-law, describing her as a person who could never relax, always striving for perfection in household tasks and "looking at me whenever I am relaxed as if she is telling me to work." Agni experienced her mother-in-law as "wrapped up with my husband (her son)" with "nothing better to do than see if he has clean underwear." I focused on Agni's sense of feeling intruded upon, and penetrated by, her mother-in-law and of her jealousies: not just her possessiveness toward her husband but also, what I believed was a bigger driving factor, her jealousy that she had not had such a mother as did her husband, a mother who was enthralled with her, and, relatedly, an oedipal rivalry with her husband that was acted out obliquely as an anger toward her mother-in-law, but was actually hurt that her mother-in-law focussed on her son instead of Agni.

Numerous other personal factors are a part of this case. However I'd like to focus on Agni's difficulties in drawing that she initially presented as "my mother-in-law who prevents me from drawing" and then moved on to "my (biological) mother who never encouraged me to draw" before it showed up in the transference. About four or five months into therapy, Agni began the longed-for drawing classes and another month later began showing me her work, reproductions commissioned by her teacher. I praised her easily, as her drawings and paintings were technically good and saturated with color. During this time period, Agni brought her very first dream to therapy. In the first dream that Agni shared, a dream that she had about an hour prior to her therapy, Agni said she was "being kissed and touched by another woman, and feeling very aroused, really enjoying this, but so surprised I was enjoying it." I made the connection to her paintings, and to my enjoying of the paintings, and to her enjoying my pleasure. She could not relate to my interpretations, but returned to her own sense of surprise at her pleasure in the dream.

The mutual pleasure in that first dream was, and is, paralleled in the sessions when Agni shows her artwork. Though I experienced this pleasure during the sessions, I found it hard to stay with the sensation, experiencing the pleasure as fleeting and thereafter unattainable as something to think about. Interestingly, the fleeting session of pleasure was mirrored in my link with Agni, which, during this period of showing me her drawings, did not sustain between the sessions. Agni struggled at my non-availability outside the therapy hour and she would frequently reach out to me via email or text asking to "repeat what you said in a session." When I could not gratify her she would lash out and attack me. After struggling to figure out what was this magic thing that I "said" in the session, I slowly realized that this was something I "did" in the session—admire her work—which was also something the representation of me had "done" in her first dream, during which she was completely passive as the woman pleasured her. I wondered also whether the praise in the session or the pleasure in the dream both bespoke a promise, a beginning of sorts, one that was not delivered on during the sessions.

A maternal tableau had been evoked by this first dream and its attendant analytic environment. The tableau was a dense composition of the homoerotic feeling between mother and daughter, and between women, but the analytic environment also held the cultural taboo against this feeling. In the months that followed, this taboo would become enacted again and again between us, while evoking the lack in the early environment that was the root of Agni's narcissistic struggles. While I was not able to comment upon all aspects of this tableau in the moment, what I did comprehend was Agni's inability—and related sense of helplessness— to give to herself the sense of eros she looked for from others in her relationships, whether her husband, mother, mother-in-law, or me.

Agni had a tendency to act out in envy and anger at those whom she perceived as doing as they pleased. However she lacked the capacity to take the initiative to do as she herself pleased. She often resented others after she spent her energies pleasing them. Continuing the theme of pleasure from her first dream, during an incident where Agni vouchsafed that she had spent several days angry and upset with her husband—despite her better intentions and logic—because he was "making himself happy with a Playboy in the bathroom," I intervened in this to ask Agni if she was able to masturbate. She responded immediately: "You know I have tried, I start trying but then I always stop quickly. Its weird to say but you know I think my mother would not like it."[6] Here I remarked on the difficulty Agni had starting "but stopping quickly" in many areas of her life, including her artistic work. I also spoke to Agni's sense of oedipal rivalry with her husband in the vying for the attention of mother. "It feels so unfair," I said, "that your husband can have a life in which he can make himself happy, while his mother still goes running after him, while you sacrifice your happiness, you miss your classes, you work in the kitchen for her happiness and his mother still does not notice you." Agni's response was to turn to me, her eyes brimming with tears as she nodded emphatically.

Six months after she began the drawing classes, Agni dropped out of them, stating that her mother-in-law did not like it. From here began an intense series of sessions in which she talked incessantly about her hate and anger toward her mother-in-law. She ignored my efforts to remind her of the parallel to her frustrated masturbation, when I repeated her own words back to her, "(you) stop (your art) quickly because you think your mother will not like it." During this period, she refused to be on the couch, choosing to face me instead, an effort that I thought aimed to recreate the eye-contact of the lost maternal tableau. It was unsuccessful. Enthralled and in-thrall collided; I felt watched and monitored, as if Agni were "keeping an eye on me" and I was without ways to imagine my way out of it. The analytic situation itself had become the thrall, the trap. I was not able to mirror Agni enough about the truncated pleasure of the earlier sessions, as I was not myself in touch with it. Nonetheless, I was able to make the link to Agni's truncated pleasure with her mother-in-law, her constant efforts to establish the erotic link between herself and her mother-in-law, and her frustration in seeing that her intended beloved was occupied by her own son. She accepted this interpretation, adding that she had dropped out of drawing in order to redirect herself to household tasks and "give my mother-in-law what she needs." I responded that she hoped for a certain kind of love in exchange for her efforts in the kitchen, and was angry and frustrated that it was not forthcoming.

The interpretations showed their effort in a regression. Agni escalated her attacks and her demands that I give to her like I "once did." For my part, I experienced a dramatic reduction in my capacity for reverie, an essential tool in the psychoanalytic way of working and making interpretations (Ogden 1997), perhaps a similar kind of blankness that Agni experienced in herself when devoid of narcissistic supplies. During this time, Agni produced a drawing; crude, unlike the sophisticated copies she made, but coming from her own imagination: a sketch of a marionette, the puppet dressed in the garb of a princess, and controlled by invisible hands that worked from behind a curtain, also decorated with sequins and gold-dust matching the dress of the princess. She submitted the drawing to me with the words: "this is how mechanized I am." Since I too felt cold and wooden during the sessions, I could relate to the drawing, but initially, could not make the link to the cultural piece of the picture.

I sought consultation for the case, finding the wooden feeling and absence of reverie unbearable. During these consultations I experienced a parallel process—and a moment of condensation—during my own experience of injured narcissism with my supervisor. During the course of the consultation, when at one point I pointed out an intervention from the process note and wondered aloud why the consultant had not praised this intervention, she made two comments: "Perhaps I've been an Indian mother, who could not say "shabash" (well done) to you" and later in the same session, almost *sotto voce*: "perhaps you and I had the same kind of mother." Following this consultation, I recalled the voice of my own mother cautioning me against the dangers of an overly rich fantasy life,, "don't be lost in your own world" and, painfully, my own shame while engaging in child-like fantasy play.

From this moment of condensation, I returned to Agni's drawing of the marionette as a picture of an ideal woman—Manu's woman—whose inner access to narcissistic supplies has been cut off, and who depends entirely on the outside—notably her husband and the domestic sphere—for narcissistic supplies, indeed for animation and movement. I understood my patient and her mother-in-law's obsessive mutual watching as a way in which unexpressed longing and eros is channeled (albeit unsuccessfully) between the patient and her mother-in-law, as well as the patient and myself, and, in the frozen space between each, I saw an unsymbolized, unacknowledged kind of mother, one who is able to unashamedly take pleasure in her own female eroticism—outside of utilitarian and relational functions—as well as in the erotically tinged pleasure between herself and her girl child, and eventually adolescent daughter (Chodorow and Contratto 1982; Irigaray 1990).

Bringing these insights back to the therapy, I made a slight shift in my approach. I started referring to the culturally dominant mother in the analytic moment. I used a slight adjustment of language, that allowed me to keep in mind not only the mothers in Agni's life, but also the ones in my own. For example, when I pointed to Agni's sense of shame about how "mother" would perceive each of these personal acts—relaxing alone,[7] drawing, or masturbating—I referred to the fact that "mother's eyes" were everywhere. I purposefully did not add the words "in law" after mother, nor did I add the possessive pronoun "your" before "mother." I found that my patient did not correct me, and that during one of these sessions she spoke for the first time of a new kind of loss: the mother she *could* have had, a mother who could see her without watching her. She spoke also of the kind of mother she could become, of her horror of becoming a mother-who-watches—whom she associated to her mother-in-law—a mother who depends upon the child for an animating function and who becomes obsolete once her child is grown up. The sessions unfolded into a series of sessions about Agni's lack of female role models and eventually the fantasies she had about my capacity to animate, to give life and pleasure. This reference was not only to her first dream but also, in my mind, to Parvati's narrative of absence, that Agni believed was always accessible for me—and envied— but in fact had become inaccessible in the transference until the consultant was able to make the link to mothers.

Agni's "mother-who-watches" is related to Kakar's "enthralled mother." As coda, I return from the individual case of Agni, back to the cultural "case" of the Indian unconsciousness to explain this link: if the mother is enthralled, she is also *in-thrall*, trapped, into a compulsive relationality with her child—and also to Indian society itself—the kind of trap that though pleasurable at times, proves a particular obstacle to a young woman already floundering with a weak narcissistic foundation. The analytic hour is an opportunity for a tale within the Tale, a chance to revisit aspects of Cultural Narratives from an individual perspective (Dettbarn 2013). Agni's case pushes for such a tale, and mourns the absence of such a Tale, the missed attendance to the inner worlds of the mothers and daughters, and the call for a different sort of mother. Her struggles could be simply seen sociologically, of course, as a new daughter-in-law trying to locate herself in her husband's family, or from the viewpoint of, say, a universalist model of psychoanalysis as a problem in regulating narcissistic states of consciousness. It is richer however, and true to the Indian terroir, to see the case culturally, from an Indian psychoanalytic viewpoint where, in Agni's struggles, we find not only individual narcissistic concerns, but also an unsymbolized mourning in the composition of the Indian daughter. Perhaps we can build on what Kakar (1995) wrote: "One of the more dominant narratives of this culture is that of Devi, the great goddess, especially in her manifold expressions as mother in the inner world of the Hindu son" (Kakar 1995, p. 355). To this I add, that in concert with her manifold expressions in the inner world of the Hindu son, an equalling culturing force in the unconsciousness is the Goddess Parvati's inaccessible, non-dominant, invisible, or absent narrative in the inner world of the Hindu girl.

The loss and covering up of the loss of female erotic subjectivity in Indian culture has been well documented, as the terroir has regarded women's erotic impulses outside of motherhood with suspicion since antiquity (Doniger 1991; Marguelis and Kakar 2014); Narayanan 2008). Perhaps not coincidentally then, women's erotic needs have not been well recognized by Indian feminists in the post-independence generation (Lakshmi 1984, 2009, 2013) at the moment when female individual needs were collectively sacrificed to the national ideal (Kumar 2011). The unmourned, unacknowledged act of disappearing the erotic mother, with her capacity for reverie, revives the control of women's physical bodies and sexual imaginations spoken of in the Manu Smiriti. The lack of this acknowledgement, has, I believe, created a social vulnerability for post-liberalization Indian woman (including my patient Agni who is part of that generation), who knows that in a neo-liberalized India, Kakar's enthralled mother risks becoming Johri's (2011) forgotten mother.

Agni's is a hesitant composition, against a backdrop where the majority of girls' primary narcissism is at risk. It is weighty with loss—and the need to mourn—the uber-leitmotif of the boy-enthralled-Indian Mother (Kakar 1978; Marguelis and Kakar 2014) and what it means for the Indian girl. Such a mourning would offer, in the Indian terroir, a pathway toward a recognition of women that nevertheless stays away from "mother-blaming," the pitfall of most feminist-psychoanalytic narratives (Chodorow and Contratto 1982). From sharing the terrors of the enthralled mother (Kakar 1995), and the forgettable mother (Johri 2011) comes a mourning, from which emerges the figure of the subjective mother, one who has an available space in her own mind, yet capable of caring for her child.

Diatkine (2015) writes that if we consider this kind of a mother one who has Bion's "capacity for maternal reverie" or Jessica Benjamin's "the third in the one," this mother may be also considered an erotic mother, whose reverie might include rest from her child alongside the resuscitating dream of her sexual partner. The Indian terroir finds agreement with Diatkine, in the oedipal narrative itself, in Parvati's fantasies and dreams that she has in the absence of both husband and children, the dreams before Ganesha was born, the dreams in the bath when the doors to the world are closed: Parvati as the erotic mother.

Listening to the great myths and repetitive family dramas of the culture in the psychoanalytic moment, I wonder if there is a possibility of a different kind of listening to the listening (Faimbeg 2010): that is, listening to the coded and patterned ways in which we hear the cultural narratives and the roles in it. In the case I briefly presented, without diminishing the layered nature of the case, and the many factors at play, I "hear" the cultural absence of the erotic mother being remembered, repeated, and worked through in the clinical moment. In the clinic—and perhaps in the polis—accessing the erotic mother, a young woman with a capacity for masturbation, a mother with her capacity for erotic reverie, an older woman who is relevant for her contribution, requires a mourning of a recessive female presence that is not represented enough in the cultural imagination.

NOTES

1. I say Hindu Indians to make clear I am not conflating the notion of "Hindu" and "Indian" under the rubric of culture. Muslim, Christian, Parsi, Anglo-Indian, and Jewish women share some of these circumscriptions simply by inhabiting the same physical polis and may find some resonance in the ways I speak of "Indians" as a consequence of inhabiting a shared polis that is often dominated by Hindu voices. They also have, of course, their own different sets of circumscriptions.

2. "Drinking, associating with bad people, being separated from their husbands, *wandering about*, sleeping, and living in other people's houses are the six things that corrupt women" (italics mine) (Doniger, 1991, p. 198)

3. "No man is able to guard a woman entirely by force, but they can be kept guarded by using these means: he should keep her busy amassing and spending money, engaging in purification, attending to her duty, cooking food and looking after the furniture." (Doniger, 1991, p. 198)

4. Name chosen by the patient at the time of requesting permission to write about her case.

5. My use and understanding of the word *narcissism* comes from Bach, 1977, who to be precise speaks of *narcissistic states of consciousness.*

6. I have discussed this interaction in great detail elsewhere in a separate paper on Indian women and masturbation (Narayanan, 2015) referencing the work of Freud (1914), and Laufer (1968) that relate masturbation to basic narcissism.

7. Agni's experience of shame about the act of relaxing is something I have noticed in other interviews, such as the case of Darshana described in Narayanan 2015.

REFERENCES

Akhtar, S. "Mental pain and the cultural ointment of poetry." *Int. J. Psycho-Anal* 81(2000): 229–243.

Akhtar, S. *Immigration and identity: Turmoil, treatment, and transformation*. Northvale, N.J: Jason Aronson, 1999.

Bach, S. "On the narcissistic state of consciousness." *Int. J. Psychoanal* 58(1977): 209–233.

Chodorow, N., and Contratto, S. "The fantasy of the perfect mother." In *Rethinking the family: Some feminist questions* edited by B. Thorne, 54–75. New York: Longman,1982.

Cusk, R. *Outline*. New York: Farrar, Straus and Giroux, 2015.

Dastur, M. "The universal truth of myths in psychoanalytic theory and practice." In *Psychoanalysis in Asia: China, India, Japan, South Korea, Taiwan,* edited by M. Hooke, A. Gerlach, and S. Varvain. London: Karnac Books, 2013.

Dettbarn, I. (2013). "Havoc comes from the mouth." in *Psychoanalysis in Asia: China, India, Japan, South Korea and Taiwan*, Gerlach, A., Hooke, M., and Varvin, S London, Karnac, 2013, 310.

Diatkine. G. "Is It Necessarily So?" Paper presentation on *The Paternal in Culture and Psychoanalysis* at the second annual conference at Fortis Healthcare, New Delhi: India, 2015.

Doniger, W. *The Laws of Manu*. New Delhi: Penguin Books, 1991.

Faimberg, H. "The Telesescoping of Generatioms." In *Reading French Psychoanalysis,* edited by D. Breen, S. Flanders, and A. Gibeault. London: Routledge, 2010.

Ferrante, E. *The Lost Daughter.* Rome: Europa Editions, 2008.

Freud, S. (1937). "Constructions in Analysis" in Phillips, A. (Ed) (2006). *The Penguin Freud Reader*. Penguin Books. London.

Freud, S. "On the introduction of narcissism." In *Beyond the Pleasure Principle and Other Writings,* edited by J. Redick. London: Penguin Books, 1914.

Irigaray, L. *Je, Te, Nous: Towards a culture of difference (Thinking Gender)*. London: Routledge, 1990.

Johri, R. "Mothering Daughters and the fair and lovely path to success." *Advertising & Society Review*, 12(2011): 2. doi:10.1353/asr.2011.0014.

Johri, R. and Sachdev, D. "Yashoda. Kaushalya. Kunti. Sunayana: Re-membering the forgotten mother of daughters in the Hindu family." Paper presented at the M(o) ther Trouble: An International Conference on *Feminism, Psychoanalysis and the Maternal,* Birkbeck, University of London. May 31, 2009.

Kakar, S. and Kakar, K. *The Indians: Portrait of a people.* New York: Penguin, 2007.

Kakar, S. "The maternal-feminine in Indian psychoanalysis." *Int. J. Psychoanal.* 16(1989a):355–362.

Kakar, S. *Intimate relations: Exploring Indian sexuality.* Chicago: Univesity of Chicago Press, 1989b.

Kakar, S. "Clinical Work and Cultural Imagination," *Psychoanal. Q.* 64(1995): 265–281.

Kakar, S. *Inner world: A Psychoanalytic study of childhood and society in India*, 245. New Delhi: Oxford University Press, 1978.

Kitayama, O. "Psychoanalysis in a shame culture: a drama based viewpoint." In *Psychoanalysis in Asia: China, India, Japan, South Korea, Taiwan,* edited by M. Hooke, A. Gerlach, and S. Varvain. London: Karnac Books, 2013.

Koshy, Mridula. "The good mother." In *If it was sweet.* Australia: Brass Monkey Book, 2009.

Kumar, M. "(Re)Locating the feminist standpoint in the practice of psychology today: A case of India." In *Handbook of International Feminisms: Perspectives on Psychology, Women, Culture, Rights,* edited by A. Rutherford, R. Capdevila, Undurti, V. Vindhya, and I. Palmary. New York: Springer, 2011.

Kumar, M. "Examining the circle of attachment trauma, shame, and marginalization: The unheard voices of young Kutchi girls." In *Marginality: Addressing the Nexus 133 of poverty, exclusion and ecology*, edited by J. Braun and F.W. Gatzweiler. Netherland: Springer, 2014.

Kumar, M. "Little girls must be seen and not heard: Examining the circle of attachment trauma, shame, and marginalization. *The unheard*, 2013.

Lakshmi C.S. Personal Communication, 2013.

Lakshmi, C.S. *Acceptance Speech for the lifetime achievement award: Tamil Sangam Garden. May 24th 2009.* Toronto: University of Toronto, 2009.

Lakshmi, C.S. *The face behind the mask: Women in Tamil literature*. Advent Books,1984.

Laufer, M. "The body image, the function of masturbation and adolescence—problems of the ownership of the body." *Psychoanalytic Study of the Child* 23(1968): 114–137.

Marguelis, A. and Kakar S. "Discussion of Culture and Psyche: A Personal Journey." Committee on International Relations for Psychoanalytic Psychology Division of Psychoanalysis (39) of the American Psychological Association, moderated by Kenneth Reich, Ed.D. April 19, 2014.

Mori, S. "The complications of the perpetrator-victim relationship for Japanese Children in World War Two." In *Psychoanalysis in Asia: China, India, Japan, South*

Korea and Taiwan, edited by A. Gerlach, M. T.S. Hooke, and S.Varvin. London, Karnac, 2013, 310.

Narayanan, A. "Goodmarks for good goddesses." *India Currents*. 8(2008):12. Berkeley, California. https://www.indiacurrents.com/articles/2008/08/12/goodmarks-for-good-goddesses.

Narayanan, A. "Psychoanalysis in Asia: China, India, Japan, South Korea and Taiwan, Psychodynamic Practice." *Individuals, Groups and Organisations,* 21(2015): 200–03. DOI: 10.1080/14753634.2015.1016648.

Narayanan, A. "Inaccessible masturbation, impossible mourning: Collective melancholia, the prohibition on female sexual subjects in India and masturbation fantasy as a zone of the strange." *Psychoanalytic Review*, 102(6), December 2015.

Offil, J. *Department of Speculation.* New York: Penguin Books, 2014.

Ogden, T.H. "Reverie and Interpretation," *Psychoanal Q*. 66(1997): 567–595.

Chapter Two

Devi Possession

At the Intersections of Religion, Culture, and Psychoanalysis

Sabah Siddiqui and Bhargavi Davar

There is "Religion" with a capital letter, but also religions. There are the big ones, the major religions followed in India, which can be arranged according to percentage of followers in the census data. This arrangement tells us nothing about how they are situated vis-à-vis each other. That is one question. By being juxtaposed against each other, they appear internally coherent. But, within each, there are break-away sects and reform movements which are trying to redefine "religion." Already the concept is decentered! And that is another question. Then there are the religious practices that evolve in their own ways, away from the religious canon, the codified texts and the priestly class. These are subaltern practices that can neither be categorized nor codified. It is difficult to label them as customary or religious. They fall somewhere, in common parlance, under superstition. And yet how many of us really follow the canonical form of religion: living by the book and dying by the doctrine? Religion becomes personalized as faith. However, in its subaltern form, religion undergoes yet another transformation since it neither frames a politics nor develops a science. It is only a religiosity, a way of living, of becoming; in short, subaltern religions are *asketic* practices, which we will come to presently.

How will psychoanalysis set up a relation with these forms of religiosity? What happens when psychoanalysis and religion come face to face? When and where do they come face to face? As a starting point, we can look to Sigmund Freud in *the Future of an Illusion* (2008 [1927]) in which he discusses the psychical genesis of religious ideas. While he concedes that religion is a deep-seated need of all cultures to safeguard themselves, the primacy of intelligence and the god of reason must hold sway over psychoanalysis. Nonetheless, Freud is struck by deep doubt, as evidenced by his preserving within the text his other voice that protests this rejection of the value of religion in culture. Thus, when he maintains that religion is an illusion but science need not be—"our science is not an illusion," he says at the end of the paper—this should be read with at least as much caution as Freud himself has used. However, the analyses of the Judeo-Christian roots of both psychoanalysis and Freud are quite comprehensive. Then what do we mean by religion *and* psychoanalysis? Are we talking about a religion other than the ones dominant in the census data in the context of Europe? Or are we talking about another form of praxis, of faith, and of healing that does not conform to what is conventionally understood as either religion or science?

This chapter re-examines these assumptions in light of the phenomenon of possession, specifically being possessed by a deity, which is a common occurrence in certain religious cultures of India. This chapter emerges from work carried out by the Bapu Trust for Mind and Discourse, Pune, on traditional healers in Maharashtra.[1] For the purpose of this chapter we have taken recourse to interviews with two respondents—Shivani Salve and Manasi Ghule, both residents of high-density, low-income slums in Pune. Salve and Ghule narrated experiences of being possessed by goddesses and therefore identified themselves as *Aradhis*. The phenomenon of Devi-possession makes us ask: what if psychoanalysis came face to face with something irreducible to what is conventionally understood as either religion or science?

Interview with Shivani Salve

Shivani Salve was married when she was in the first standard to her father's sister's son. At puberty (12 years), she went to live with her husband's family in the village[2]. By the time she was 14, she had one child—a son who lives with her to the present day. The next year, there was drought in the village and the family was suffering, when her husband was advised to marry another girl who could bring money into the family. Salve left her husband and returned to her parents' house in Kashewadi (a slum in the inner city of Pune). Her description of her married life in the village is bleak and full of strife, and when her mother died a few years later, even after being pressured by her father, she refused to return to her *sasural* (father-in-law's house). When her brother got married, her father forced her out of the house. She was supported for a brief while by relatives and friends, before it was suggested to her that she buy her own house. Borrowing from her employers in 1984, Salve bought the house she is currently staying in for Rs. 2500. In that house she raised her son, educated him till the 10th-11th standard, and, at the age of 20, arranged for him to be married to a cousin's daughter. She has a grandson now who is seventeen years old. Her son has been unemployed for three years now and is given to drinking in excess. She has described their relationship as very difficult (*chatees ka akda*) since he is uncooperative and demanding. Until a couple of months ago, she was the sole wage earner in the family, although recently her daughter-in-law has been working as a domestic help to earn a little money. Her relationship with her daughter-in-law seems to be more supportive. Salve is over fifty years old and is concerned about aging and the effect it will have on her ability to work. For the last twenty years, she has been working in the *anganwadi* in the morning. At the time of the interview in 2011, she was also engaged with nursing patients in the evening.

Salve is from the Matang caste, a Scheduled Caste of Maharasthra. She brought the goddess into her house and her life seventeen years ago, after a series of fortuitous events. She was handed, for safekeeping, a bronze idol of Tuljabhavani[3] which her Muslim neighbor had found on the ground. She started to worship the idol, since Tuljabhavani was also her parents' clan goddess. However, she did not believe in the gods very much at this time, perhaps because times were very hard on her at this point. Her daughter-in-law was undergoing a very difficult pregnancy around this time as well. Salve was being supported at this time by Datta-*bhau,* a *Jogati*[4] who recommended that they should at least visit the Mira Datar Dargah in Ravivar Peth. Some days after her daughter-in-law lost the child, an *Aradhi* who had come to collect *Jogwa* (offerings for the deity), under the direction of Datta-bhau, indicated that Salve also had the favor of Tuljabhavani for four years, although she was not a believer. To understand this better, Salve went on a pilgrimage to Tuljapur. Listening to the other devotees, she also wanted to offer flowers to the goddess in the temple there. The event (that sounds almost mythic) that kindled her belief in the goddess is best recounted in her own words:

> There was 10 minutes left for 8 PM, and at that time, the temple gets closed. The person over there said that everybody should go out as this is the time of closing the temple. I said to God, *I don't bend (namaskar) in front of you. I make fasts for you and worship you. Now I am going from your place, but once I go from here, I will not turn back to you. If you are true then the priests should take me inside the temple.* Saying this I went outside the temple but the priests announced that those who wanted to put flowers for the Gods could come inside. So two other women and I went inside. The priest took two frangipani flowers—one yellow and one white and he said that whatever you want to ask, think about any one colour flower and keep that wish in mind. So I selected the white colour flower and I said (to the Goddess), *since last year I am not able to prepare one cup tea in my home, I have not called you in my home, I have*

> *not urged you to my help. But somebody else has given you to me so I took it, placed it in my home and started worshipping you, but you put me in trouble. If you really want me to be happy and contented and you want to come to my house then you should say it clearly, here and now. And within 40 days you will have to show the result to me. Then only will I really establish you in my house and I will perform a big function for you.* I put my wish on the white flower and the priest said that keep your hand below the statue of Goddess and stand here. I did that and the priest put both the flowers on the Goddess . . . two times and both the times the flowers rolled down from the sari of the Goddess. How it will stay on the Goddess? It is bound to come down. So the priest said that you have not wished from your heart, you should say it from the heart. So I put my head on the feet of the goddess, and I rubbed my nose on it and again made the wish. The priest put the two flowers on the goddess and I kept my hand below the statue. The yellow flower fell into my hand and the white flower remained on the sari of the goddess. So the priest said that whatever you have wished for will come true.

With this, Salve decided to bring the goddess home, and in the procession back from the temple, she had her first experience of possession by the goddess. While singing the *aarti,* her legs started shaking: "At that time I was trying to control myself very much and pressing my leg hard that it should not shake but I felt it was like fever and my legs were shaking continuously. How you shiver with the cold in the fever of Malaria? I felt like that. Then there I got possessed for the first time." However, the celebration for this was carried out in her brother's place in Indapur, rather than her own home, some months later. In doing so, she had neglected the resident goddess of Indapur—"Shiva-chi Aai" or Mahalaxmi. Being possessed by two goddesses was hard work:

> While I was getting possessed by Bhavani-Aai, the *malas* around my neck would get thrown around. Not a single mala used to remain on my neck. Once I had an episode of possession that I could not even sit or stand for eight days. All my muscles from head to toe used to get stiff. I couldn't even move my neck an inch from here to there. I used to suffer a lot. That time my *Guru-Aai* said that as she is suffering so much, which other goddess does she have now? Then she observed me closely, she saw the *mala* and said that I also have the goddess of Shiva-chi Mahalaxmi, 'As you hadn't offered her anything that time she followed you.' I was not ready to accept the Shiva-chi Mahalaxmi and fell sick for four months due to cold and fever. I used to take Crocin tablet everyday and then used to go for work.

It would seem that possession by gods/goddesses can be both a boon (*var*) and a punishment. Salve says in the interview, "God doesn't go to anybody like this. The God goes to them whom he/she likes. Those people who want (God) to possess them surely do not get that. [But also God goes to] those who don't believe in the God, who criticize the God, those who became angry at the name of the God, those who deny the God . . . God definitely follows such people." She herself is an example of someone who did not believe but, in time, came to be possessed by not one but three goddesses, although she is most dedicated to Bhavani-mata. While the gods chose their mediums, the Aradhis also choose the god they wish to institute in their houses, based on whether or not they believe, as well as more practical concerns about if they can provide for the needs of the god. Thus, Salve carries the *mala* and *pardi*, ritual ornaments, for Tuljabhavani, but not for Mahalaxmi of Kolhapur or Shiva-chi Aai.

Interview with Manasi Ghule

Manasi Ghule is a 28-year-old woman (in 2011), also belonging to the Matang caste. She lives in a house in Lohiyanagar, an inner city slum of Pune, which is next to her *maher* (her mother's house), with her husband and three children (two daughters are studying in the eighth standard, and the sixth standard and a son is in the fifth standard). About five years previous to this, she was living with her marital family in a slum in Dharavi, Mumbai, but it was demolished for the sake of real estate construction and they were offered a flat in the building. However, since they had financial difficulties (especially her brother-in-law), they sold the flat and moved back to Pune. Her husband was able to buy their present house with that money, which is a great relief for Ghule since she reports that not having their own house, having to worry about rent, etc., used to be a source of great tension (*traas*) for her. Since then her husband's job has stabilized as well, and things have been proceeding more smoothly for them. Her sister-in-law also participated in the interview and would speak for Ghule, often embellishing the details. They seemed to share a cordial and supportive relation.

Sometime after moving into their current house, during an *aarti* in a neighbor's house in the honor of a son in that family who was also undergoing possession, Ghule experienced possession for the first time. However, she was not unaware of these matters since her mother is a medium herself, to whom people come for answers to their problems. Her older brother used to be a *Potraj*[5], the tradition being carried on after his death by his son. Some months after her brother's death, Ghule fell ill and since even the doctors could not diagnose what had gone wrong; she felt that the treatment was ineffective and no improvement had been made. They began to consider other possibilities, outside of those offered by medicine. She says, "After his death we did not look after the goddess. Even my mother didn't. At that time I didn't cry at all . . . I was swollen so they took me to hospital but there was no relief, so we went to a woman who looks into matters of the goddess (*bai baghate devache*). And the woman said, 'She (Ghule) has the goddess, it will come and then only she will be fine,' so we promptly submitted to the goddess (*patkarun dile devache*). Meaning, we said that let the goddess come, we will accept it and do it properly . . . we will worship the goddess." Nonetheless, when asked directly, Manasi does not connect the loss of her brother to her first intimation of the approach of the goddess, in the way of her inexplicable sickness.

As a medium to the goddess, Ghule seems to be happy and confident. She is respected by those around her. When she is menstruating, all the work is done by everyone else in the house. When the other women are menstruating, they maintain her sanctity by voluntarily not coming close to her. Her husband will also not beat/kick her (as she claims happens in marriage) since he has to consider that the goddess resides within her (*angamadhe devaahe*). Nor will he demand sexual intercourse of her too frequently or impudently. As a young woman, Ghule is content that the gods are looking after her and her family. When she acquires a *Guru*, she will gain more knowledge (*vidya*) and will become somebody, like her mother, to whom others may come for help.

POSITIONS ON POSSESSIONS

The languages of expression in the interviews were Marathi with a smattering of Hindi. Translated into English, the terms may appear deceptively similar to regular English. However, attention to language is all the more important in a culturally different text. One instance of vernacular terms not being easily translatable is the term *hijra*. Salve speaking of Datta-bhau, says, "No, he is *Jogati*. You know those *hijras*? So he is of that kind. Those are different. They belong to Yallamma Devi . . . *hijras* are of Yallamma Devi. They break their bangles and become widow every year. They follow different science all together." The *hijra*s *do* follow a different science or logic, even of gendering, being neither male nor female.

In fact, the very word "possession" itself should make us pause. The *Aradhi* of Tuljabhavani characterizes her experience as "*angamadhe devaahe,*" the deity inhabiting the body. Possession has connotations other than this apparently simple statement. In the clinical context, for decades since the growth of psychiatric diagnostics, such phenomena were routinely diagnosed as "hysteria" involving high degree of "suggestibility" and "attention seeking" (Davar 1999). More recently, Indian psychiatrists have identified it as a distinctive, culture-specific symptomatic cluster, which they refer to as the possession syndrome (Addlakha 2008). With its entry into the lexicon of the

DSM—via the Culture-Bound Syndromes—it has been interpreted as a form of dissociation. This phenomenon has also been called, more specifically, the Devi syndrome (Sebastia 2009). The Devi syndrome can be observed in "sacred" spaces of different religious persuasions sprinkled generously throughout India that, for the lack of a term, have been grouped under "faith healing." However, this diagnostic and clinical formulation is neither descriptive, nor prescriptive; this is the fate of the "culture-bound syndromes" or in other words that which does not quite fit into the Western nosological system of pathology. These new syndromes however still get accommodated into the psychiatric lexicon far too easily as petty variations of more universal conditions. An in-depth analysis of these cultural patterns is required to explore their differences from the model proposed by psychiatric diagnostics, for even in the domain of the "abnormal," these do not quite fit. On the other hand, being so neglected by the American Psychiatric Association may not be entirely a bad thing, since the phenomenon does not get immediately reduced to a psychiatric abnormality. Before the setting up of containment of the phenomenon in carefully defended categories of illness and disorder, we can still ask some different questions, which may open up another imagination of psychosocial health or distress.

Psychoanalytically, though, possession has been understood as an episode of neurotic outbreak. Freud in *A Seventeenth-Century Demonological Neurosis* (1957 [1923]) is reading the phenomena of possession, indeed all religious experience, as strategies of the neurotic to access some safety and comfort from threat, either internal, as in wishes that cannot be owned up to, or external, as acceptance of a cultural prohibition on seeking out unlawful libidinal satisfaction. He starts with the declaration that the neuroses of earlier times came in "demonological trappings" and goes on to explain:

> The states of possession correspond to our neuroses, for the explanation of which we once more have recourse to psychical powers. In our eyes, the demons are bad and reprehensible wishes, derivatives of instinctual impulses that have been repudiated and repressed. We merely eliminate the projection of these mental entities into the external world which the middle ages carried out; instead, we regard them as having arisen in the patient's internal life, where they have their abode. (Freud 1957 [1923]: 3996)

For Freud, possession is simply a case of pathological neurosis, the projecting of an inner reality into the world, which was a commonly accepted exposition of the distress experienced by the person in times of yore, but has since then been surmounted by scientific explanations as offered by psychoanalysis. The question for us is that, in the post-colonial consciousness, where both psychiatry and psychoanalysis are not without their problems of translation and representation, how does one look at possession, specifically Devi-possession?

THE HOME AND THE WORLD

Within the set of interviews presented here, *Aradhis* or the women possessed by the Devi experienced possession, in time, as a benevolent relation with their resident "spirits," while the reactions of family members and neigbors around them were different, which affected and altered their own experience of possession. They identified themselves as belonging to the Matang *jati,* identified by the Indian State as a Scheduled Caste. According to Dr. Machhindra Dnyanu Sakate in his unpublished doctoral thesis *A sociological study of Matang community in Maharashtra* (2010), *Matang*[6] is considered to be etymologically related to *Mang*,[7] its Sankritic root. He states that "the Mangs who were adivasis earlier and who lived a tribal life quite for sometime and who were settled at the outskirts of the villages were incorporated in the list of Scheduled Castes in 1961" (Sakate 2010). Matang religious practices seem to contain several indications of their *adivasi* origin: "various practises and beliefs in deities, Bhagat, impact of magic, method of sacrifice, method of last rites after the death, all this goes very close to adivasi life style" (Sakate 2010). Indeed the Matang women have a sizable number of *Aradhis* amongst them and the festival honoring Tuljabhavani in the month of April sees huge numbers of pilgrims from this community making their way to Tuljapur.

Salve and Ghule found social support and encouragement in their journeys as mediums to the goddess Tuljabhavani. They were prepared culturally for the experience of possession, especially since possession brings the body to the public domain, breaking gendered barriers. Before, during, and after possession, the warmth of a helping hand is required and these women receive it from the women around them. For instance, when Ghule is under the throes of possession, her sister-in-law will straighten her *saree* and open her hair to ease her movement. Like grooming preparations for a wedding or other such public occasion, women assist in preparing the body for the possession. There are usually people around to ensure that the Aradhi comes to no harm.

There are various ways of looking at the phenomenon of the body in a trance. Trance for the Aradhis, very often, involves rigorous exertion of the body, and many Aradhis report a feeling of being "refreshed" by the experience (Davar and Lohokare 2009). At the end of trance or possession, the body has been put through strenuous exercise and there is a feeling of both lightness and fatigue. A burst of concentrated body activity has the beneficial effects of trauma release and the positive emotional changes related to it.

There is also the need for a *Guru* in becoming a medium fit for the gods. The *Guru* is one, in Ghule's words, "[O]ne who is good, who has knowledge, and one who teaches well." In the case of Salve this is the presence of her *Guru-Aai*, a spiritual guide who is usually an older woman more experienced in the matters of possession. The *Guru-Aai* directs her disciple in the matters of the gods as well as *vidya* (knowledge or science), and the disciple responds with reverence as well as *dakshina* (a tribute offered to the Guru/Guru-Aai for their teaching). When Salve was undergoing an episode of possession for the second time, lasting for more than a week, it was her *Guru-Aai* who diagnosed the nature of the affliction; it was another goddess inhabiting and dominating Salve in order to receive her due homage. In other circumstances, where people do not have recourse to such explanations, Salve could well have been referred to a doctor—a general physician or even a psychiatrist. The presence of a second mother, in the absence of her own mother, stood Salve in good stead. Similarly Ghule, who had not yet found her *Guru*, had her own mother who was already knowledgeable about the ways of possession. So, when Ghule fell ill, although they travelled through the medical route, they could look for other explanations for the disease and accept that it was being caused because of the ways of the goddess.

In this manner, a new social organization occurs inside the community around the one possessed. It is a kind of sisterhood within the women of the community, which also takes into consideration the Indian concern of wisdom in relation to age and thus the importance given to the *Guru-Aai*. The *Guru-Aai* and the other women in the community are there to support the one possessed during moments when the goddess descends and takes control of the body of the medium. Thus, possession creates around it a new network of social support and local knowledge.

In the case of Salve and Ghule, being possessed provided them with something valuable in another way. Their resident spirits are venerable female goddesses and thus not coming into conflict with their husbands (or the patriarchal world that the signifier "husband" stands for). Salve had in fact left her husband more than thirty years previous to this and had fended for herself and her family on her own all this time. Her status as an *Aradhi* allowed her to exist in society as a *savashani,* as married to the god, especially since Tuljabhavani and Mahalaxmi are both symbolic representations of women who are married and performing their household responsibilities. It facilitated her movement in a society that privileges married women. Salve says that she does not usually attend big functions because people say a lot of things, unless she is invited as *savashana*. In this way, being the medium for the gods increased her social capital, just as Ghule's possession by the goddess ameliorated her position in the family and the community.

This draws our attention to the relation of the self of the one possessed with the larger community and is important in understanding two processes; one, the position of the possessed one in society, which includes how the vicissitudes of gendering is negotiated, as well as the more important question of how the experience of possession increases or decreases the social capital of the medium (this is something we have been analyzing in the narratives of the women up to this point); two, the ways in which a community organizes the experience of distress and the management of crisis. How does a community deal with individual expression, eccentricity, personal or social calamity? We must also turn our attention to the function the one possessed plays in the community.

Ghule speaks of the way in which the goddess's shrine in her mother's house becomes the meeting place for many women who come with different wishes, "Like mother's colleagues come here and pray like, 'may this happen with me or that happen.' Then after they pray and when they go from here, it (the wish) gets fulfilled. Then they come of their own will and tell me, 'I said this to the goddess and it came true.' [And] so on their own, they bring coconuts and all as offerings for the goddess."

Thus, while there are differences in individual experiences of possession, there is also the shared experience of being the one marked, even specially chosen, by the Other World where beings of preternatural status reside. This is also something that needs to be taken on board to understand the phenomena of possession; what we are referring to here is a human search for the esoteric and extraordinary, and to bring it into the fold of everyday and ordinary experience. What emerges is the way in which the mundane and the transcendental are very much this worldly, rather than other worldly. That gap is somewhat bridged through their grounded experiences that bring the self, other, community, body, mind, spirit, etc., and all such divisions into the same shared performance arena. Possession is very mundane in that sense, blending into the everyday routines of the woman, family, and her local community. A hyper-separation of the human and the divine is rejected in these narratives of possession. For us, what has been interesting is the very "worldliness" of gods, angels, *jinns*, demons, spirits, *devis*, etc., giving a more habitual ritualized scope of incorporating the moral and spiritual, maybe also creative, ways of dealing with life. Faith *is* healing in itself, and Devi-possession is one moment in the practice of faith-based healing. Faith healing, in turn, is part of the corpus of the indigenous traditions in India geared toward understanding and responding to pain, distress, and crisis. Belying the assumption that such practices occur only in "backward, illiterate, rural or remote areas where there is no development," they are prevalent at large in urban spaces.

TECHNOLOGIES OF THE SELF

What connects the narratives of the *Aradhis*—Salve and Ghule—is that being possessed allows them to feel that there is someone who accompanies them wherever they go and can support them in whatever challenges of life they face. Their resident spirit is a buffer between them and the misfortunes of life and the spite of people around them. Salve expresses it very well,

> I feel that I have somebody for me. What I can't talk or share with anybody, I can share in front of god. Sitting in front of you I can't talk to you but I can talk over there (in front of god), the thoughts I can share with her (god). Every word of mine doesn't become into reality, out of 10 times it may be true only for once. If I am suffering a lot and if I say 10 words, then out of that one word will come true. Or if I say something spontaneously to somebody, then it might come true. [But] it is not the case that every utterance of mine will come true. God has to look after the whole world, we are not the only ones.

It is particularly interesting to note that each of these women is more than one *in herself* through her experience of possession. That is to say that her experience of her own selfhood is manifestly plural; Davar puts this as the *Aradhi* being a 'virtual society of one person.'[8] The medium is hosting one or more spirit/deity and the relation of her conscious self to each inhabitant spirit/deity is different. In fact, many mediums really do host more than one spirit or deity within. To be inhabited by other perceived beings gives a relief from self-responsibility all the time. To be somebody else, a more exalted, powerful being, to occupy another ego for a while, is all part of the selfing process. This was clear from Salve's story; she hosted three goddesses inside her body but had dedicated herself to the service of Bhavani-Aai first and was less likely to perform all the rituals and *puja*s for Lakshmi-Aai and Shiva-chi Aai who had come to her later. Thus, she would exert herself more for Tuljabhavani but her expectations of this goddess were also more demanding. From this we can imagine that the multiple selves of the one possessed are also constantly in flux or are in transition depending on which stage she has reached in realizing and expressing her relation to the Self. There have been several theories proposed to discuss the relation of one to the Self; what it amounts to is, in Michel Foucault's words, a "Technology of the Self."

Greek Askesis

Foucault calls the technology of the self that "which permit individuals to effect by their own means or with the help of others a certain number of operations on their own bodies and souls, thoughts, conduct, and way of being, so as to transform themselves in order to attain a certain state of happiness, purity, wisdom, perfection, or immortality" (Foucault 1997). According to him, there were two Greek principles in late antiquity that, although different, blend into each other:

- *Epimelesthai sautou* or "to take care of yourself," "the concern with self," and
- *Gnothi sauton* or "know yourself."

Over time, in the west, these two principles were sundered and the second stricture of *gnothi sauton* or "know the self" passed on into philosophy through the Christian elucidation of it as exomologesis or "a ritual of recognizing oneself as a sinner and a penitent" and thus the condition of knowledge was asceticism. This is one route, while Foucault would like us to consider one more that travels through "care of the self." He says,

> In Christianity asceticism always refers to a certain renunciation of the self and of reality because most of the time your self is a part of that reality you have to renounce in order to get access to another level of reality. This move to attain the renunciation of the self distinguishes Christian asceticism.
>
> In the philosophical tradition dominated by Stoicism, *askesis* means not renunciation but the progressive consideration of self, or mastery over oneself, obtained not through the renunciation of reality but through the acquisition and assimilation of truth. It has as its final aim not preparation for another reality but access to the reality of this world. (Foucault 1997: 238–39)

Foucault is inviting us to consider *askesis* as it comes to us from the Stoics, as the philosophical burden of the subject, rather than the Delphic pronouncement of "Know thyself" that becomes the theological burden under Christianity. *Askesis* does not necessarily mean the practice of self-denial. The technology of the self that came to be almost exclusively practiced as self-renunciation was the development of Christian asceticism. However, in its other Greek context, the word simply meant *exercise*, as in training, practice, or development. Foucault points out that exercising meant perfecting oneself, developing one's capacities, becoming who one is.

Buddhist Askesis

Obeyesekere (2002) develops the notion of the Buddhist *askesis* as a way to both enrich and challenge Western thought, not because Western thought can be overthrown in the social sciences to usher in the era of Asia by a simple turn to culture, but because it can be revised and ameliorated. The Buddhist ideal, mirrored in the Buddha myth, is theorized by Obeyesekere[9] as a renunciatory one in which deep meditative asceses[10] open the way to salvation (2002: 150). But what would social sciences do with salvation? It is necessary here to disaggregate the concept of salvation and the actual phenomenon. Obeyesekere uses Freudian psychoanalysis and Buddhist religion to open up conceptuality, which is the very *stuff* of the social sciences.

According to Obeyesekere, the Buddha gave "primacy to knowledge acquired through concentration which requires the abandonment and emptying of the mind of discursive knowledge and its re-adoption after the experience is over when he has to describe his experiences to his disciples or congregation" (2006: 20). The Buddha is a perfected being who willingly chooses to live in the lower realm of the humans so as to impart his knowledge revealed to him in visions, first when he observed the reality of the world and its suffering through his own eyes in his foray outside the royal palace, and then as a mendicant meditating under the Bodhi tree (the Peepal tree). These events are two awakenings—one to the external reality and the other to an internal reality, both of which come through the experience of visions. Obeyeskere is conceptualizing that in the visionary experience of the Buddha, there is a move from "it-thinking" to "I-thinking." He turns to Nietzsche (1956: 24) to conceptualize this move:

> A thought comes when 'it' wishes and not when 'I' wish, so that it is a falsification of the facts of the case to say that the subject 'I' is the condition of the predicate 'think.' It thinks: but that this 'it' is precisely the famous old 'ego' is, to put it mildly, only a supposition, an assertion, and assuredly not an immediate certainty. (Obeseyekere 2006: 21)

There is an assumption that the "I" thinks and therefore there is the positing of an ego as the agent that performs this function. It-thinking is characteristic of only certain vital moments, like dreams and visions, hallucinations even. In moments, it-thinking is like the function of the unconscious itself, but it-thinking is the conceptuality of thinking itself, the thought of the thought. This is the condition of the subject, which Lacan speaks of but in different terms: "Even this between-the-two that opens up for us the apprehension of the unconscious is of concern to us only in as much as it is designated for us, through the instructions Freud left us, as that of which the subject has to take possession" (Lacan 1977: 72). But what is "it"? It is not a being or an entity, nor a location or a structure, very much like the mind. It is a function that happens—it happens, thinking happens—outside of the subject's agency, or rather that agency isn't the discourse of the subject[11]. This challenges the Cartesian *cogito, ergo sum*: I think, therefore I am. At the least, moments of it-thinking interrupt the (Cartesian) subject of its certainty of "being," a being that is premised on the condition of cogitation or conscious thinking. Obeyesekere's intervention in this field, through the example of the Buddha, thus displaces the conscious subject of the Enlightenment but also the unconscious subject of Psychoanalysis.

Subaltern Askesis

This section argues that when psychoanalysis comes to India it confronts something that does not conform to the canonical versions of religion, which psychoanalysis has always left out of its analyses. It shows that psychoanalysis comes face-to-face with not Spirit but Self; not the transcendental Spirit but the care of the self; not asceticism in the Christian tradition but subaltern *askesis*. This is perhaps an opening to chart a relation between psychoanalysis and religion in the cultural context of India, which is marked by a sensibility that cuts across the usual ways of looking at religion and science, which have become as if the questions of the East and West, respectively. We have tried to read Devi-possession as a form of subaltern[12] *askesis.*

The Aradhi's possession of/by the Devi does not need to take recourse to renunciation of desires and other earthly considerations but to negotiate with them; rather than casting away her human bonds to other people, she becomes a vital force in the community.

Thus, the Buddha as the Awakened One who moves between it-thinking and I-thinking is a far cry from the narratives of the ones discussed in section II, but we can see that in the case of the narratives of Salve and Ghule, (Devi) possession is caught up in the discourses of mental health and illness. Juxtaposed on the tropes of the "mad" and the "divine," how can we understand possession? Sudhir Kakar invokes the transcendental and mystical aspects of "the spiritual" in *Mad and Divine: Spirit and Psyche in the Modern World* (2008). Transcendence has been traditionally ascribed to the great "Awakened Ones" like the Buddha or Osho. The Awakened Ones, to borrow the term for Obeyesekere (2012), have grasped the reality of *karma* and rebirth, and use it to bring our attention to the momentary point in time and space when we have the choice to act virtuously, thereby changing forever the course of moral actions. In his work on such personages, Kakar positions the psychic as against the spiritual, which

> "Incorporates the transformative possibilities of the human psyche: total love without a trace of hate, selflessness carved out of the psyche's normal self-centeredness, a fearlessness that is not counter-phobic reaction to the fear that is innate part of the human psyche. Yet spiritual transformation is not a once forever achievement, even in case of enlightened spiritual masters and saints. It remains constantly under threat of the darker forces of the psyche. One is never *not* human. (2008: 5, italics in original)

In the narratives of the *Aradhis*, one could trace the negotiation between the sacred and the profane being enacted, which is also the move between spiritual striving for transcendence and the human condition of being bogged down by the "darker forces of the psyche." In the case of Salve and Ghule, they would casually refer to the devotional work of an *Aradhi*; mediums to the goddess must devote a great deal of time and labor to the care of the goddess, from dressing her to feeding her, sometimes for several hours every day.

The realm of the sacred demands exact care and promptitude. Furthermore, the *pujas* and rituals may require financial resources that are already scarce within the family. There are also other prohibitions and restrictions the devotee must adhere to; the medium may not remarry, and during holy times of the year not indulge in sex with their husbands. Menstruation in women can cause a great deal of disturbance in their lives. Ghule tells us what happens if she inadvertently touches another woman who is menstruating:

> If suppose someone is menstruating and touches me, then what happens is that my body starts itching, my head will ache, I will behave like mad, I will fight again and again, will not talk properly to anyone till they bathe me with rose water, *gomutra* [cow's urine], neem leaves, *haldi kumkum* [turmeric]. Then I feel very light, relieved that everything is gone.

This is the realm of the profane. Even the shadow of the woman menstruating must not fall on the idol of the goddess, for the sake of maintaining her purity and sanctity. The *Aradhi* shifts between moments of transcendence (the experience of possession by the goddess) and moments of immanence (menstruation as defiling). Her transcendence is never complete since the monthly cycle of menstruation will bring back to the mundane matters of this world; "one is never *not* human." Nevertheless, her attempt at transcendence is so valuable to herself and the community that the women around her will voluntarily not intrude upon her when they are menstruating.

Kakar brings the psychic battle within the subject to the spiritual quest of the human. He distinguishes between "unitive imagination" and "connective imagination"; unitive imagination succeeds at uniting the knower and the known and constitutes "an end point of a spectrum, accessible only to individuals with extraordinary spiritual gifts" (Kakar 2008: 154) but it is connective imagination that is the attraction of religious practices in which "[an] imaginative world is created [that] is both shared and public in that it is based upon, guided and formed by the symbolic, iconic network of [. . .] religious culture" (p. 155). Thus connective imagination can be linked to the phenomenon of possession that is an integral part of everyday occurrences of India, reminding us that there exists "a god of small things" as well as subaltern practices of possession in a slum in Pune.

Nonetheless, Kakar sees spirituality as a possible expression of creativity and wonder. However, for the practice to be *asketic*, transformation of the self is meant not only as the result of the quest but the *ethical* condition for the subject-medium of possession. What if the experiencing of possession of the *Aradhi* is their relation to the question of Self and not Spirit? Within the West, there are two trajectories as Foucault has shown—one that goes the route of asceticism and will contend with the concept of the Spirit, the other that follows the route of *askesis* and will deal with the concept of the Self. We would like to suggest that these cultural and religious practices living and thriving in one corner of the East are one form of *askesis* that is geared toward transformation of the Self of the medium-subject to access the truth of her being in the world. If *askesis* is transformatory work on the self, the *Aradhi* is performing this exercise by hosting more than one self and speaking in other voices, which also means to host the differences and contradictions multiplicity brings. The Self of the *Aradhi* is as chaotic as the body politic of the nation.

CONCLUSION

Does the subaltern practice of Devi-possession come within the fold of religion? This is a religion without a canon or the text; the *Aradhi* herself speaks to the community in the voice of the Goddess. In this woman-to-woman relation, Aradhi–Guru-aai–Devi, the priestly class cannot intervene. The power dynamics between Aradhis and their husbands are reconfigured. There is another relation to the Other and the Self. At once, the practice sets up a religion without Religion as it has been understood, as well as a politics of relating that will not become the politics of the University, Science, or the State. It will require perhaps the birthing of a psychoanalysis that can respond to the woman's work on the self, the care of the self she is evolving. This is a psychoanalysis that will need to orient itself to technologies of the self hitherto overlooked. Or is psychoanalysis itself a technology of the self, as Foucault (1982/2005) suggests in *Hermeneutics of the Subject*? How does psychoanalysis make sense of subaltern askesis in India? What are the conceptual detours psychoanalysis itself requires to make sense of such subaltern askesis? What psychoanalysis does subaltern askesis give birth to?

NOTES

1. The interviews were conducted between August and September, 2011, by Deepali Deshmukh, and Swati Shinde through the help of an interview guide prepared by the co-author of this chapter, and as a part of a larger project on "Mental Health and Development." The project took into consideration the profile of the respondents from basic demographics to a more nuanced inquiry into the respondent's social network. The interview guide focused on the journey the respondent underwent in her experience of getting possessed, in terms of the personal (bodily and emotional), the familial, and the communitarian; the attempt was to understand how the experience of possession interrupted and intervened in the life of the respondent, its positive and/or

negative consequences as well as the ordinary and/or extraordinary aspects of being possessed by a being considered superior to the self. There was also a preliminary attempt to tease out the legends and myths that surround such beings and the part they play in human affairs. This chapter discusses some of the ideas that were exchanged between the authors to this chapter, over several months.

2. Names have been changed to protect identities of those cited in the interview.

3. The goddess Bhavani whose temple is in Tuljapur, Maharashtra, is called Tuljabhavani by devotees.

4. The *Jogatis* in Maharashtra are devotees to the goddess Yellamma, a *Hijra* community whose tradition of being dedicated to the goddess has been likened to the *Devadasi* tradition.

5. *Potraj* in Maharashtra are devotees of the goddess Lakshmi who perform acts of devotion in public spaces or community events to earn a living.

6. "The real meaning of the term Matang," according to researcher [Sakate], "is the son of the earth—the one who is brave and powerful. However, with the passage of time the meaning is degraded and Mang is taken to be the one who indulges into unfair deeds and the one who asks for food" (Sakate, 2010).

7. Sakate (2010) recounts the origin myth of the Matang people: "A myth goes like this, when the lord Brahma started creating the universe, his work was hampered by the winged horses. Consequently the making of universe was impeded. By that time the Lord Mahadeo created the first 'Mang.' He was 'Madhya' [medium] after which the whole universe was created. In short, the Mangs have contributed in the creation of universe and he was created by the Lord Mahadeo himself." This myth requires to be fleshed out, the task of another research project in the future.

8. Voice-hearing people who have supportive or comforting voices do speak about the "blessing" of being more than one within oneself, and to have "on call" support so to speak!

9. This is the form of Buddhism popular in Sri Lanka, more particularly the Sinhalese.

10. Obeyeskere has styled the spelling as *ascesis.* However we will be using *askesis,* from the Foucauldian tradition, also to differentiate conceptually askesicism and asceticism. The Buddhist *askesis* is ascetic and renunciatory according to Obeyeskere. Asceses thus seems to combine askesicism and asceticism.

11. For instance, Oedipus's predicament is not an issue of agency. In trying to escape the prophecy of the Oracle, Oedipus fulfills it. To see this as the problem of whether the human has free will or not misses the psychoanalytic moment of the unconscious.

12. Subaltern, in the words of Gayatri Chakravorty Spivak, is a position without identity, or where social lines of mobility, being elsewhere, do not permit the formation of a recognizable basis of action (*An Aesthetic Education in the Era of Globalization*; Harvard University Press; 2012: 431). She warns us that we should not be too quick to classify the subaltern: "Subaltern content takes on identity, names itself "people." People becomes a slogan too quickly. [. . .] outside of such politics, subalternization does not stop" (p. 432–433). I heed this warning as that subalternity cannot be made into a political call for action, or at least not the political in any conventional sense.

REFERENCES

Addlakha, R. *Deconstructing mental illness: An ethnography of psychiatry, women and the family.* New Delhi: Zubaan, 2008.

Davar, B. V. and Lohokare, M. "Recovering from Psychosocial Traumas: The Place of Dargahs in Maharashtra." *Economic and Political Weekly* 44(2009): 60–68.

Davar, B.V. 1999. *Mental health of Indian women. A feminist agenda*. Sage Publications, New Delhi. 1999.

Foucault, M. *The hermeneutics of the subject: Lectures at the College de France 1981–1982*. Burchell, G. (Trans.). London: Palgrave Macmillan, 2005.

Foucault, M. "Ethics: Subjectivity and Truth." In T*he essential works of Michel Foucault (1954-1984)*, Robert Hurley (Trans.), edited by Paul Rabineau, New Press: New York Press, 1997.

Freud, S. "A Seventeenth-Century Demonological Neurosis." In *The standard edition of the complete psychological works of Sigmund Freud*, edited by James Strachey (Trans.). London: Hogarth, 1957 [1923].

Freud, S. *The future of an illusion.* London: Penguin, 2008 [1927].

Kakar, S. *Mad and divine: Spirit and psyche in the modern world.* New Delhi: Penguin, 2008.

Lacan, J. *The four fundamental concepts of psychoanalysis: Seminar XI.* London: W. W. Norton, 1977.

Nietzsche, F. *Beyond good and evil: Prelude to a philosophy of the future.* R. J. Holligdale (Trans.). New Delhi: Penguin, 2003 [1956].

Obeyesekere, G. "Asian Studies and the Discourse of the Human Sciences." In *What about Asia: Revisiting Asian Studies,* 15–29, edited by Josine Stremmelaar and Paul van der Velde. Amsterdam: Amsterdam University Press, 2006.

Obeyesekere, G. *Imagining karma: Ethical transformation in Amerindian, Buddhist, and Greek rebirth.* Berkeley and Los Angeles, California: University of California Press, 2002.

Obeyesekere, G. *The awakened ones: Phenomenology of visionary experience.* New York: Columbia University Press, 2012.

Sakate, M. D. *A sociological study of Matang community in Maharashtra.* Doctoral dissertation. 2010. Available on Indian ETD Repository @ INFLIBNET. Retrieved from http://hdl.handle.net/10603/10010.

Sebastia, B. *Restoring mental health in India: Pluralistic therapies and concepts.* New Delhi: Oxford University Press, 2009.

Spivak, G. C. *An aesthetic education in the era of globalization.* Cambridge, Massachusetts: Harvard University Press, 2012.

Chapter Three

Of Mothers and Therapists

Dreaming the Indian Infant

Urvashi Agarwal

This chapter brings to focus two ideas central to the work with patients with severe pathology, for example, psychotic and borderline states.[1] Before I put forth the ideas, I would like to add that I see this chapter as a continuation and an elaboration of an earlier paper, The uncomfortable subject: Observing the Indian girl child (Agarwal & Paiva 2014) which focused on an experience of infant observation. The paper explored how the observation of the mother-daughter couple brought up acute emotions for the observer and how she was able to use these feelings to understand not only what was happening between the mother and the infant, but also could come to an understanding of her own infantile parts. That paper, apart from highlighting the girl child in India, touched upon the idea of the formless, nonverbal, infantile feelings and the importance and value of counter-transference in working with these kinds of feelings. I also see this work as a precursor of, and a foundation to, a work which would address the centrality of the body, and how it is through our bodily experiences that we begin to get located in our minds. I will briefly come back to this point toward the end of this chapter.

In this chapter I will explicate the idea that infantile feelings are raw, formless, acute, and cannot be represented. They often elude language and, in this sense, the body and bodily expressions and enactments become the only way to present, represent, and access them. The second idea that I will take up is that of the value and integrity of counter-transference in working with borderline and psychotic states. These states are regressed states, and the anxieties and needs of the patient are heavily infantile. In order to make sense of, engage, contain, and possibly work through some of these feelings, the therapist must not only be in touch with her own infantile feelings, and be constantly attuned to her own bodily reactions and responses, but also be open to *not knowing,* and allow herself to be changed by the therapeutic process that takes place between her and the patient.

For this, I will describe how the experience of infant observation helped me understand the nature of infantile anxieties and feelings and come closer to them in my own self. This experience helped me to make sense of, and changed my work with my patient(s) who presented psychotic and borderline states. I will describe some of my clinical work with the patient(s) to show how, when I became aware of my own infantile parts, I was able to receive those patients differently, and more importantly, show how work with them changed me as well.

THE INFANT AND THE BODY

As infants, the care that we receive and need is mostly of our physical and bodily self, in terms of feeding, bathing, diaper changes, and sleep. In carrying out these tasks, the mother or the primary caregiver holds the baby, soothes her, touches her, and it is through these interactions between the mother and the baby, that they come to recognize each other. Thus at the earliest stage, the body is primary and is the medium of communication between the mother and the baby, for example through the skin and the mouth. Thus what we remember is not images but textures and sounds and smells and tastes and these remain embedded in us. These memories are bodily memories, hard to access.

One of the foremost thinkers about early infancy is Donald Winnicott (1991). Winnicott, a pediatrician trained as a psychoanalyst, has described infancy in detail, exploring the unique relationship between the mother and the infant, and its importance for healthy emotional development and the maternal function. Winnicott writes that the self of the infant develops through a handling and holding of the infant such that the psychical and the somatic become intricately linked. For Winnicott, the fantasy, abstract ideas, and the self all had somatic origins. "[T]he basis of self forms on the fact of the body which, being alive, not only has shape but which also functions" (Goldman 1993, p. xvi). When I read Winnicott, what becomes clear is how the somatic and the psychical are not separate and how not only does the somatic feed the psychical but "every function is elaborated in the psyche, and even at the beginning there is fantasy belonging to the excitement and the experience of feeding" (Winnicott 1991, p. 53). His writings bring to us how infants might experience their bodily needs. For example, he says that at the time when the baby is hungry, "he is a bundle of discontent, a human being to be sure, but one who has raging lions and tigers inside him. And is almost certainly scared of his own feelings . . . if you fail him it must feel to him as if the wild beasts will gobble him up" (Winnicott 1991, p. 23).

Thus, Winnicott describes the infant as a bundle of instincts and it is only through the relationship with the facilitating presence of maternal care that the infant begins to develop his ego and eventually a self and relationship to another. In the beginning, the mother, by her perfect attunement to the infant, allows the baby to deal with the unthinkable anxiety that it stays at the edge of because of the experience of an infiniteness of the anxiety. Slowly, the matrix of the maternal environment allows the infant to begin to deal with the failures of attunement, and it is in these gaps that reality potentially emerges.

THE PSYCHOTIC AND BORDERLINE STATES, INFANTILE FEELINGS AND THE BODY

In the earliest phase of life, the infant and the mother form an inseparable dyad. For the infant, any break in continuity of its being, whether it is hunger or any other kind of impingement, is experienced as acute anxiety. This anxiety is too much for the infant to bear and it is the mother's body and mind that serve as containers for his anxiety. The warmth of the mother's body, the textures, and the smells, all serve a containing function. Andre Green refers to the mother's body as a "framing structure" (Deloumel 2013) that contains and gradually allows for the development of thinking, and for a thought process to develop. The infant projects his or her needs and anxieties onto the mother, who holds these for the infant and reflects feelings back to the infant, in a way that she or he is not overwhelmed by them. This communication between the mother and the infant is a felt communication. It is this that the infant internalizes slowly, and this forms the basis of healthy emotional development, and builds in the infant, and later the adult, the capacity to manage feelings and anxieties.

In my experience with patients who present psychotic and borderline states, there is usually a history of disturbance in early relationships. These disturbances can take various forms, whether it is premature separation from the mother, separations which were felt to be abandonments or rejection of the self. For others, despite the maternal presence, the mother's mind was inaccessible; something that is often true with mothers suffering from postpartum depression. In such cases, there is no active engagement with the mother and the mother is unable to hold the infant in her mind. Without this sense of being held, not just physically but psychically as well, the infant is left to manage his or her own anxieties. At the same time, many times the mother's presence is overbearing, such that the child continues to be an extension of the mother in a way that his or her own self fails to take shape.

The nature of infantile feelings is such that, though they are present in all of us, they are nearly impossible to represent. However, in working with psychotic and borderline states, we find ourselves in the presence of these feelings. Winnicott has written about this and he says "the intensity of infant feelings recurs in the intensity of the suffering associated with psychotic symptoms. The infant's preoccupation with feelings of a certain type, at a certain moment, reappears in the ill person's preoccupation with fear of grief." (Winnicott 1991, p. 50).

In my clinical work, I have found that for some patients to put into words what they are grieving is impossible. Very often, these patients come with dissociated states or blankness and an inability to be alive to experiences and feelings. The experience of the loss itself remains unlived, undreamt.

Working with patients who are non-neurotic is fraught with many difficulties. I have had experience of long-term work with two such patients and a shorter ongoing relationship with two more patients, all of whom can be considered to fall in the category of borderline and psychotic. Here I am using the definition of "borderline" defined by Green (Kohon 1999, pg. 37) as the patient who belongs neither with the neurotics nor with the psychotics. Due to constraints of confidentiality, I am unable to present in full my experience with these patients. This was also my first engagement with anxieties which were psychotic in nature and through the work, I grew much in my understanding of not only these states but of myself as well.

In this work and through my subsequent engagements with these states, I came upon a particular fantasy in these patients. They find it difficult to have a relationship with another person, and often the relationship that is formed is tenacious, denies the reality of another person, and is based on a fantasy of fusion with another. Separation is impossible to conceive, and there is a great fear of it, as if separation means a loss of parts or an annihilation of themselves. At the same time, there is a fear of loss of identity through fusion, and dependency is terrifying to acknowledge and accept. The experience of maternal containment, of mirroring, as well as curiosity and engagement—all essential for us to *know* the self and to develop a relationship with our own subjectivity—were missing for these people. Further, in order to relate to other people, it is important to recognize one's own subjectivity and to see the other person too as a subjective being and not as an object. Thus, each separation, whether it is the end of a session, or a vacation break, is hard to negotiate and can be felt as rejection and abandonment. The security that the other will keep them in mind is not there, and the internalization of the therapist's continuing presence also takes a long time to develop, if ever.

Along with the fantasy of fusion, there exists a fantasy of omnipotent control. For example, just as we imagine the baby to have the fantasy that it has created the breast to meet its need, the fantasy here is that the therapist is, and should be, available at all times. Contact outside of sessions is often sought. In such cases, establishment of boundaries and maintaining the setting becomes foremost and it is most often attacked. Any reminder, whether implicit through the setting or stated in words, that the therapist and the patient are two separate beings is terrifying and can lead to anger and rage, often expressed through devaluation of the work and the therapist, and through missing of sessions.

The self, as well as the other, are experienced as split into good and bad and thus there are constant shifts between idealization and devaluation. There is also a movement between experiencing the self as bad, toxic, and having paranoid anxieties of being attacked, watched, and manipulated by the outside world. Often these stem from perceiving one's own feelings as acute and overwhelming—since the capacity to contain and hold these anxieties is not developed—having never had a good experience of containment. I also feel that these patients experience their own feelings as so destructive that they feel convinced that they could destroy the other. At the same time, they might believe that their existence is only to the extent of being an object to the other, to being used. At the root of this fantasy is often the experience of having had to deal with the mother's own overwhelming and unheld anxieties and feelings, and the infant-child had to adapt their being in a way that suited and held the mother, rather than it being the other way around.

I realize that patients with borderline and/or psychotic features are formidably attuned to the emotions of the other and their ability to identify the other's feelings is nearly uncanny. Whether it was sometimes my feelings of anger or irritability, or when I would become defensive against the questions about me, the patient would know the feeling. Yet there is a near blindness to one's own feelings. What I did realize was that rather than protect the analytic space from these emotions and feelings, and to keep them away, I had to use them as tools to understand the patient's world of emotions, which was without words and had no form. Many patients, especially those who are neurotic in their presentation, have a story to tell about their lives, memories to share and remember, and some sense of themselves that they carry. However, psychotic individuals have lost the relationship to their own inner world, such that what they present is a certain *blankness*—about their feelings as well as memories. The feelings that I was experiencing in the sessions were often feelings that the patients were unable to feel, or were feeling but were unable to know or recognize as theirs, and to accept them.

Every individual is unique. Even if we might categorize a patient, his or her struggle will remain unique. Thus, what gets evoked in us with each person is different and unique. I may have explored many parts of myself and yet find myself in unknown territory with every new patient. In my work I discovered my own states of blankness, withdrawal, and a desire to numb myself to the onslaught of emotions. I always had difficulty in trusting my knowledge of my emotions and, when one of the patients came for the first time with the presenting problem of *not feeling,* I knew deep down that this work would be a challenge for me, for someone like me who too struggled with not feeling. However, at a conscious level it seems that I was unable to recognize the similarity that lay between the patient and me. How could we be similar? Now, I see how many of the fears and fantasies I have come upon are fantasies I can identify in myself.

At the beginning, I often found myself at a loss. The setting and rules often became a source of refuge. At other times, I found the therapeutic space to be like a battlefield. Through my hurt, anger, sadness, confusions, boredom, and feelings of being intruded on and manipulated, I realized how often we also play into the patient's fantasy of being available and to meet every need. My defensiveness also arose from my guilt, as if the patient's accusations that I was not good enough, that I was like the devil and was purposely torturing them, were actually true. As if I did have the power to give all that they need. Writing on the dependency needs present in such patients, H. Searles puts it as a wish for an omnipotent control that leads to feelings of grandiosity such that what the patient might be saying is "if you would only give me enough, I could assume my rightful place of omnipotence in the Universe" rather than saying "I need you as a little child needs its mother." (Searles 1965, p. 121)

Searles also says that "to the schizophrenic there is no distinction between feeling and acting in the sense that he assumes that a dependency desire on his part, for instance, to suck on the therapist's breasts or penis will inevitably lead him to attempt this in action. He senses that the therapist would respond with hostility to such a move." (Searles 1965, p. 121) Taking from Searles's thought, I would say that there were many occasions in my sessions when fantasies did not remain fantasies for the patient, and were felt as concretely real. My understanding of many of the fantasies, anxieties, and feelings that I understood and have elaborated above, came through how I felt in the sessions with the patient, where the transference was heavily erotic and the needs acutely infantile. The feelings that were felt by me, my own and the patient's dissociated, undigested feelings, were felt even before I could come to thinking about them. The patient's need for and demand on me was often physical, in terms of touch: a need to touch and to be touched. I did not remain a whole person but it was my parts of my body, clothes, and objects, that became erotically charged, and which I saw as the desire for the mother's body, without there being a representation of it.

Another patient brought abstract thoughts, philosophy, and theories to the sessions. My feeling with her was that I did not matter. Often I felt intimidated by the iron-clad control she displayed. For a long time, I felt that nothing was happening in the sessions. In the sessions that followed, I can only recall a few sessions where I could see her *feel* any of the emotions which she was talking about. She would talk about times when she was so distressed that she could cry, but would not. Many times I felt that I was getting sucked into an intellectual, abstract vortex with her and colluded with her desire to not come very close to feelings. *Understanding* came too early, too fast, and left little space for her own feelings. I said to her *"I have not heard the angry you. I am curious to know that person. Maybe others also wonder who this larger than life person is."* She said that she was not being *fake* but she would still put on a smile for the other and not let her true feelings show. I felt that this is what was happening even in the sessions. I felt that what she also conveyed through her smile was that "*I am perfect and fine and the madness lies in you, who is the other.*"

And many times this is how I would end up feeling—somewhat mad. Other than the boredom, I would usually find myself confused and slightly disoriented in the sessions. Trying to keep track of what she was saying was not always easy, not because the content was too much or there was something in the manner of her talking, but I felt that there was a general disconnect between the things that she spoke about. I think it was also likely that there was a disconnect between what she was feeling and what she was expressing, or, more likely, that the content was stripped of feelings. Often in the sessions, I found her using the phone. In these moments, I would feel that she did not really care for what I was saying and I wondered if she even heard what I was saying to her.

For this patient there was a history of continuous sexual abuse at a very young age. No one in the family was aware of it. These memories were present but were lifeless and stripped of all emotions. My sense in the sessions was that attempts at thinking were actually being blocked. Sometimes analysis can itself feel like an invasion, and the disorganization that we keep ourselves in, is in the service of fending off any organization that may lead to an elaboration of thinking and feelings, and possibly reawaken memories and associated feelings of trauma. As our work progressed, my continuous feeling was that there was something happening in the sessions, but I was unable to know what it was. I felt that it was like a pressure cooker waiting to be released. While there were many missed sessions, what I began to note was that she was seeking out a large number of boys for sexual contact and intimacy. Most of these contacts were virtual but with some of them, she also had a sexual relationship. She went from one relationship to another, without any acknowledgement of its effect on her, and as if one was easily replaced by another. It was not about the persons as much as about the body. So much was happening outside the sessions, and I felt that this was an acting out of that which was not getting addressed and lived out in the sessions. The turning point of the work was when I, in one session, wondered if what she was feeling for me, was anger at not recognizing and responding to her need to be seen and held. She said that she experienced me as cold and indifferent and what she was not getting in the sessions from me, was what she was seeking outside.

The confusion I felt in the sessions with her was perhaps the confusion she was also living daily. The indifference that I felt in her toward me was how she had experienced the world around her as a child. Indifferent and unable to *see* what was happening to her. Despite the helplessness that she felt in the sessions, she was anything but helpless. Her control unnerved me. The will and tenacity that she showed in her communications was, I think, her way of overcoming the absence of her mother. In what she spoke about the mother, she repeatedly pointed out that the mother never took any decisions and always referred everything to the father. What I sensed was a frustration she felt in seeing the mother as being voiceless. But her own identity was fragile. Both separation and fusion were acutely anxious positions and she struggled to be indifferent and invulnerable to the world around her, even though it was at a heavy price—at the cost of her own sense of feeling real. Reality would destroy the other, but in this process she had given up a relationship to her reality.

THE "UNLIVED" AND "UNDREAMT"

Toward the end of his life, Winnicott wrote a paper, possibly an incomplete one, "Fear of Breakdown" (1974), that was published only after his death. Winnicott's paper is a beautiful piece of writing that is tentative, exploring, and talks about a fear of a breakdown, but is not clear what this breakdown is. Through his reading and re-reading of this paper, Thomas Ogden understands this to mean that what Winnicott is referring to is to a "breakdown that has *already happened*" (Ogden 2014, p.7), but has "*not yet been experienced*" (Ogden 2014, p.7), that is to say that "we have ways of experiencing or not experiencing the events of our lives" (Ogden 2014, p. 7).

What makes these papers remarkable is that they address early life trauma and experiences that were too much for the infant's psyche to elaborate and represent and were subsequently repressed. The impact of these experiences is, then, not always possible to "remember." As Ogden points out, Winnicott in his paper is trying to extend the conception of the unconscious to include "registrations of events that have occurred, but *have not been experienced* . . . (and refers to) the aspect of the individual that carries one's unassimilated traumatic experience, one's 'undreamt dreams'" (Ogden 2014, p.9). As long as the ego is not able to gather the original experience into its own present-time experience and into omnipotent control, the experience cannot be *forgotten*.

The therapeutic setting is one space where the *living and dreaming* of the experience can happen, with the analyst. As long as we carry a sense of an unlived life, we will not be able to feel complete, and all of us, according to Ogden, carry this universal need in ourselves to "re-claim, or claim for the first time what he has lost of himself and, in doing so, take the opportunity to become the person he still holds the potential to be" (Ogden 2014, p. 10). In this sense, Winnicott's conception is closer to the French Psychosomatic School, who believe that unlived experience, that which is not elaborated in the psyche, is relegated to the body and may manifest as a somatic illness or perversion.

This process of claiming the unlived parts of one's experience is a painful process because it involves experiencing the pain of the breakdown and of the primitive agony that results from the breakdown, which had not been experienced the first time, and had caused the person to become a stranger to himself or herself, to lose important aspects of self. While we may appear to others and ourselves to be psychologically healthy, "there are important ways in which we are not capable of being alive to our experience, whether that be the experience of joy, or the ability to love one or all our children, or the capacity to be generous to the point of giving something highly important to us, or the capacity to forgive someone (including ourselves) who has done something that has hurt us profoundly, or to simply feel alive to the world around us and within us" (Ogden 2014, p. 11).

All of us make compromises in living. To live, we sacrifice some knowledge of pain and suffering that we go through in the ordinary moments of life. If we were unable do this, living itself would come under threat. But for some people this compromise is too heavy. What they sacrifice is not just pain but a relationship to the self, a continuity that makes them know themselves, an aliveness that allows them to feel human, and a relationship to reality that validates and creates experiences. What we are left with is a living that feels incomplete, where experiences fail to come alive and the sense of self not only comes under attack but is constantly questioned and felt to be without an authenticity.

AN EXPERIENCE OF INFANT OBSERVATION

As part of my training program I was expected to do infant observation for two semesters. Infant observation involves observing an infant in his or her family. It is recommended that we start observation from birth up to about six months or a year. This involves setting up observation with a family and visiting them once every week at a fixed time, and then afterwards writing in detail what one observes of the baby. The experience of infant observation was particularly difficult for me. It felt to me that the mother, for whom this baby (Jaya) was the second child (her first was a son), was less attuned to Jaya's needs, and it seemed that she had a difficulty in keeping the baby in mind. There were various factors which perhaps affected their relationship, including what I thought was the gender of the baby, the mother's own infantile anxieties that came to the forefront in looking after a baby girl, and the lack of familial support. However, infant observation is based primarily on the observations of the observer and on how she feels while she is observing. The observer becomes a container of many projections and at the same time her own infantile anxieties may be powerfully evoked.

I experienced difficulty in setting up observations, and each week felt like starting all over again, introducing myself over and over again. Eventually after the first three visits, I did not go back to the house for four months and it was only when I was able to process my distress at being in the house, because of what I observed, that I was able to contact the family again. I realized that I had felt ignored; I felt the mother did not keep me in mind. When I look back at my experience of the observations, I have this gnawing sense that my presence in the house was barely registered. When I explore this feeling further I realize that this feeling is most acute vis-à-vis the mother.

I think this experience then was significant for me in several respects. The profound distress that I experienced during the observations and my subsequent inability to go back to the observation setting came to my notice more sharply because of the persistent discomfort and irritability that I felt during the infant observation seminars and later in writing about it. Clearly, there was a reason this was becoming so difficult. I knew I was identifying with the infant—the helplessness that I experienced her as feeling and her rejection, which was reflected in her mother's lack of attunement. For the first time, I became aware, acutely so, of the infant that I was. That before I became an adult, I was an infant. But this is a matter of fact. Why then do I need to state it like this? Maybe because the infant me feels like another existence—another person. As I become curious, I search for memories—what I come upon is only a mass of sensations, formless yet full.

Winnicott says early descriptions of body states also become like early descriptions of emotional states. There is no thought and they exist at the level of sensations (Winnicott 1991). So these parts exist in me, so familiar yet so forgotten, in my bones and in my body and it is this which has allowed me to think about the infant that I was, the girl child that I became and the woman that I am.

Rustin says that "where the choice has already been made (to be a therapist), the exposure to intense feelings, the impact of feeling oneself drawn into an emotional force-field and struggling to hold one's balance and sense of self, the encounter with the probably unfamiliar confusion and power of infantile emotional life, are especially valuable aspects of infant observation for beginning therapists" (Rustin 1989, p.8).

Antonella Sansone in her book *Working with Parents and Infants: A Mind Body Integration Approach* (2007) writes that one of the most important aspects of infant observation is the impact it has on the observer's emotional life. In newborns we see the most vulnerable state of a human. This can make infant observation a hard experience, but also valuable, as it prepares the observer for re-experiencing the intense feelings of primal life . . . The capacity to "feel," to "listen" to the body's feelings, to "think" about them, and to give them "meaning" leads to an integrated psyche soma in the observer and the prospective clinician. (Sansone 2007, p.139) She further writes that "you can think about feelings if you can truly experience them with all your body. This kind of mental frame requires a capacity to tolerate anxiety, uncertainties, fear, helplessness, and discomfort. A therapist needs these capacities to make the psychotherapeutic work effective" (Sansone 2007, p. 142)

(AT)TUNING IN AND USING THE COUNTER-TRANSFERENCE

In work with severely disturbed patients, as in infant observation, the transference and counter-transference matrix is swamped with primitive, infantile feelings. Just as the presence of the maternal mind is essential for the digestion and internalizing of these feelings for the infant, the therapist's mind also has to become an accessible maternal space to hold the infant patient. Psychoanalysis is a unique form of treatment. In treatment, the therapist-patient's relationship becomes the route for the powerful fantasies, patterns, and feelings to emerge, to be felt and in course to be thought through. Adam Phillips, in his introduction to "Wild Analysis," a collection of papers written by Freud, writes "psychoanalysis is about what two people can say to each other if they agree not to have sex" (Phillips 2002, p. xx). However, for the most part Freud considered counter-transference to be something that interfered with the treatment process and something that needed to be kept out of the therapy. As psychoanalytic understanding and writing has grown, there has been a recognition of counter-transference as being integral to the treatment process. I feel that in working with patients, especially those who are severely disturbed, whose sense of self is poorly developed, patients who can be categorized as psychotic or borderline, counter-transference becomes the key to gaining awareness of the psychic self of the patient. In these patients, it is not only that the link to the reality and self that is broken, but more often the self is not there to be found. In other words, the task of therapy is no longer to uncover the unconscious, but it needs to concentrate on helping the patient form representations for that which is present and that which is absent.

In psychoanalytic therapy, it is through the unique relationship with the therapist that many of us find ourselves finally being able to mourn. Inside the therapy room, time moves differently. The means and end of the work is affects. The past and the present intertwine, like the many creepers on the forest floor. Feelings that have become muffled and lost in the present are dangerously, longingly, alive in the past. Therapy seeks to unearth these feelings and to help the person in the here and now *feel the person he or she was in the past*. The task of the therapist is balancing the health and the madness of the patient, to see the meaning behind madness, not to take away the madness. It is in this process that we help the patient to form a relationship to his own madness and through that to himself. Often the trap we fall into is to *explain away the madness* and in this process create a further dissociation between the patient and his or her inner world. As a patient myself, I have often expected therapy to help me *recover memories* that would *explain* how I was, and therapy becomes a *search for answers* or a process of *forming links*. However, while therapy is both, a search as well as a process of forming links, I think it is more than anything else a space that allows for feelings to be *lived*. Therapy is as much about the story the patient brings to us as about how he talks and does not talk of the story.

Delourmel, writing on Green's work, says that the work of analysis and the patients' incapacity to use this work is a traumatic experience, and one which is kept at bay by "resistances which immobilize their psychic life and which they will maintain as long as they are convinced that only this state of non-life has the power to prevent the danger of a mental breakdown" (Delourmel 2013, p. 153). He further writes how the traumatic experience is actually a repetition of infantile reactions and "the traumatic return of this return of the past stems from the fact that the traces inscribed in the mind at a time when 'the infant could hardly speak' could not be constituted into memory traces, and have therefore remained unpresentable and inaccessible to memory" (Delourmel 2013, p.153).

Ogden (2014) says that Winnicott (1974), in his paper "Fear of Breakdown," has written how the only way to allow the patient to *experience breakdown* is through transference and counter-transference. Winnicott says that only a therapist, who has experienced her own madness and known it, can help a patient to live the unlived (Ogden 2014). Further, Fisher (2006), writing on the K function, says "the opening up of the analyst to the emotional experience of wanting to know the patient, thus making possible by the patient's internalization of this relationship, a wanting to know, and being able, to know oneself, is surely the essence of psychoanalysis." (p. 1235)

In this kind of work, it is not only coming to an insight, but the process that develops between the therapist and the patient, the therapeutic alliance, that leads to understanding and growth. The setting—in terms of space, time, and fees—protects this process and makes the work of therapy possible. However, more than the outside frame that is needed, what affects the work is the internal frame of the therapist, which refers to the therapist's counter-transference, their own analysis, and the theory that the therapist roots her work in.

Andre Green "recommends using the setting as a transitional space" (Delourmel 2013, p. 154). For him, the analyst-patient couple forms the heart of the treatment and he "suggests that the transformational processes of the session are intersubjective as well as intrapsychic" (Levine 2009, p. 247) and he assumes that there is a difference between that which can be represented through language and that which cannot yet be represented, and which manifests as impulse and action. The therapist's role becomes integral to making sense of what cannot be represented in speech. Green (Levine 2009) suggests two concepts—transference onto speech and transference onto object. The capacity for transference onto speech is a consequence of good enough attunement, availability and responsiveness of the object, and repeated good experiences which allow for binding and representation. On the other hand, transference onto object occurs as a result of an inability to create representation, and can result in enactments, raw feelings, and somatic reactions, in relation to the analytic relationship. This "disorganization is a result of repeated and/or traumatic experiences of failed drive satisfaction and when there is a "failure of representation, object attachment and associative links maybe weakened or severed and the fabric of the psyche may be torn, so that self continuity, object constancy, and meaning itself may be severely disrupted" (Levine 2009, p. 248). Thus, taken together, "transference includes not only the repetition of the past but also a creation of that which has not yet been *fully experienced*, that is, that which has not yet been or only weakly been represented or symbolized" (my italics, Levine 2009, p. 248).

Therapy is difficult. It brings us close to parts of us that are most painful and to realities that render us helpless and are impossible to change. I saw my patients' difficulty with therapy as a resistance, and something that we needed to work through. While this is also true, I think it was only when I could form a relationship to loss in my own life that I realized how slow and subtle this process was. It could not be evoked, it had to be borne. Separations are acutely painful, especially when they are premature. Sometimes, the separations are felt as losses. And very often we do not even know what is it that we have lost. The loss, the absences, though sometimes subtle in themselves, leave a deep impact on us. Through the experience of infant observation, I understood that, despite my effort to locate the exact nature of this absence, what I had was only feelings. Feelings that had to be felt and not understood. I had to be patient with myself, to wait for them to unfold in me. As I worked with a patient toward termination, I realized that I had to analyze my own relationship to separations. Many separations that happen in our lives are not out of choice, whether it's weaning from the mother's breast or later, separations from family, friends, school, and college. Most of these separations we don't process. Now as I looked, I saw how my body had become a medium to express the acute anxiety that I had felt in some of these separations, whether through an upset stomach, headaches, fever, body ache, uncontrollable crying, restlessness, and even panic attacks.

As infants and children, the process of separation comes after a period of good-enough contact with the mother. The comfort and security that we receive and internalize of the mother's body forms the blueprint for the holding that we often search for in later adult life. Sexual experiences are so powerful because they are reminiscent of our first most intimate contact with a body, the body of the mother. The heavily erotic transference that my patient had toward me, as well the search for sexual contact outside the sessions for another patient, were, I think ways to recover the lost mother and to deal with premature, painful separations and losses that they had not processed.

When I was able to come close to my own feelings, it helped me not only in understanding what was happening with my patients but also allowed me to open myself up to the patients' feelings and projections. Where often the relationship to the loss itself was lost, what the work had to be was not only to recover memories, but also to begin to know the feelings and create a representation of them in the psyche. I became deeply aware how this kind of work requires a great deal of capacity for the therapist herself to stay with *patience, not knowing, misunderstanding, being with uncertainty, and not being in a hurry to know and understand.* The therapist too has to wait and then wait some more. Feelings cannot be hurried and like a deer in the forest, they flee at the smallest signs of danger, here the danger being a threat of fragmenting.

The intensity of feelings that borderline and/or psychotic patients feel is often overwhelming. However, in order for the patient to reach any kind of awareness it is essential for the therapist to allow for the fusion to happen. If we ourselves are terrified of it, for the patient to come to his own differentiated and whole identity is impossible. A perception of the self and other, actuality and fantasy, inside and outside, develops only with time and, to start with, there is no absolute differentiation. I am helped in my formulation by Marion Milner's classic work *The Hands of the Living God* (1969) and the subsequent commentaries on her work, particularly by Nina Farhi (2010), and the symposium held on her work by others like Dodi Goldman (2010). What Milner puts very clearly for us, and what is highlighted by Farhi's works, "the rhythm of oscillation between submergence and emergence, the reciprocity between differentiation and fusion, is what animates new insights. This involves perceiving something common in structures that beforehand had been seen as only different and discovering difference in what previously had only been perceived as the same. When the mind settles into one position, be it differentiation or its opposite, no growth can occur" (Goldman 2010, p. 509).

It is worth thinking about how so many of us chose to work with patients that invade and affect us. I wonder what is it about us that makes us seek such a contact, and are we also then not looking for something with these patients? The work of psychotherapy is around suffering. We are all carrying parts in us that elude expression, elude meaning and which remain elusive until found, and sometimes even despite being found, whether as patients or therapists, only the degree of suffering is different. In therapy, the patient is the center but the work is created in between the two people and without the involvement of any one person, the work will fail to come alive. Within the boundaries of the psychoanalytic setting, the boundaries between the two people become hazy, taking various forms and sometimes merging. The relationship formed is like no other and its impact becomes a part of the being—like the mother's touch—never to be forgotten.

CONCLUSION

Through this chapter I hope to have emphasized the central link between the psyche and the soma and how the capacity to experience and reflect belongs to an integrated psyche-soma. Effective clinical work, especially when working with severely disturbed patients, depends on this integration. To come to an integrated psyche-soma requires us to be open to our own feelings, to have the capacity to bear uncertainties, not knowing, helplessness, anxieties, and fears. Only a therapist who has been able to stay with her madness and mad anxiety will be able to help the patient come to his own, to not be scared of it and to live it, mourn the loss that may be felt despite remaining unknown.

In psychoanalysis, the mother and the maternal function is given a special place, with the therapist's role often being equated with that of the mother. The emphasis on the mother in psychoanalytic theory, and the primary role that she plays in the health of the baby's emotional development, has often led to placing an undue burden on the mother and the full responsibility for the child's emotional health at her doorstep. In this chapter, I have tried to highlight the need for the therapist to be attuned to her own infantile anxieties and to allow her to be used and changed by the patient. Furthering this thought, I would like to say the crucial need then is for us to listen to the mother and her own infantile needs. In order to look after the baby, it is essential for the mother to have an integrated sense of herself and to have the capacity to deal with her own anxieties that flood her when she becomes a mother and has to take care of her baby.

Sudhir Kakar has provided us with a description of the mother within the Indian ethos. Through his writings, that draw not only on clinical experience but that also depend heavily on Indian mythology, legends, and folk culture, he brings out a coherent description of the Indian girl and woman and then highlights why and how motherhood is an imperative and seemingly inevitable choice for the Indian woman. According to Kakar, an Indian woman, irrespective of caste, class, age, and regionality, "knows that motherhood confers upon her a purpose and identity that nothing else in her culture can. Each infant borne and nurtured by her safely into childhood, especially if the child is a son, is both a certification and redemption." (Kakar 1997, p.56) The Indian girl is born a daughter, and once married she becomes a daughter-in-law, a wife, and finally a mother. Cultural anthropologists universally have noted how there is an obvious improvement in an Indian wife's social status once she becomes pregnant and the belief is that pregnancy is a woman's ultimate good fortune.

To be the mother of a girl child in India is often a matter of shame, guilt, and depression. For a mother to look after an infant is a challenge, but even more for the girl child since her identification with the baby is more and evokes her own anxieties and fantasies. Amidst the idealization of motherhood, the mother as a woman having her own identity and needs is forgotten. And, in all the celebration associated with birth, the mother's depression is overlooked and she is expected to think only about her baby. What I suggest then, as further research and an elaboration and continuation of my present thinking, is to explore maternal depression in India, to look at the mother-daughter relationship, how she is differently affected in giving birth to a girl versus a boy, and to imagine possible interventions at the earliest stage in the mother-infant dyad. The shame and depression that the mother feels are unknowingly passed on to the daughter and the vicious cycle that develops shatters hope for being different and for any real change to happen not only in individuals but in a society as a whole. I feel that there is a significant link between the mother's depression and the daughter's sexuality and unless we can address the mother and help her recover her own relationship to herself, the body and the mind will remain split, and the sexual and the maternal aspects will always remain split aspects of the culture. We all then become carriers of this melancholic depression—so intimate, yet so strange.

Lastly, I would like to say that, in India, mental health and seeking help remain shrouded in shame. One of the most acceptable forms of expression of suffering is through the medium of the body. The hospitals here are full of people walking in with unexplainable symptoms and diseases. Research on the psychosomatic disorders, where thinking and feeling are evacuated into the body, is bare. Psychosomatic disorders are the most radical and extreme form of psychic reduction that not only affects the emotional well-being of the individual but his physical well being as well. I feel that in order to address that which is silenced, that which has not been mourned, we need to listen to the bodies that are talking. Otherwise the body and the mind will continue to be split and the idea of emotional suffering always shameful.

NOTE

1. This chapter in a modified form was presented before publication at the First Annual Psychoanalytical Conference, 2013, New Delhi, as "Remembering, Repeating and Working Through: The Indian Girl child."

REFERENCES

Agarwal, Urvashi and Paiva, Nupur Dhingra. "The uncomfortable subject: observing the Indian girl child, Infant Observation." *International Journal of Infant Observation and Its Applications* 17(2014):151–166 DOI: 10.1080/13698036.2014.937925.

Deloumel, C. "Andre Green: An introduction to the work of Andre Green." *International Journal of Psychoanalysis* 94(2013): 133–156.

Farhi, N. "The Hands of the living god: 'Finding the familiar in the unfamiliar.'' *Psychoanalytic Dialogues* 20(2010): 478–503.

Fisher, J.V. "The emotional experience of K." *International Journal of Psychoanalysis* 87(2006): 1221–37.

Goldman, D. "Letting the sea in: Commentary on Paper by Nina Farhi." *Psychoanalytic Dialogues* 20(2010): 504–509.

Goldman, Dodi. *In One's Bones: The Clinical Genius of Winnicott.* New Jersey: Jason Aronson Inc., 1993.

Kakar, S. *The Inner World: A Psycho-analytic Study of Childhood and Society in India*. New Delhi: Oxford University Press, 1997.

Kohon, G. ed. *The Dead Mother: The Work of Andre Green.* London: Routledge, 1999.

Levine, H. "Representations and their Vicissitudes: The Legacy of Andre Green." *The Psychoanalytic Quarterly* 78(2009): 243–62.

Milner, M. *The Hands of the Living God: An account of a psychoanalytic treatment,* (Reprint). London: Routledge, 1969.

Ogden, T. "Fear of breakdown and the unlived life," *International Journal of Psychoanalysis 95*(2014): 205–23. DOI: 10.1111/1745-8315.12148.

Phillips, A. "Introduction." In *Wild Analysis,* edited by S. Freud. London: Penguin Books, 2002.

Rustin, M. E. "Encountering primitive anxieties." In *Closely observed infants.* Edited by L. Miller, M.E. Rustin, M.J. Rustin, and J. Shuttleworth. London: Duckworth. 1989.

Sansone, A. *Working with Parents and Infants: A Mind-Body Integration Approach.* London: Karnac, 2007.

Searles, H. F. "Dependency in schizophrenia." In *Collected Papers on Schizophrenia and Related Subjects,* edited by H. F. Searles. London: Karnac, 1986[1965].

Winnicott, D.W. *The Child, the Family and the Outside World.* (Reprint). London: Penguin Books, 1991.

Chapter Four

Myth, Misogyny, Matricide

Nilofer Kaul

In Figure 4.1 we see the mythological figure *Putana*, who suckled the infant Krishna with poisoned breasts, an act which led to her own death. The birth of Krishna was a threat to his uncle, a father surrogate, Kansa. The word "putana" in Sanskrit literally means "putrefaction," "smelly," and also "the one without virtues." Several versions of this myth exist, as the tale is told and re-told in Hindu scriptures. In some versions, she is sent by Kansa on a mission to kill; in others, murdering infants is her own mission; and in yet others, it is her longing for suckling an infant.The Putana myth recurs in several texts across centuries.In the earliest textual version, *Harivamsa*, of late third century C.E, she comes to the child as a bird. She is often depicted as a bird, in sculpture as well as myth. In the *Bhagwat Purana*, between the sixth and tenth century C.E, there is a fuller account of her assuming the form of a woman (Gordon White 2006, 52). She is closely associated with pustulence and the sores of chickenpox, and owes her name to the smell associated with the disease. She is mentioned in medical texts and is also supposed to have gotten a boon from Shiva to eat little children (Gordon White 2006, 51). One can see her, amongst other things, as a personification of the dangers that beset newborn infants. What is significant is the way in which this threat resembles the mother. Sudhir Kakar (2002) in his work on Krishna myths draws attention to a whole spectrum of interpretative possibilities that emerge from locating this at a later phase in Krishna's life. He suggests for instance, that the Putana tale can be read as incestuous fears experienced by the child who feels himself caught in a threatening stranglehold with his mother who entangles him in this erotic, hostile, part-seductive, part-sacrificing relationship, from where he finds himself unable to move out (424–5).

What emerges through all the different versions and interpretations possible is the idea that Putana represents an undesirable aspect of the mother, and

Figure 4.1. Putana with the baby Krishna, mid-twenieth century.
Reprinted with permission from Crafts Museum.

Figure 4.2. Putana with the baby Krishna, mid-twenieth century.
Reprinted with permission from Crafts Museum.

the interpretation would depend on in which phase of Krishna's life Putana appears. The repetition of the figure is in itself significant as echoes from the unconscious that will not fade. In most versions her poisoned breasts are to end the threat the infant Krishna poses to his uncle's empire. In an omnipotent twist to this oedipal tale, she dies after suckling the infant, who "aggressively consumes the cruel mother" (O'Flaherty 1982, 102).

What is interesting in this particular rendering of the myth is the way it condenses sequence: it is rather "action-packed." But it also creates a peculiar frisson between splitting and fusion. The sequence here is not self-evident. It could be read in the reverse: the dead mother who comes alive while feeding is an obvious mis-reading that the image lends itself to. The most obvious and repeated idea in both the myth and its representation here is of "splitting," but almost equally suggestive here is the darkness of the story, that in fact they are fused, the "hateful siege of contraries" is eloquently dramatized (Milton 2003, *Paradise Lost*, Book IX, 121–2). That even as Putana is the "dark and demonic" aspect of the mother who needs to die, she is suckling the baby, bringing him to life, holding him not with hate, but tenderness and intimacy. The representation belies the splitting that certain versions of the story enforce.

Melanie Klein (1946) persuasively imagines the infant's universe as not sanguine, but troubled, where helplessness is coupled with neediness. The infant needs the breast but experiences its powerlessness over it. The bigness and the potency of the breasts are replete with fantasies of its magical properties—it can poison, drown, choke, as well as give life, fullness, beauty. This makes the infant apprehensive of the breast. Confronted with an object that seems indecipherably desirable and sinister, the infant deals with this unexpected situation by keeping these two sets of feelings apart from each other and this is how Klein understands splitting. The good breast that feeds it needs to be kept very far from the bad one that deprives it or chokes and suffocates it. If these two come close, he fears losing the good with the bad. Putana is the bad mother who poisons the baby and this is an embodiment of the infantile fantasy of the poisoned breasts (Klein 1948; O'Flaherty 1982). This would entail the idea that this is a demonic, bad aspect of the mother, which is split-off; and by implication, there must be a good mother tucked away somewhere.

MYTHS: PSYCHIC TELEGRAPHS

Myths, like dreams, may be read as condensed carriers of unconscious messages. The oedipal myth (Freud 1900) is the one that remains paradigmatic to psychoanalysis and if we put that at the center, we can see both diachronically and synchronically how it plays itself out in Greek gods, in Satan and God, in Adam and God. Here and elsewhere, in Freud it is the murder of the father which is usually the best kept secret, akin to the secret attic of the gothic novel, the origin of the taboo (Freud 1913). Repression—intrapsychic or cultural—was the key to his reading of myths and their equivalents. Repression is the word Freud uses almost synonymously with defense: unconscious ways of disavowing parts of the self that threaten the coherence of the self. If we follow the economic model of the psyche, then we might argue that the psyche maintains its equilibrium by bearing down on certain unwanted parts. On the basis of what Freud says here, as well as the way in which they have been read, it may be fair to surmise that myths are narratives that carry echoes of a cultural unconscious, and that is how they get repeated, retold, reinvented.

A.K. Ramanujan (1971), writing about the oedipal myth in India, points out the absence of the actual patricide, and how Indian variants run along the negative (son surrenders to father) rather than the positive (son kills father) oedipal pattern. For instance, the Putana myth is an offshoot of the oedipal scape of the Kansa-Krishna rivalry which has resonances with not only Oedipus Rex but also Kronos-Zeus, Christ-Herod, and Satan-God amongst others. Yet we note that Kansa is not Krishna's literal father; but he stands for the law of the father. About the absence of the real father, Ramanujan admits this as an unresolvable question even if we "explain away the Indian pattern as only a projection, a reversal, a transformation of the Greek one; or assert that Indian tales manifest a cultural repression . . . so deep that the killing of the father is entirely absent; or insist that the child projects its own desires . . . on to his or her father or mother . . . if that is the case, we still need to ask why it is that Indian tales are more like 'screen memories' and the Greek one is so straightforward" (p. 393).

Ramanujan gets to the horns of the dilemma here when he poses the chicken-and-egg riddle of culture and psyche. What shapes who and how and why? Certainly as long as we pose it like this, it remains unresolvable. All too often, we theorize the universal and the cultural in an either/or, losing sight of the intersecting and perhaps even concentric, nature of the two circles.

However the idea of invoking this essay here is with an eye to making a connection between the presence of matricide and the absence of patricide. There emerges a possible connection between the need for a castrating father and an incontinent, incestuous, lawless mother. Extrapolating from Kakar's argument that Putana represents a threat from the lawless mother, the child desires an omnipotent father who will defend him from (his) incestuous desires. Without really questioning the centrality of the oedipal myth, one can ask the question as to how as psychoanalysts, we strain to find the oedipal trellis under the overgrown thicket of human relationships. Amber Jacobs quite persuasively argues that the dominance of Oedipus has also relegated the *Oresteia* to the margins. That silencing can be read symbolically as matricide. I would like to suggest that perhaps, what Ramanujan is pointing toward is the inadequacy of repression as a key to opening all locks; that in fact, Putana harks back to a pre-oedipal psychic structure where splitting and projection rather than repression appear to be psychically more consonant. In psychic history, more primitive defenses appear before repression.

Any story that gets preserved and retold (hence reinvented) must carry echoes of what one may term "dangerous knowledge"—of which the forbidden tree is the best-known signifier. As opposed to a generalized notion of repression, I am going to argue that this kind of splitting is a pre-eminent defense used in myths, particularly when it comes to women. In splitting, the emphasis appears to be on keeping things far apart, very much visible and present, but located outside. Semantically, one may say that splitting is the equivalent of an oxymoron which coincidentally recurs constantly in poetry that laments the coldness of the woman. In poetic traditions ranging from Petrarchan to Urdu, the inaccessibility of the cloistered woman is interpreted as coldness; who being "icy fire" causes the man to "burn and freeze." (Forster 1969). Coldness, being a manifestation of hate and cruelty, is projected into absence and inaccessibility. Could we see this as continuous with the figure above, for instance, which can be seen as representing an imagined moment in the psychic life of the infant?

BREAST MOTHER, TOILET MOTHER

The informed viewer here already knows that Putana is not the mother. She is a usurper, a demoness masquerading as a "breast mother." Here I use the term to indicate yet another way of articulating the split that the infant/child performs. The breast mother is the good mother who feeds, while the toilet mother is the one for whom he leaves his dirty, fecal parts, the degraded mother (Meltzer 1967). One kind of splitting is already in existence in the myth. The good mother—in Krishna's case this is complicated because he has a biological (Devaki) and a foster mother (Yashoda)— is preserved through the split. What this particular image does is embody unconscious split-off wishes. By fusing together both the poisonous and the poisoned bad mother, it participates in dyadic intimacy and its dangers. The sequence is not self-evident, which complicates our reception of the image. As mentioned before, the demonic figure is both split and fused. It is therefore both a vanquishing of the danger as well as a lingering on of it. That I feel is the power of this image. However this chapter is not an analysis of this image alone, fascinating though that may be.

By emphasizing splitting and projection, Melanie Klein reduced the ubiquity of repression. As opposed to the hydraulic implication of repression, she went to more primitive states that were more expulsive, chaotic, evacuative: the unconscious in more primitive states throws out, splits off, projects states of mind and objects that it cannot own. It is not a psyche that has arrived at the capacity to repress, but throws the bad parts out, expels them into the other and thereby keeps those parts very much alive, not bearing down on them, but actually casting them out, vomiting them, putting them out into another. Here I use the term "matricide" to include the real, the imagined or the symbolic killing of the desired mother. And that this ultimate enactment of hate can be seen as a retaliatory response to the projected hostility of the mother, that is, the violence of emotion stirred up in an immature psyche is experienced as emanating from the other, and such an object must be snuffed out along with Othello, with the rageful "Put out the light, and then again, put out the light!"

BREAST GODDESSES AND TOOTH GODDESSES

Ramanujan (1986), as he emphasizes the plurality and cross-currents, the dialogic encounters in the landscape of Indian myth and religion, plots at least two broad influences that run counter to each other. He sees Sanskritized literary tradition as being contrapuntal to folklore versions that democratize the same narratives or use often the same form for a different content. The Sanskritized narratives abide by the law of the father while they grant a domesticated status to the women deities—"breast goddesses," as opposed to "tooth goddesses" of folklore. The distinction between what Ramanujan refers to as "tooth goddesses" and "breast goddesses" is another instance of splitting. He seems to indicate that if culture is a whole, a gestalt, like the psyche, then scriptural and oral, or more accurately, the Sanskritized and the folk, become split parts of this whole object. In Sanskritic myths the male gods give the goddess her powers, while in the oral traditions this need not be the case. In Sanskritic myths, father figures lust after daughters; in folklore, women too have their share of desire. Goddesses in anthologies are consort goddesses, like Lakshmi and Parvati; their shrines are subordinate to their spouses. These goddesses are mild. But village goddesses are often cheated into marrying untouchables, raped by a local villain, killed and buried by cruel brothers, and require animal sacrifices (498).

This fierce aspect of the feminine seems to have affiliation with the Matrikas: the cluster of goddesses that were worshipped together, and represented frightening aspects of the feminine. Kinsley (1998, p. 151) notes how, in their earlier avatars, these goddesses had more threatening aspects which changed over a period of time. There is an assimilating of these inauspicious female deities that seems to divert their violence outward, directed toward protection of the family, rather than to devouring it. Nevertheless, these savage aspects require appeasement. They are known to murder babies, drink the blood of the dead, dance on corpses, and cause smallpox. Their physical appearance varies from being beautiful and soft, to savage with protruding teeth, long nails, carrying corpses around their neck. The different Puranas offer varying accounts of the origin and function of these female deities. That they are distinct from consort goddesses is common, but what differs in the stories is whether they serve a protective or a destructive role. Their potency for, and affiliation to, destructiveness is never seriously in doubt. Once again, this lurking presence in the midst of the pantheon is a reminder of the dark, uncanny force that resides in the woman and must be placed far away from the "good" mother.

In Ramanujan's instance of Kannada folklore which is discussed next, the savagery is, interestingly, very much located in the mother. This primordial, rather threatening figure, is exorcised by the scriptures—those texts that acquired authority. In fact, while I agree with Ramanujan, that the variants on the oedipal story do end up differently in Indian versions, and that the castration actually is carried out by the father, what I would like to focus on is how this exorcising—this hushing of plurality and the dominance of the ur-text—is not only to uphold the authority of the omnipotent father over the unruly sons, but also to exorcise the disquieting, unruly aspects of the mother, feared and fantasized by the infant.

WHO'S AFRAID OF INCEST: SETTING THE MOTHER ON FIRE

Ramanujan (1988) speaks of one such Puranic folk song which is sung ceremonially in Karnataka every year by several bardic groups. This begins with a creation myth, and we can see how antithetical its shape, form, and texture is from the Edenic story of creation. I will recount this briefly. The primordial goddess is born three days before everything else, which indicates the primacy of the womb, hinting at a matriarchal, rather than a patriarchal society. This goddess grows up very quickly, attains puberty, and wants a man to satisfy her. Finding no one around her, she creates one out of herself, and this one is Brahma the eldest. This incestuous, unboundaried, lawless mother in the absence of father, asks him to grow up quickly and sleep with her. He pleads with her invoking the incest taboo. She calls him a eunuch and burns him. This cycle repeats itself next day with Vishnu. Then finally on the third day, Shiva is born. The wily Shiva outwits the mother. He buys time and asks her to let him grow up. Finally he plots the murder through the powerful dance of seduction and destruction. It is the fantastic cosmic dance. Matching him step for step, she bursts into flames. Incestuous desires are experienced with horror by the primitive psyche and must be expelled and cast into the m/other. A matriarchal society is rife with dangers.

I am going to cut to the chase: interestingly, once the mother is got rid of, Shiva sets about work, establishing a world. For this he revives his brothers and recreates the world. Women are now needed for the womb function, to populate the world. How do they get them? Shiva now goes to the heap of ashes he had reduced his mother to, and creates consorts by dividing the ashes of the mother. The domestication is also through the splitting of the mother. One reading of this would be to see how the authority of scriptures is built upon an edifice of destroyed mothers, or, more accurately, the demonic mother is split off and evacuated. It can also be read as how ordered, civilized, patriarchal society must be founded upon matricide: in the hands of Shiva, the world is felt to be safer. He takes charge of the mother who is unruly in her sexuality and therefore law-less. Patriarchy seems to restore order which is under threat from the essential but law-less matriarchy that precedes it.

Matricide, in this context, is the murdering not of the mother, but projectively of the incestuous and matricidal desires that will otherwise destroy civilization. But these desires are not owned, they are not repressed; they are cast out, violently put outside, into the desired—and therefore feared and hated—other. If along with Klein, we imagine the infant's universe to be turbulent and frothing with incomprehensible but overwhelming emotion, it follows that this infant has no capacity to keep this within himself. He must cast them out into the object which evokes these in him. The historical primacy of the relationship to the maternal object casts a shadow over the future of the infant's dyadic relationships to women. The immature psyche, yet unable to bear the strain of violent emotion carries this ghostly pall, often shaping future relations with women in general. What I am reiterating here is that misogyny (and one of its most primitive expressions, matricide) corresponds with the unpreparedness of the psyche to contain.

RESURRECTING FROM THE ASHES

Putana is vanquished and she is not really owned as a mother; she is demonic, like the stepmother of fairy tales, like the surrogate father Kansa—she too is cast away, an aberration. The Kannada creation myth appears bolder in its acceptance of the incestuous, murderous mother; however, matricide leaves a cavity, which must be filled again. Then while she is partially resurrected, she is pared down, reduced, contained: a pale, domesticated shadow of the fiery original. In certain pockets we have versions of her local female deities who are protective but also terrifying, castrating like Shitla mata, the small-pox deity. She is worshipped, appealed to, deified and then immersed, laid to rest. So the contrast I am drawing here is between Putana split-off part of the mother, killed off by the omnipotent, suckling infant—and the mother of Brahma-Vishnu-Shiva, who is killed and then re-invented through dividing her into three lots. This relatively obscure version of the myth seems to bear the weight of acknowledging the terrifyingly bad mother who must be outwitted by Shiva and reduced to a heap of ashes. The incestuous, promiscuous, murderous mother is resurrected, but in order to build civilization, her scattered ashes must be divided. Depending on the vertex from where we interpret the myth (preoedipal or oedipal), the maternal seems fraught with dangers that seem almost too terrifying, and patriarchy with all its concomitant constraints seems almost preferable. This choice seems to reverberate through the absence of patricide as much as it does through the misogynistic figures that are either devouring or devoured.

The Kannada creation myth is an interesting variant on the omnipotence of Krishna, who unabashedly kills the bad mother and introjects her goodness (milk). In fact one can see how the baby Krishna embodies oral greed and hunger for the mother by being a butter thief; butter itself being a concentrated and enriched form of milk/breast/mother.

MADONNA AND THE WHORE

In the final section of this chapter, I am going to discuss the dream of a patient A. The specific details of the case are really irrelevant to the purpose here, as I felt while listening to his dream, that it carried within it a collection of whispers from many dreams and myths:

> *I was in a room with M and she starts pushing her bum on me, like a lap dance on me. She then takes off her clothes and becomes Beyoncé. It is as if she were saying: Is this what you imagined me to look like? I was quite surprised. Then the show's over. Does a show and then it's over. There's no sex. She's back on her computer. She's telling me 5 guys and I'm done. Now you and one more. I ask her why, why does she need to do this? She says to earn money. I say, but not like that! Then O walks in. M gets up and gives him a lap dance. It seemed so plausible. He's not malicious at all. He exits. She starts screaming at me:*

what are you going to do? How would you react if during the world cup, I were supporting my ex-lover's team? It would make you feel I am thinking of him. I'm confused and angry. She's the one that's angry with me. Her shouting is how the dream ends.

In his associations M represented someone erotically desirable but unattainable. O in all probability represents the patient's father who is seen as more endowed and with whom he has a deep rivalry.

This tantalizing girl is withholding her Beyoncé-like sexiness. She is only offering a lap dance and does not actually allow sex. This in fact makes A furious, and he needs to degrade her by saying she is a whore after all, providing the same service to other rivals. The dream catches the connection between the inaccessible and the reviled: the wish to degrade the rejecting object.

It seems as if this dream condenses the male fantasy of the enigmatic woman: she is the Madonna (does not have sex) and the whore (renders the same service to several). What is interesting about the dream is the way it both retains and discards the splits. The woman he desires and thinks of as sublime disappointingly turns out to be whorish. This echoes the discovery of the oedipal child: but my mother does not love me alone, there is/are others. This is almost too painful and the dream endeavors to make this pain bearable, by giving voice to the woman. The woman M turns to him at this point and her words are consoling, even if the tone appears not to be:

"*no matter what I do, you will always suspect me of being unfaithful!*"

The dream attempts to make containable what is experienced as uncontainable. The pull toward the prohibited woman/mother is experienced with unbearable intensity and the dream suggests different containing jars that might help to make this desire bearable: she titillates everyone by offering lap dances indiscriminately, she withholds from everyone including the ultimate rival O (so that I am not the only rejected suitor), she is whorish (she does it not for pleasure but money), and she has a history that predates my existence (but that does not mean she does not love me).

This dream brings together different aspects of the mother experienced by the desirous, overwhelmed child. While this patient was a young man, it is not by any means exclusive to men. Here are threads of different, often irreconcilable feelings that lie in close proximity but which, in our conscious minds we attempt to keep apart. Several feelings—fear of the woman's unknowable sexuality, her prehistory, her desirability as well as her arbitrary boundaries perplex the little, terrified infant who has several kinds of fantasies. This dream is singularly eloquent in the way it brings many of these fantasies together.

CONCLUSION

My bringing it up in this section of the chapter is to foreground the enigma of the mother, as experienced by the child who is confronted by a larger-than-life figure with an incomprehensible rhythm that appears cruel, perverse, terrifying, and also perhaps extraordinary, magical, beautiful, or perhaps a peculiar combination of both. Whatever its response may be, the infant can barely fathom this presence. This unfathomable other—perplexingly terrifying and seductive—seems connected to misogyny. The linguistic register that is used for women is all present in this dream: she is a virgin, a whore; she is omnivorous, indiscriminate, frigid. There may be different ways of understanding this. One is to see misogyny as a way of dealing with the projected hatred that is provoked in the infant at what must feel like a rejection by her in the fantasies. Another way of looking at it would be, to use Donald Meltzer's term, an apprehension of beauty (Meltzer 1988, p.16). From the moment of its birth, the infant is drawn not into the battle between life and death instincts but into the conflict between love and hate for the mother Meltzer terms the "aesthetic conflict":

Winnicott's stirring little radio talks of many years ago on The Ordinary Devoted Mother and her Baby could just as well have spoken of the "ordinary beautiful devoted mother and her ordinary beautiful baby." He was right to use that word ordinary, with its overtones of regularity and custom, rather than the statistical "average" (16).

The infant is struck by the ordinary, beautiful mother and responds to this with fear and even terror. This magical, beautiful mother evokes an excessiveness of unmetabolized feelings in the tiny infant who can respond only with awe, itself an experience which combines terror and beauty. Yeats (2008) incantatory refrain from "Easter 1916" captures this dimension as every stanza ends with the oxymoronic refrain "a terrible beauty is born." The capacity for tolerating a psychic paradox may emerge later if all else goes well. But I might hazard here that the disposition of the infant coupled with the mother's capacity to contain this excessiveness shapes the baby's capacity to relate to others, and misogyny is frequently a consequence. In sum, I am suggesting along with Freud, Klein, and Meltzer, that hate is perhaps easier to accommodate than love as a response to uncertainty and perhaps the awe. And also that loving brings with it depressive anxieties of losing the loved object; the infant's recourse to the paranoid-schizoid position—to hate—is a way of fending off the unconscious fears of loss. The seed of misogyny may well lie here, and later on, other fears of incest and castration may contribute their bit to this form of "othering" of the woman.

REFERENCES

Forster, L. W. *The Icy Fire: Five Studies in European Petrarchism*. New York: Cambridge University Press, 1969.

Freud, S. *Interpretation of Dreams. The Standard Edition of the Complete Psychological Works of Sigmund Freud.* Vol. 4. London: Hogarth and The Institute of Psychoanalysis. 1900.

Freud, S. *Totem and Taboo. The Standard Edition of the Complete Psychological Works of Sigmund Freud.* Vol. 13. London: Hogarth and The Institute of Psychoanalysis. 1913.

Gordon White, D. *Kiss of the Yogini: "Tantric Sex" and in its South Asian Contexts.* Chicago: Chicago University Press, 2006.

Jacobs, Amber. *On Matricide: Myth, Psychoanalysis, and the Law of the Mother.* New York: Columbia University Press, 2007.

Kakar, S. "Cults and myths of Krishna." In *Indian Literary Criticism: Theory and Interpretation,* edited by G.N. Devy. Orient Blackswan: India, 2002.

Kinsley, D. *Hindu Goddesses: Vision of the Divine Feminine in the Hindu Religious Traditions.* Delhi: Motilal Banarsidass, 1998.

Klein, M. *Contributions to Psychoanalysis 1921–45*. London: Kluckhohn, 1948.

Klein, M. *Envy and Gratitude*. London: Hogarth Press, 1946–63.

Meltzer, D. Harris Williams, M. *The Apprehension of Beauty: The Role of Aesthetic Conflict in Development, Art and Violence.* Perthshire: Clunie Press, 1988.

Meltzer, D. *The Psychoanalytical Process*. London: Heinemann, 1967.

Milton, J. *Paradise Lost.* Book IX, 121–2. London: Penguin, 2003.

O'Flaherty, W.D. *Women, Androgynes and other Mythical Beasts,* 101–2. Chicago: University of Chicago Press, 1982.

Ramanujan, A.K. "The Indian Oedipus." In *The Collected Essays of A.K. Ramanujan,* edited by Vinay Dharwadekar, 393. Delhi: OUP: 1971[1999].

Ramanujan, A.K. "Two Types of Kannada Folklore." In *The Collected Essays of A.K. Ramanujan,* edited by Vinay Dharwadekar. Delhi: OUP, 1986[1999].

Ramanujan, A.K. "Who Needs Folklore?" In *The Collected Essays of A.K. Ramanujan,* edited by Vinay Dharwadekar. Delhi: OUP, 1988[1999].

Yeats, W.B. *Easter Rising*. Collected Poems. London: Vintage, 2008.

Chapter Five

Sita Through the Time Warp

On the Ticklish Relationship between Renunciation and Moral Narcissism in the Lives of Young Indian Women

Shifa Haq

Sudhir Kakar's works, such as *Culture and Psyche* (1997), *The Inner World,* and *The Indians,* have built a corpus of knowledge on psychoanalysis in India.[1] I find myself to be a rich heir, astonished by the enormous wealth of ideas. Yet in the stories I tell and the stories I hear, I find myself at a loss when considering the experiences and the psyche of young Indian women. As a woman born in the wealth of Kakar's ideas and the wealth of her own doubts, I would like to delve into one such concern—the inheritance of the "Sita Ideal" in young Indian women. Kakar establishes the Sita ideal as a powerful cultural motif in the Indian psyche, producing patterns of choices and behavior through which ideal feminine qualities and expectations are rendered eternal. What happens when the "ideal" enters the clinic and leaps out of the unconscious like a wandering ascetic? How do we listen to the presence of Sita in the voices or experiences of young women, their preoccupation with the notion of "good woman," and the "will to renounce"? The paper re-reads the renunciatory principle of the Sita Ideal, written most persuasively by Kakar in *The Inner World* (1981), in hope of reflecting on the undisclosed riddles of the internal battleground borne by women.

KAKAR AND THE SITA IDEAL

For Kakar (1981), as for Winnicott (1971), the sensory presence of the mother, marked by a devoted involvement in the care of the infant, is the hallmark of human relationships. Whether held in deep regard by psychoanalysts or in myths and folklore, a child's relation to her mother is an indivisible shadow against which many adult aspirations take shape. Kakar notes that childhood in India is an idealized part of the cultural imagination and, to an Indian woman, motherhood confers a purpose and an identity that nothing else in her culture can, especially if that child is a son. The gestalt of mothering in India is a complex interplay of the mother's own unconscious repository and her place in the social matrix that inscribes on her identity roles and expectations, so that she exists in her relationships with others. A young woman I worked with, Amrita, described her childhood in a village on the outskirts of Delhi as follows, "There was my brother, who had a glass full of goat's milk, and my younger sister was little so she needed nourishment too. As the middle child, the milk for me was diluted to make the glass full. It felt like I was being punished. At other times, I thought my body did not need so much. I thought I needed to support my brother and my sister." On listening to this, I felt deeply troubled by the leaps her mind had made in a few swift movements. At the age of 24, she came for therapy for she did not know how to respond to her lover who had slept with her close friend. She said that though she had many mature responses to this event, she was looking for "appropriate" anger. [One could ask why not "proportionate," "legitimate" instead of "appropriate." For the time being, let us preserve these gaps.]

Kakar, in *The Inner World* (1981), writes, "one would expect the preferences for sons, the cultural devaluation of girls, to be somehow reflected in the psychology of Indian women. Theoretically, one possible consequence of this kind of inequity would be heightened female hostility and envy towards males, together with a general pronounced antagonism between the sexes . . . I do not have sufficient evidence to be categorical; yet my impression is that these phenomena do not, in general, characterize the inner world of Indian women" (p. 59). While there may be proclivities within Indian women, raised in a patriarchal society, to turn the aggression inwards into feelings of worthlessness and inferiority, strong identifications with the mothering persons and the secret passage to spheres of femininity through domesticity or cultural ideals offer an alternative to young girls so that their silences take on puzzling meanings.

The Sita ideal, in the psyche of Indian women and men, represents a powerful presence. Standing as an epitome of chastity, wifely devotion, and self-surrender, it runs deep in the psychic substratum. We are familiar with the legend of Sita—her marriage to Rama and the adventures and hardships of their exile. The Ramayana narrates Sita's kidnapping by the demon-god Ravana who is slain by Rama. Doubting Sita's fidelity, Rama puts Sita through the *agni-pareeksha* (trial by fire). The fire god himself testifies to her purity and they return to Ayodhya. Unable to put his suspicion to rest, Rama banishes Sita again. Dejected, Sita embraces an ascetic life and gives birth to twins. The twins grow up and return to their father. On seeing his sons, Rama repents and asks Sita to return to Ayodhya. However, he asks her to take the trial by fire again, to prove her purity, leaving Sita to embrace her death wish; she calls upon mother earth to swallow her.

While her faithfulness and chastity are celebrated in many social and religious interpretations of the myth, the myth influences the identity and character of Hindu women regardless of their caste, class, or education. The internalization of the ideal, notes Kakar (1981), makes the repudiation of desires, including the rebellion against "the constraints of impinging womanhood," possible (p. 63). In other words, the subject learns to govern her own behavior to guarantee other's approval of her (Kakar, S. and Kakar K., 2009). She must therefore be the guardian of her morals and pride. I am concerned with Sita and her "will to renounce." I will refer to this as the renunciatory principle of the Sita ideal.[2] I am interested in the Sita ideal not as a motif emblematic of the moral order it perpetuates in the Indian psyche or the social functions it establishes such as the construction of femininity in Indian culture, but the will to renounce as I have come to see it in the lives of Indian women, where wanting and feeling are experienced as violent invasions in the serene waters of the feminine. I wish to approach the Sita ideal not from the perspective of the dharma of a devoted wife but as the depressed Sita who actively abandons.

While, in the Valmiki Ramayana, Sita is said to have been discovered in a furrow by King Janaka who adopts and raises her, in *Adbudht Ramayana* (2001), Sita's birth is elaborated and describes her mother's torment.[3] Ruth Vanita, in *Gandhi's Tiger and Sita's Smile* (2005a), narrates this legend as follows:

> Mandodari, Ravana's wife, neglected by her unfaithful husband, tries to commit suicide by drinking the blood of sages that he had collected and told her was poisonous. But the blood impregnates her instead of poisoning her. Afraid that she will be accused of adultery, she aborts in a field. The foetus develops into the baby Sita, who is found and adopted by Janaka. Thus, Sita is the product of a neglected and suicidal wife's despair. The male element in her birth is an ascetic one (p. 230).

Sita, then, carries the autonomous principle of feminine creativity as well as suicidal despair. There is a potential to realize the ascetic ideal as well as the tendency toward dark crevices of depression—like two strings in the dotara, the folk instrument, running parallel to one another.

While many thinkers, including Kakar, have written about the enlivening presence of the Indian mother whose sensory presence is legible on the psyche-soma, my attempt is to throw light on the experience of maternal depression in Mandodari, who abandons Sita, and Sita, who disavows her rage at devaluation. I wish to trace the relevance of psychic deadness and moral narcissism as defense against anxiety caused by sexual impulses and maternal failures as they are illuminated inside the clinic. Let us consider a fragment from a life, which may help uncover this grand cultural schema a little further.

DEVIKA: A CLINICAL VIGNETTE

Devika came to me when her short but intense relationship with Manish came to an end. She explained that she carried an intense urge to cry and broke down often when she was with him.[4] This troubled Manish deeply. On being asked by Manish about what made her cry she offered no answer. In therapy, she introduced herself similarly. She came to sessions but was unable to utter a word. It took us a few months to understand her need to cry in the ambit of wordlessness. She recalled that soon after her relationship began, she felt restless and confused. She cried whenever Manish left for work, went out of the city, or when a beautiful evening together came to the expected end. This astonished and challenged Manish to a great extent. Devika was not behaving like the girl he wanted, "independent, confident and sure of herself," his first impressions of her. On the contrary, she appeared deeply dependent, unhappy, and ill. Ironically, to Devika, her not voicing the unbearable pain of separation offered a veneer of independence and self-respect that she held on to precariously. Unable to deal with Devika's bouts of tears, he became less and less affected by her states, and chose work over her until he could no longer live with her. I struggled to understand Devika's difficulty in expressing longings and the need for dependence to her lover. Being in love had become an impossible affliction and an exercise in exile.

At the age of 12, Devika had lost her mother to what seemed like a sudden hemorrhage. She rarely reflects on the loss of her mother. According to Devika, her death was "nothing new," for her depressed presence cast a heavy shadow on their relationship. Recounting one of her earliest memories, she shared, "I remember going with my mother to a park outside our house. I was perhaps 4 or 5 years old. I fell from the gate I had climbed. I looked to my mother as I hit the ground. She did not come to pick me up." With no word uttered or feelings exchanged, the child learnt the grammar of a depressed mother. Many years later, Manish mysteriously echoed the same indifference preserved in the memory. For Devika's mother, marriage and motherhood did not become an inspired labor of love but a natural or pre-ordained turn for women. She recalls feeling a deep unease when at home, and escaped to neighbors and friends for refuge. Therapy became an occasion to understand and rework the story of her mother's depression, while she asks hesitatingly, "Is it important?"[5] In the wake of the mother's death, Devika became a "helpful" child to a grieving father who relied on his "little soldier" to rebuild their lives.[6] She views this as a natural progression and when touched upon in therapy, she asks "so what?" While words escaped us, her body communicated unambivalently through severe fatigue, panic, restlessness, insomnia, and shifting pains. These states are reminiscent of intense primitive anxieties of a baby, needing a devoted container or the facilitative environment expressed in Winnicott's thoughts and Jamini Roy's paintings—held in the warm embrace of a mothering person who nourishes and protects the baby from primitive anxieties let loose by rejection and abandonment.

A year into therapy, Devika sat overwhelmed with regret for having had sex with a suitable man she met two days before. She announced, to him and to me, that it was a mistake and that it shouldn't have happened. She added that she acted "like someone else," someone she did not know. Contrary to her admission, the man reminded her that he did not force himself and that she was the same person he made love to the night before. Swamped with guilt, she asked me what I thought about it. It seemed to me that she was waiting for my reproach or disapproval that it was too risqué or too reckless of her. Instead, I responded, "You are getting to learn new things about yourself." She was relieved as well as disappointed by my response. A little later, emerging from deep thought, she added, "It wasn't that I had sex with a man. But that I do not want him in my life." I asked, "Like it never happened?" She was quiet. During the silence, I was reminded of another patient I worked with a few years ago who experienced cuddling with her lovers as far more sensuous and intimate than sex. I reflected back to Devika, "Sometimes sex is not as intimate as we think," communicating to her that perhaps she hasn't betrayed her private self, which is unwilling to allow entry to the man in question.

There is a lot to think about our interaction here. By becoming a permissive object, I came in conflict with the immaculate Sita, incapable of impure feelings. While renouncing the pleasurable delights of adult sexuality comes to her as an obvious choice, one might ask whether psychotherapy is complicit in freeing (or alienating) the subject from her traditionally held values, into the horizons of modernity and its disputatious internal revolutions. Am I freeing sex from the burden of "true love" or puncturing the taboo subject of women's sexuality that, through repetitive cultural performativity, in the lives of mothers and daughters, conceals the lack of, as well as the desire for, mutuality, tenderness, and love? We find that Devika carried a sense of guilt and the fear of discovering a sexual self, but more importantly, she was bent on renouncing any possible connection with a real object. What does the wish to expunge a possible relationship imply?

In the course of therapy, a pattern emerges. She yearns and struggles to form lasting bonds. She has begun sensing the intensity of her need to belong to someone, to make a home, but her neediness remains unexpressed in the façade of maturity. She gravitates toward nurturing women, feels restored in these relationships but, unfortunately, her wish for closeness, in the context of these relationships, is experienced by her as illegitimate "demands." She fights bitterly to not repeat the mistake or give rise to expectations within. Instead, she chooses to withdraw; that is, to renounce the need to have or to belong, until wanting seems alien and its fulfilment unnecessary. In therapy too, she actively recreates the *fort-da* between us, with episodes of disappearances, abating my feelings of love and concern for her[7] (Freud 1920). Her predominant feeling remains that of homelessness, which breaks her down, yet at the same time liberates her. In therapy, she is able to articulate the wish to be independent and free from the bonds of love. In an uncanny improvisation, she becomes the independent woman of Manish's desires. She articulates this as: "One should not have to ask to be taken care of. The other should know. It's humiliating to have to ask. Now I don't even want it." She continues to describe her feeling as: "I feel as if I am floating. I am either on a cloud or behind a thick fog. I feel that something crawls into me and it sucks in all that there is—like a black hole."

In one session she struggled to describe the feeling she knows too well but cannot speak of. She said, "I feel choked and constricted, like there is something around me, holding me down . . . restraining me." At this point, she gestured with her hands, making a circular motion. I responded, "Like a serpent coiling itself around you, squeezing and breaking your bones." Relieved to get a metaphor, Devika replied, "The serpent is not squeezing me. It is more like it is right there and one cannot do much about it."

I reflected on that and said, "So the serpent is a disciplining force? The baby wants to explode, be spontaneous, but the serpent hisses and controls."

Devika retorted, "Why do you think it's a baby?" and I replied, "Why not? Why do you resist being a baby?"

"I have a friend who is mollycoddled, often indulged by everyone around. She enjoys it and complains about being made into a baby. But that's not the case with me. I am seen as extremely responsible, mature and independent. I wish somebody saw the baby in me. (pause) You should be careful. I am over-demanding."[8]

Seeing her articulate the conflict of wanting and fearing the emergence of the child, I prodded, "That's very judgmental of you, just like the serpent disciplining the baby. Whose side are you on?"

With much relief, she added, "I am on the side of the baby."

The fragment of the session carries significant questions in its labyrinth. How do we make sense of the serpent in the room, a silent presence that she feels around her all the time? Is the serpent coiled around her, a symbol of wordless dread, the image of maternal depression that constitutes Devika's inner world? Green (1986a) suggests that a chronically depressed or emotionally absent mother transforms the inner vitality of the baby into a psychically dead child. The coils of the serpent do not nourish like the umbilical cord connecting the baby to her mother, but become a punishing maternal presence refusing to acknowledge the baby's narcissistic needs. Green imagined this as "murder without hatred" (Green 1986a).[9] The serpent and the baby together allude to the failure of mutual recognition through which autonomy and relatedness become a vital source of play (Benjamin 1988). Furthermore, the image of the serpent as a disciplining figure is a testimony to the abridged childhood of a girl child in India. It is an allusion central to the gendering of the baby. The restraining or binding experience, through the use of domination and consequent compliance, forfeits embracing a spontaneous exploration of the self, which Winnicott (1965) referred to as the "true self."[10] It is within the feminine identity formation in the Indian context to make peace with the cultural ideal while changing the force of her instinctual life. Kakar, in *The Inner World*, writes, "Any inner shift towards, or desire for, autonomy arouses the most severe of the culturally supported anxieties: the fear of isolation or estrangement that are visited upon the completely autonomous human being" (p. 36). At one level there is the patient's individual history, the story of her mother's depression and her inability to mirror the growing child's vitality; on another level, there is an ever-looming imprinting of the Sita ideal. The hissing snake also represents Devika's disavowed anger at empathic failures, living side by side, incommunicado, while she loves and laughs. What would it mean for her to let it be seen, to be known not for her patience and care, but for her poisonous fangs, indiscriminate in their ruthlessness? Will my women patients wish to find out this side to them?

RENUNCIATION AND MORAL NARCISSISM

Much has been written about submission, masochism, and women in psychoanalytic literature. Instead of recreating the polyphony of voices from what seems like a rich dialogue between psychoanalysis and feminism, I would attempt to argue that, in the constellation of observations I have tried to illumine through the clinical case, there is a creative tension between what Freud called moral masochism and what Green developed as moral narcissism.[11]

What does it mean to renounce pleasure? Similarly, what is the relation between masochism and renunciation? What guides the will to create a sovereign self, free of its dependence on the object? What is the predicament of lives where the ceaseless erosion of the self or the disappearance of desire is held as an ideal? Freud in "The Economic Problem of Masochism" (1924) writes, "If pain and unpleasure can be not simply warnings but actually aims, the pleasure principle is paralysed—it is as though the watchman over our mental life were put out of action by a drug" (p.159). What one sees is not a simple co-occurrence of two forces—life and death—but their "fusion and amalgamation" in varying proportions (Freud 1924, p. 164). Our proclivities and "taste buds" for the complex fusion of instincts is developed through early experiences (Eigen 2010). Freud considered that the destructive instinct, guided by pleasure-unpleasure, seeks mastery either by the will to power, sadism, or the will to submit, masochism. A masochist pursuit, through the negation of pleasure and a passionate search for unpleasure, rediscovers a rich tie to the object. In the fantasy of submission or domination, there is an unrelenting and near impossible search for surrender. Ghent (1990) suggests that object usage, transitional experiencing and the "longing for something in the environment to make possible the surrender, in the sense of yielding, of the false self" are deeply intertwined (p. 109). Just as for Ghent, surrender is possible in the presence of another person who devotedly creates facilitative conditions; renunciation, the way I see it, is a repudiation of the desire for the other's presence, where self-overcoming or disbelief in the other is the *raison d'être.*[12] While true surrender may remain elusive, object relating may still happen through submission, resignation, and, I believe, through renunciation. Rosenfeld (1971) observes this shift as a narcissistic state of defused destructive impulse seeking to destroy "the caring self, his love, forever and there is nothing anybody can do to change the situation" (p. 173).

While a masochist, according to Freud, "always turns his cheek whenever he has a chance of receiving a blow" (p. 165), there is, however, another kind of self-punishment that seeks not the pleasure involved in masochistic fantasy, but the punishment involved to save one's honor, a substratum of narcissism called "moral narcissism" (Green 1986b, p. 118). According to Green, "the true moral narcissist always volunteers himself whenever he sees a chance of renouncing a satisfaction" (p. 119). While masochistic fantasies revolve around being beaten, dominated, or reduced to passivity in relation to an "other," for a moral narcissist, it is matter of being pure or free of pleasure and displeasure through the active renunciation of one's ties with the other. Here, the vow of endurance and willing absorption in solitude, destitution, and poverty or even hermitage is held dearly.[13] While Freud imagined the masochist as the one who desires to be treated like a child,[14] the aspiration of a moral narcissist is just the opposite. He desires to imitate the parents who have no trouble dominating their instincts. The megalomanic self overcomes instincts and surrenders only to the ego-ideal.[15] What we have is not a child tormented by desires but a grown-up, held together by impressive wisdom and principles. Compared to a masochist who maintains a rich tie to the object passionately involved in producing the pleasure-unpleasure in the masochist, a narcissist tries to abandon it.[16] Here, the pain is bound to the knowledge or the experience that one's satisfaction runs through a "willing" object and frustration arises when the object disappoints. Green adds, "To resolve this conflict the narcissist will attempt increasingly to impoverish his object relationships in order to reduce the ego to its vital object minimum, thus emerging triumphant. This attempt is constantly frustrated by the instincts which require that the satisfaction pass through an object. The only solution is a narcissistic cathexis of the subject, and we know that when the object withdraws itself, is lost, or disappoints, the result is depression" (p. 121). Seen from this position, the rise of excitement is better left untasted, the push and pull of desire better left undiscovered.

The renunciation of attachments to the object, or the reform of the ego with asceticism as a mode of being, forces the ego toward a progressive shrinking, replacing the excitement of wants with a logic of needs. The subject evacuates pleasure and embraces survival. Like a devoted worker, engaged in the passion of labor, the self or the body is immersed in work, of caretaking, removed from the trappings of the exciting object (Fairbairn 1952). Interestingly, the use of renunciation may operate as an ego ideal not only for the subject torn by desire, but also for cultures that privilege the ascetic self or ascetic living. It is important to situate the two shades of renunciation here. Renunciation, or the willing abnegation of material comforts and attachments, has been considered an important resolution in many religious societies. Renunciation, in the Indian worldview, is believed to be an act of giving up or relinquishing one's ties with objects of possession toward a spiritual pursuit of joy in transcendence. Considered within the frames of the spiritual realm, the abandonment of worldly pursuits, objects of desire or possession, and the self defined in relation with others, is actively sought to present liberation or *moksha* and inner tranquility. In the Indian cultural imagination, the state of abandon is a powerful fantasy for individuals, whether they nurse it into reality or are deeply guided, in their psyche, by its romantic escape. The renunciatory ideal that I am interested in resides not in the streets, the holy banks of great rivers, or a hermitage in great mountains and their forests. It is the secular ascetic ideal, the quest for a sovereign self, carried in the crevices of the psyche, to accomplish a world devoid of connections or instinctual gratifications. Women's identification with the ascetic ideal, defined here by the renouncing Sita, makes the admission of instincts into their consciousness dangerous and frightening. As Green points out, "there is a refusal to see the world as it is—that is the battle ground upon which human appetites indulge in an endless combat" (p. 125). Unlike the spiritual renunciation through which surrender or the transformation of the self is sought and desired, renunciation, in moral narcissism, repudiates desires, the object's presence, and the recognition of mutuality in the service of a defensive sovereignty of a pure self (Benjamin 1988).

There is, of course, a prevalence of asceticism in the Indian cultural context wherein women's opting out is a legitimate question. Ruth Vanita (2005b) cites a curious case of a woman who left marital unhappiness to join the Brahmakumaris. The vow of celibacy, taken under the ascetic order, brought a closure to conjugal relations with her husband. She lived amongst her family while incorporating the changes brought by her vows. Soon the family found the special food she cooked unpalatable and she started cooking only for herself. Despite clear resentment about her new lifestyle, they found it hard to forbid it. Ascetic life, surprisingly, brought access to mobility, as well as a way to imagine life unconstrained by filial trappings. While there are women who, through a strong religious identification, come to embrace asceticism, the modern subjects who frequent psychotherapists are, however, largely unmoved by passionate religious ideals and renounce not the worldly affairs but love affairs with desired objects. Their quest is not a spiritual one through which overcoming the self is transformed into splendid joy; it is rather an impressive domination of the cauldron called instincts.[17] Renunciation, as my work with young women shows, implies that a loved aspect of the self is surrendered or repudiated in the service of the ego-ideal. This is an inevitable journey for many young women, mothers and daughters, whose lives witness repetitions, if also a possibility of remembering and working through, of Mandodari's renunciation of her daughter and the beginning of an ascetic self in Sita.

In the portrayals of the mother–daughter bond, their connection to or the inheritance of the ascetic ideal, there is an opportunity to understand generational continuities and fractures. For Kakar, the image is a hopeful one where the young daughter, through her identification with the women, internalizes the Sita ideal to negotiate with the new—marked by challenges of identity transitions, sexuality, and relationships, and the search for the self—thereby finding her roots through the many fluctuations in fortune (Erikson 1964). But is this journey to renunciation, the submission of desire in a young girl, experienced as the tender caress of the maternal tethering of the self, circumscribing spontaneity?[18] We have, for long, admired Sita giving up worldly pleasures and comforts; but Sita, the one enamored by the golden deer, still awaits our approval and compassion. The journey I hope to attempt in psychotherapy with young women is the one where "giving up" and disavowal are questioned before their fortuitous idealization.

A daughter's familiarity with maternal depression, such as we know in Devika, and the theft of the self that ensues this mutative experience, acts as a veil concealing feelings of hurt, disappointment, and deep depression (Bollas 2012). An empathic exploration of young women as daughters can unlock currents of mourning if one waits long enough and bears the affliction of "wanting" for both the daughter as well as the mother.[19] The isolation of mothers in the confines of urban cities and the lack of contact with other female kin deprive the young girl of other possible secure mothering presences. Nancy Chodorow (1999) adds that the extreme need of emotional support in daughters in an ambit of very few intense relationships distorts the expectations from a romantic relationship into an ideal of total emotional sustenance.[20] Love is experienced as a menacing affliction. On the one hand is the wish to possess a loving object for one's psychic survival; on the other, wanting is experienced as humiliating. Phillips (2012) asks, "Which of them is the tyrant, the mother who doesn't deliver, or the frustrated child? What are the preconditions for tyranny? How does it become such a handed-down misery? Does the proud will frustrate, or is it the product of frustration, pride being a state of mind, a way of being organized as a self-cure for certain kinds of frustration? It is to this first deception and making void that we need to turn" (p. 16).

CONCLUSION

To return to the beginning of the chapter, Amrita, in her third year of therapy, found herself overcome by fatigue and pain in her body. The unsettling pain was not a testimony to depression but a consequence of malnutrition and calcium deficiency, as exposed by the elaborate medical examination undertaken by Amrita to get to the root of the problem. Relieved to learn that the pain was not a prelude to an illness but a case of severe deficiency, she shared the news with her family. Her father expressed disappointment in her spending money on tests only to find that she had no illness. From the asymmetry of father's devaluation of her and a self not so pulverized, she replied, "If I go through medical tests and find out that I don't have a disease, it is *not* money wasted. It should be a moment of joy." Through the therapeutic journey, from not knowing how to react, to confronting the father's devaluation of her, she learns to choose *enunciation* of the self over renunciation.

I ask to consider what it might mean to dream the "poorly conceived" Indian women. How can psychoanalysis contribute to their lives, made and un-made by "narcissization" ensued by new cultural shifts (Alizade 2010)? The staccato in the not-yet-free associations asks the therapist to invite the asymmetry of lived and unlived lives so that one day the neuroses and the ideals may begin to converse with each other. To make culture audible to psychoanalysis, as suggested by Kakar, requires new wanderings. It calls for a departure from the politics of the "inherent" to a space of "inheritance." Sita will perhaps remain inimitable for the Indian psyche but, as she travels time, will she appear different?

NOTES

1. Parts of the chapter were first presented at a symposium organized by the Psychology Department, Christ University, Bangalore, January 2015.

2. In the "will to renounce," one may find an uncanny re-occurrence of Nietzsche's "'will to power" through "self-mastery" or "self over-coming."

3. The birth of Sita, as recounted in *Adbhut Ramayana*, offers the possibility to imagine a complex mother-daughter relationship which we do not find in other versions about her birth. Sita, through this tradition, is both an abandoned child and also a goddess with female powers or *Shakti*. In foregrounding this version of the popular myth, I wish to locate inner unrest in Sita's character.

Adbhut Ramayana is traditionally attributed to Valmiki and carries 27 chapters in which Valmiki narrates the story to Rishi Bhardwaja.

4. The case presented here is an ongoing clinical work at a university-based low-fee clinic, Ehsaas, run by CPCR, Ambedkar University Delhi. Through the low-fee clinics, the center hopes to provide psychoanalytic psychotherapy to socially and economically challenged sections of the society.

5. Maternal depression, to me, is a complex phenomenon not only for the baby who is deprived of the capacity for mutual recognition in the mother-child dyad, as emphasized by relational psychoanalysts, but also for the mother who is a subject in her own right, as suggested by Jessica Benjamin and Adrian Rich, stifled or supported by circumstances.

6. Devika continually feels talking to her father about the states of anxiety and panic as difficult. She felt that it was more important that she worked on these states in therapy with me than give a hint to the father and "add to his worries." Her choice to live in another city provided a neat separation precluding his involvement. Here, the migration to another city is reminiscent of the childhood escape from the "gloomy house," carrying the promise of happiness and uprootedness, both at the same time.

7. While in many relationships her wanting and needing remained unfulfilled, it is now, in the third year of therapy, that needing my presence is becoming a source of pleasure and delight for Devika. In the transference, she sees me as an indulgent maternal presence, biased and protective toward her desires and blind to her faults. I

see this as an interesting caricature of me which she both ridicules as well as enjoys. It's a site of playfulness—a potential space for self love and self-cohesion.

8. The word "over-demanding" is a reflection on the perceived illegitimacy of her desires or feelings in the absence of empathic recognition from the caregivers. One hears similar echo in psychoanalytic theory about gratification, when excessive or lacking, in usage such as "over-gratification" or "under-gratification." Such a conception mystifies self-other relationship by reducing the baby to passive receiving of caregiver's ministrations.

9. Larkin in his poem, "This be the verse" (collected poems, 2001), offers his rendering of what Green calls 'Murder without hatred' in utterly uncomplicated fashion as:

> They fuck you up, your mom and dad.
> they may not mean to, but they do.
> they fill you with the faults they had
> And some extra, just for you.

10. Here, it is important to ask whether the journey to the true self, in the analytic treatment, means the same for different genders. Masculine and feminine experience of spontaneity and aliveness are shaped and reinforced according to the sexual hierarchy prevalent in our societies.

11. I am grateful to the contributions made by my colleagues from the Psychology Colloquium, Ambedkar University Delhi. Their ideas and insights helped me during the writing of the working document, I hope I have been able to attend to some of our "collective ranklings" pertaining to the questions of gender, culture, and psychoanalysis.

12. Ghent (1990) suggests that inability to surrender is akin to failure of faith or failure of object-seeking.

13. Anna Freud (1936) was also interested in this profound asceticism and saw this as a defense mechanism common to adolescence in the normal development of an individual.

14. Also, a "naughty child" (Freud 1924).

15. Freud (1924) wrote "the sadism of the super-ego and the masochism of the ego supplement each other and unite to produce the same effects" (p. 170).

16. Kundera, in the novel *Life is Elsewhere* (2000) writes about the careful premeditation of the one who abandons, " . . . he must not take part in the rigged game in which ephemeral passes for the eternal and the small for the big, that he must not take part in the rigged game called love" (p. 64)

17. The inner world of Indian patients, women and men, is replete with presence of sages and saints. In clinical work, these figures are invoked in their associations as an unfailing, boundless maternal presence. The ascetic life of the sages and saints inspires and provokes them to reflect on on relationships, unbearable conflicts with greed and attachment as well as offers the fantasy of relief from suffering.

18. Benjamin, J. (1988) writes, "The psychic repudiation of femininity, which includes the negation of dependency and mutual recognition, is homologous with the

social banishment of nurturance and intersubjective relatedness to the private domestic world of women and children" (p. 185)

19. The surfacing of little girl's unconscious anger and bitterness toward her mother is an important juncture in psychotherapy. It is through this slow process, of working through, in which the sacred tie with the mother is risked, ambuscaded, and repaired. The journey to mother's subjectivity, particularly in psychotherapy, cannot be completed without empathy for the self that feels deserted, unmothered, or carries what Adrianne Rich (1986) calls, fantasies of the "unhealed child" wishing to have "an infinitely healing conversation with her, in which we could show all wounds, transcend the pain we have shared as mothers and daughters, say everything at last" (p. 224)

20. The works of psychoanalytic thinkers such as Juliet Mitchell, Adrianne Harris, and Susie Orback point that there may be other domains too, such as body, autonomy-separation, and morality, where the feminine experience carries the stamp of a complex gendered developmental trajectory.

REFERENCES

Alizade, M. "Trauma and Positivity." In *Psychoanalysis and Positivity.* London: Karnac, 2010.

Benjamin, J. *The Bonds of Love—Psychoanalysis, Feminism and the Problem of Domination.* New York: Pantheon Books, 1988.

Bollas, C. *The Christopher Bollas Reader.* London: Rutledge, 2012.

Chodorow, N. *Reproduction of Mothering—Psychoanalysis and Sociology of Gender.* Berkeley: University of California Press, 1999.

Eigen, M. *Madness and Murder: Eigen in Seoul.* Vol 1. London: Karnac, 2010.

Erikson, E. "Identity and Uprootedness in Our Time." In *Insight and Responsibility.* New York: W. W. Norton, 1964.

Fairbairn, W.R.D. *Psychoanalytic Studies of Personality.* New York: Rutledge, 1952.

Freud, A. "The Ego and the Mechanism of Defence." In *The Writings of Anna Freud,* Vol.II. London: Hogarth Press, 1936.

Freud, S. "Beyond the Pleasure Principle." In *The Standard Edition of the Complete Works of Sigmund Freud.* Vol. 18, 1–64. edited by J. Strachey. London: Vintage and Hogarth Press, 2001[1920].

Freud, S. "The Economic Problem of Masochism." In *The Standard Edition of the Complete Works of Sigmund Freud.* Vol. 19, 1–64. edited by J. Strachey. London: Vintage and Hogarth Press, 2001[1924].

Ghent, E. "Masochism, Submission, Surrender-Masochism as Perversion of Surrender." *Contemporary Psychoanalysis* 26(1990): 108–136.

Green, A. "The Dead Mother." In *On Private Madness.* London: Karnac, 1986a.

Green, A. "Moral Narcissism." In *On Private Madness.* London: Karnac, 1986b.

Kakar, S. *The Inner World.* New Delhi: Oxford University Press, 1981.

Kakar, S. *Culture and Psyche.* New Delhi: Oxford University Press, 1997.

Kakar, K. and Kakar, S. *The Indians: Portrait of a People.* New Delhi: Penguin India, 2009.
Larkin, P. *High Windows.* London: Faber and Faber, 1974.
Kundera, M. *Life is Elsewhere.* London: Faber and Faber, 2000.
Nagar, S. ed. *Adbhut Ramayana.* New Delhi: B R Publishing Corporation, 2001.
Nietzche, F. *Will to Power*. Translated by Walter Kaufmann, edited by R. J. Hollingdale. New York: Vintage, 1968[1901].
Phillips, A. *Missing Out: In Praise of the Unlived Life.* London: Penguin Books, 2012.
Rich, A. *Of Women Born: Motherhood as Experience and Institution.* New York: W.W. Norton & Co., 1986.
Rosenfeld, H. "A Clinical Approach to the Psychoanalytic Theory of Life and Death Instincts—An Investigation into the Aggressive Aspects of Narcissism." *International Journal of Psychoanalysis* 52(1971): 169–178.
Vanita, R. "Thinking Beyond Gender in India." In *Gandhi's Tiger and Sita's Smile—Essays on Gender, Sexuality and Culture*. New Delhi: Yoda Press, 2005a.
Vanita, R. "Sita Smiles: Wife as Goddess in the Adbhut Ramayana." In *Gandhi's Tiger and Sita's Smile—Essays on Gender, Sexuality and Culture.* New Delhi: Yoda Press, 2005b.
Winnicott, D.W. "Ego Distortions in terms of True and False Self." In *The Maturational Process and the Facilitating Environment: Studies in the Theory of Emotional Development.* New York: International UP Inc., 1965.
Winnicott, D.W. *Playing and Reality.* London: Tavistock, 1971.

Part II

FAITH, RELIGION, AND VIOLENCE

Chapter Six

Terrors to Expansions

A Journey Mediated through Faith

Shalini Masih

THEORETICAL FOUNDATION

Hailing from a family of healers and exorcists, and having formed a life-long relationship with psychology, I often wondered if the domain of psychology would ever be able to expand enough to include, and cater to, those experiencing terrors ensuing from loss of agency over mind and body, culturally understood as spirit possession. My journey in the enchanting yet terrifying terrain of spirits was initiated through Kakar's (1982) work, which offered windows into insecurities and vulnerabilities that plague the Indian psyche, and for which, perhaps intuiting a need for some kind of resolution, culture makes available a language populated by the "supernatural." I wondered if such a person would ever walk into my clinic, or if the clinic could reach out to such a person. What would be challenges that one would face? Would psychoanalytic technique remain the same? If not, in what ways would it alter? If the possessed person's self is broken, how can a therapist "work in the trenches"?

In the lives of possessed individuals, early maternal abandonment, abuse, physical punishment, and punitive presences in the household were common features. I noticed that before a healer diagnosed them as possessed, many patients reported experiencing dread, nightmares, and night-terrors. Terror has a certain brutal suddenness or abruptness. I wonder if it is abruptness of an experience that makes it brutal and evokes terror. I have found help in the thoughts of various psychoanalytic thinkers who have reflected on terror as ensuing from loss of distinction between subject and object, and consequently an inability to carry on psychological work. Whether terror forecloses thinking, or is set off because of the inability to think, is a question which cannot be easily answered. I am counting on you, the reader, to ally with me in this state of terror, where it is as if all capacities to think are eaten up, and there is a desperate groping for an Other, from whom some comfort can be received. By giving credence to the "baby" (which still lingers in all of us), psychoanalysis keeps the fear of being eaten up and swallowed as basal. More actively, Winnicott's (1971) pursuit of the baby in us has explained that the mother, by intuiting what the baby wants, gathers the scatter and the inside processes can be formed. Without the mother's facilitating presence, "the infant's experiences take place in a psycho-social void, and his development is likely to be severely disturbed." (Kakar 1981, p. 54) It is in this "void" where terror envelops, germinating from a failure in gathering; from mis-links, mis-alliances, or mis-recognition of an infant's state on the part of the mother. Drawing on Winnicott, Green wrote, "If the mother is away over a period of time which is beyond a certain limit measured in minutes, hours, or days, then the memory of the internal representation fades. As this takes effect, the transitional phenomena become gradually meaningless and the infant is unable to experience them. We may watch the object becoming decathected." [Winnicott 1971, p. 15, quoted by Green 1999, p. 209] Eigen (2010) elaborates on the same line of thought and writes about a Z dimension which a child enters if the mother returns after X+Y+Z time. It is in this dimension or state where he "undergoes a change, a permanent alteration, damage. Something tight, angry, something wrong, something withdrawn. Spontaneous recovery doesn't happen. In therapy with certain people more than others, it's the Z dimension we focus on, a dying out we don't return from, that we live around, develop paranoia around, or anger around, or withdrawn around" (p. 28). Kristeva (1982), and later Mitrani (2001), as quoted in Akhtar 2009), through their notion of the "abject" and the "jettisoned object," talk about states of ruptured omnipotence, following brutal separation with the subject, where the distinctions between the subject and object are lost, and subsequently adhesive identifications emerge, throwing the self into a state of collapse. The object, rather than eliciting desire or hate and thus forming a link with the subject, creates a pull toward a terrifying gaping void between them. This dread that one will fade away in the object's eyes is best reflected upon by French psychoanalysts Botella and Botella (2005) who go a step further with their theory that trauma lies in imagining one's own absence in the object's eyes, that one is not invested in.

Who contains the terror? Bion's (1962) imagination of the mother with her transformative alpha-function answers this question. In the lives of research participants[1] with foundational experiences that evoked difficult feelings and with a failure of the environment to contain and process the same, whatever was evoked seemed ego-alien. States evoked remain unthinkable, inchoate, ghostly, and, like an apparition, evoke fear and revulsion, and are to be evacuated via splitting, projection, or in body and actions. "Non-representation is experienced by the ego as an excess of excitation; and if the mind does not arrive, by virtue of a transformation, at an experience of intelligibility accessible to the system of representations, the ego will experience it as traumatic" (Botella and Botella 2005, p. 113).

Kakar's (1982) thinking helps in understanding that the first feeble attempt at representation of terror is facilitated by culture, and begins to happen in the form of *bhuta* or *samkat.* Ordinarily, we do not know how to move closer to the terror. How to touch someone who is absent to herself? Who can touch this blazing *vacuum* of the unthinkable? In its attempt toward wholeness, psyche, with whatever slim capacities and accompanying ambiguities, does try groping for *it*, with psychic limbs giving *it* whatever form they can. Among the feeblest forms is a nightmare, the space where that which had been banished from "psychic work" is brought in purview. Based on my reading and experience, I like to think of a nightmare as an implosion caused by the emerging ego, bringing the psyche, to confront its limits and also "perchance," to notice the "unthought knowns" (Bollas 1987).

Although experiencing, let alone working with, part of the *truth* of one's being can throw one off balance, Eigen (2004) stands to remind us that "the horrific has its own beauty, its own ecstasy and we ought not walk around it as if it were not there, no more than we should become one with it" (p. viii). Religion, too, urges us to confront the truth. Christ, for instance, said to the Jews who believed in him, "know the truth and truth shall set you free." It is, however, part of coming to terms with our own human-ness, when we recognize that although our own truth liberates us but it does so not without scaring us. It is not easy to confront that which has never been represented, thought about, and so remains un-assimilated. How can psyche work with that which is not represented and so cannot be formed into images or thought? Botella and Botella (2005) accord a "conceptual place to the experience of absence of representation" (p. 31). by showing that in meeting the terrors in the autistic gestures of a child at the end of the hour, the analyst meets the terror by being forced to think about circumstances in his own life. He recalls his life experiences in a mode of thinking but is unable to extend them to create a meaning and communication between patient's terrified gestures and analyst's own attempt to connect, heal, receive. In this struggle a playful enactment is created which is completely involuntary to the analyst's judgment.

> Faced with this pale, immobile, haggard-looking child, the very picture of terror, the analyst himself had, as it were, a nightmare. He then said to Thomas: 'Grrrr . . . grrrr! Are you afraid of the wolf?' And without thinking about it, he spontaneously imitated the nasty beast that bites and claws. Terror stricken, Thomas signaled to him to stop, but his disarray disappeared and he was able to

> leave. The intervention was 'a flash of the analyst, a work of figurability' giving a meaning to Thomas' terror evoked by separation and his limited capacities for elaboration. 'By naming and mimicking the wolf, the analyst was not evoking the meaning of a phantasy in the face of loss, but was soliciting in the child a psychic work comparable to his own.' The 'wolf-image' served the function of containing distress that had not been represented and was provoked by the menace of losing the object. In the absence of the function to elaborate, the intervention entailed expansion of 'preconscious formations susceptible of attracting, one day, other representations, of serving as manifest content. (Botella and Botella, 2005, p. 33)

Their work was revealing of nightmarish states into which one can get thrown when engaging with fragmented states in others. Tested, attenuated and disturbed by the non-representation, the therapist's ego will react. The image of wolf from fairy tales was "created found," facilitating some work of representation in the patient-child. "From the terror of the nightmare to the marvelous world of the fairytale, the fundamental distress of *non-representation* is demolished" (Botella and Botella 2005, p. 34).

One way we reach our truth/s is through the other and the other through us. We are always reaching out and being reached. The caregiver functions as a double, who validates, accepts, and calmly reflects the child's states. In an analytic setting some analysands come with a lack of narcissistically stabilizing childhood experiences of similarity and affinity with parents. This double echoes with oneself and one has no hesitation in echoing more than what the double echoes. It can be a best friend we are possessive about, a lover, or a guru. It picks on, unbeknownst to itself, that which remains non-represented and so, not thought. He is similar enough or in tune enough with one's states to echo parts of self which one did not even dream existed in oneself, he is different enough to articulate or represent what one cannot. It is more like a divine task that one came upon this person who was not there. Freud (1938) wrote, "Psyche is extended; knows nothing about it" (p. 299). The idea of an analyst working as a double to a patient struggling with the sense of void has found elaboration in the work of the Botellas. The double may be said to emerge in response to the fear of psychic death, in response to the risk of confronting the meaningless void. "A feature of this mode of relating is that an area of the psyche of which the subject was hitherto unaware strives to find its way into consciousness" (Botella and Botella 2005, p. 67). The double, by validating our experience, opens psyche to possibilities, to fresh perspectives on relationship with self and the other.

Confronted with and receiving primitive states as *Ruhi's* double for a possessed girl I will be calling Ruhi in this paper, I was required to give up my frantic attempts at rationalizing and interpreting, with a faith that sooner or later, the "god-head" of emotional truth would rise. Sitting in "next-ness" with culture, the interventions were elicited while leaning on the cultural, appealing to the preconscious, which Kakar (1981) has informed, is largely constituted by one's culture.

CASE STUDY

I sat under the Peepal tree, taking in the climate of vibrant *Samadhi Sthal*[2] of the *Balaji* temple. A young girl came and sat next to me. She swayed mildly, watching me from the corner of her eye, pale face partially visible behind a cascade of pitch dark scattered hair, lips curled into a sinister grin. Terrified and disgusted by the *bhuta* in her, I averted my gaze. My first encounter with Ruhi was with her grimacing face, swaying toward and away—drawing me in one moment, pushing me out the next. Carrying fears tinged with curiosities, I treaded toward knowing her. Twenty-five years old, Ruhi belonged to a middle-class Hindu family in Amritsar. Extremely talkative, beautiful, and delicate, Ruhi had sharply chiseled features and managed a small beauty salon. Her father worked in a transport company, was extremely authoritative, and did not allow Ruhi's mother to work after marriage. The mother remained a silent presence and rarely surfaced in narratives. The sexually bold elder sister eloped from the confines of home and got married to her lover. The younger brother, as interfering as the father, is preferred and given freedom by parents. At the age of two, Ruhi was displaced by her younger brother's arrival. The birth of the desired son after two daughters was celebrated with great fervor. Thereafter, the mother began to remain unwell and was advised to rest. The repercussions of the mother's early unavailability were found in the little girl Ruhi's persistent whining and clinging, cognitive lag, and destructive aggression. Father and brother persistently controlled Ruhi's life, not letting her even stand close to the window, and mocked her attempts at being independent. Her symptoms surfaced when her elder sister eloped with her boyfriend and Ruhi too was developing fondness and closeness with one of her teachers. The hurt father threatened Ruhi that he would "break her legs" if she dared follow her sister's footsteps. Consciously, Ruhi was determined to focus on running her salon, or else "parents' money would be wasted." Throughout possession, sexual images and sensations were denied and attributed to *samkat*.[3] According to her, her aunt (the father's sister) was envious of Ruhi's beauty, and her growing career as a beautician and caused her to be possessed by making her consume *kheer*[4] infused by black magic. That very night Ruhi began to experience excruciating pain in her body. One day she was working in her salon when suddenly her body turned cold and she fainted. On becoming conscious she resumed work and fainted again. Her hands contorted and froze. She was scared. She did not know what was happening to her or why she could do nothing to control her body. Her work suffered. She became irritable and withdrawn. Many medical investigations were done over three years. On a doctor's advice the family took refuge in *Balaji* temple. When she first drank a few drops of *Balaji's* holy water, images flashed before her eyes—a couple in intercourse followed by an extremely ugly child[5] wandering inside her body. She was diagnosed as being possessed by a *Masan.*[6] Possessed, Ruhi spoke in a baby voice, hurled abuses, got violent, threw tantrums, and became gluttonous. Often during a possession state the *samkat* repeated that its *buddhi* (wisdom) was blocked—it did not remember anything about its whereabouts, like Ruhi who faced difficulties of memory and thinking. The aunt and sister were envied (although the envy remained unconscious) because they were closer to their needs—the aunt established her luxurious life based on help she extracted from her brothers and sister was sexually expressive. Both had the drive to get what they desired, an attribute Ruhi lacked and was not allowed to nurture.

For the purpose of this chapter, through three crucial moments in my relationship with Ruhi, I will try to depict shifts and expansions in her and also in me. The first moment was when I met her after my marriage. For a long time she kept admiring my looks and body. I was surprised to know that she perceived me to be a *Sardarni.*[7] She then moved to sharing her fear—*"If I ever get married . . . so the relation that is to be established after marriage with the husband . . . I feel I will not be able to fulfill it . . ."* This happened just before the evening worship. I eased her anxieties and told her that we would talk about it in detail later. In the evening worship she entered the frenzy state with me right behind her. The temple bells rang, the climate became charged with devotion, and echoes of hands clapping and cries of *"Balaji Maharaj Ki Jai"*[8] filled the atmosphere. Ruhi stood with her back to me, opened her hair, held the barrier, and began swaying slightly. Her eyes were open and glassy, gazing up at and beyond the evening sky, her hair being tossed from one side to the other and her face pale. Almost suddenly she entered a state of frenzy. Her body twisted beyond recognition and rhythm. Watching her body-container crumble, scared, I wished for a goddess-like-omnipotence. If only I had multiple hands (like the Hindu Goddess *Kali,* with a ferocity to equal Ruhi's) so that I could catch hold of all the crumbling pieces and put the Humpty-Dumpty back together again, back from formlessness into some form. I stood there, receiving her, as her body fell on me, at me, against me. It was, as if I became the couch she could fall on repeatedly, enact her misery and frustration, and, perhaps, see if I could withstand the magnitude of her emotions. The body that otherwise looked timid and constrained, now seemed like a cauldron exploding with aliveness! Although communicating her refusal for active relatedness with me and her self, like a child's back held against the mother's arms and body, perhaps, her self sought holding. After this experience, I had a series of dreams in which I saw myself as a man. While, surprisingly, a corresponding shift in her was—*" . . . recently something happened . . . One day I was alone at home . . . I felt, as if, something was walking behind me . . . standing next to my bed . . . it was a Sardarni . . . she stood on the threshold of the door . . .* " Her admiration and compliments were, as if they were directed toward someone who, like a *Sardarni,* had the drive to successfully establish sexual intimacy in marriage. Her deepest fear coincided with a bodily sense, which was perhaps that the penis would enter the body, tear it apart, and damage it, like the baby-*samkat* who, she felt, ate her insides. A *Sardarni* could handle the feared penis. This *Sardarni* haunted, but also tempted with a chance for sensuous and alive body experience that opened the body to numerous sensations and the mind to exciting images but also to corresponding palpable fears. She represented attributes Ruhi lacked and desired. By entering a bodily experience with me, the *Sardarni*, was she trying to evoke in me the *Sardarni* she perceived me to be? Receiving her need at an unconscious level, I sensed a certain loosening in my own body and mind as well. I threw my limbs while walking, became more vocal, upfront, opening in our conversations various vistas of experiences which I could invite her to experience and talk about. While Ruhi experienced heaviness in body, fainting spells, aches, but with space given to body in *peshi*,[9] and our conversations, the ability to work, returned as she felt empowered and stepped out to attend beauty seminars and trainings. At this point, there emerged a promise of the metabolizing of destructive impulses, as *Bal Brahmachari*[10] *Balaji* announced that only Goddess *Kali* can consume the sexual and hostile *samkat*. Subsequently, *samkat* emerged in the form of a penis, shifted layers below, from inhabiting the stomach to pulsating her genitalia with sensations of aliveness, trying to force itself out during urination. Her forbidden desires were opening up. Now she was not holding herself back.

A second moment came with a surge of sexuality in images and sensations, and there was unleashed a deeper sense of being damned, worthless, good-for-nothing. In my attempt to contain this part, I offered a maternal lap to the *samkat,* to connect with the lack of parental love. Shoving my attempts aside, *samkat* said—*"It says . . . I don't have parents . . . I am an orphan . . ."* I then tried to enhance her self-feeling, binding the damning force with life, while this devilish force persisted, posing a difficulty for me. Bypassing all my attempts she jumped to narrating an incident where accidently her envy was lived out by making a to-be-bride customer ugly, resulting in panic, soon replaced by guilt and self-spoiling. I had reached my limits and listened to her helplessly. I told myself—*We had to patiently wait for Balaji to unlock her "buddhi."* Entering the state of a faithful devotee, I gave up frantic attempts at helping her. For me, this faith meant what Bion considered a "psychoanalytic attitude," faith in stream of unconscious to take us where emotional truth would raise its head, when frantic attempts at mastery, at helping, are given up. In prematurely appropriating what was felt as ugly, the price I had to pay was in the limits I came to face in myself. Two nightmares emerged at this turn. In the first one, I experienced that a force possessed me making me immobile. I had reached a psychotic moment, not moving or screaming, no sound or words. Through this dream, I came closest to being possessed as opposed to "knowing" possession. The next night, I dreamed, "I am in a strange village as a researcher to understand the lives of the children there. I formed a bond with one boy who managed a shop of candies. We walk the entire day talking about his life. In the evening we reach his shop and he gives me some candies. From a distance two women—one young, the other old—are watching the two of us interact. The younger one says to the older one—*'We told her not to venture in this village. We told her not to come. Now she would need to be taught a lesson.'* In the dream I woke up startled and went on scanning the house. I stepped out of my room to find a woman feeding on a little boy's corpse. She raised her head. She had my face." I woke up again, terrified, disoriented, and not knowing if this time I woke up for real. Momentarily the distinction between reality and dream was erased, causing me to experience terror I had not known until now. In internally letting go and shifting from "knowing" to "being," (Eigen 1993) I was confronted with my own split-off part—the young boy. While I could not make sense of these nightmares and grappled with sheer meaninglessness and terror, some representation began to happen in Ruhi—*" . . . Last time . . . two days after talking to you I began to see a child . . . he was very filthy . . . dressed only in underwear . . . looked starved and from a poor family . . . When I am asleep he stands beside my bed . . . it is a very filthy thing . . . and shows filthy images . . . "* Was it a mere co-incidence that a boy emerged in my dream, was eaten up or assimilated by me, and now appeared in Ruhi's images? Through the image of this split-off boy part, both I and Ruhi had become intertwined in our histories. It was this male-part, split-off, that caused both of us to feel damned and cursed, perhaps as being born as women in a culture which favored male-children. When, in the nightmare, I turn to the corpse and eat up parts of the body, in life this male part helped me to venture to healing sites alone, carry on the research work in a site where, as a woman, I was constantly exposed to threats of various kinds. This is, insofar as my dreaming comes to become the first imprint, the first layer where the terror of the possessed person, coursing through the images, as the communication between the two of us happening, is yielding some images in me through which the dream is formed. Mediated by the male-part in me and our close relationship, in which she was allowed to talk about anything, some assimilation of the split-off male-part, began to happen in Ruhi—" . . . *the other day samkat began to act, throwing tantrums, 'I don't have a mother . . . I don't have a father . . . I am three years old . . . celebrate my birthday . . . My name is Ranjeet Kaur . . . I am both a girl as well as a boy . . .* " On another occasion —"*Didi, my samkat has revealed a new form . . . one day after dinner everyone was just sitting . . . a girl began to speak from within me . . . began singing—"My name is Chameli, I have come from far far away" . . . Oh Didi, she began hailing filthy abuses at papa, mummy, brother, Balaji . . . papa made me sit in the temple . . . she abused all the deities . . . She had a heavy voice.*" The feared penis-*samkat* was now procreative-penis, taking many forms, indicating that the process of psychological work was ongoing at some level. In emergence of *Chameli*,[11] who was as bold as the character in this song, challenging the hostile father-*Balaji* himself, there was a movement toward evolution, as the child-*samkat* now took form of a seductress. Eros had begun to be embodied, which facilitated in her taking the stance of an analysand, questioning her motives—" . . . *the day samkat showed its new form, it was abusing me as well . . . sometimes I think —Do I say these things on my own?*" At this point I eased her doubt, saying that it was okay even if she did.

The final moment came when, after having understood my dreams and driven by my wish to nudge her toward healing, I sought help from culture, as represented in a *bhagat*[12] I knew. The image of couple in intercourse, boy-child, my nightmares, and *samkat's* wish to transform into a *duta*[13] made me wonder if this couple would ever transform into peaceful coexistence of the parental (and the tendencies bound with it) as seen in religious iconography; for instance, of *Hanuman*[14] revealing his heart to Lord *Rama* as proof of his love, the image of *Rama-Sita* (the ideal Indian parental couple) residing within him. The elaboration in Ruhi's experience was describable and left a tension to be metabolized by me. It was only after becoming familiar with the work of Green (1986) and Botella and Botella (2005) that I understood that primal scene images bring into frame the logic—"*Mother not there because of the father*" (Botella and Botella 2005)—and make the mother's disappearance thinkable. The image became "thinkable" for me. I think it was my internal letting go in faith that led to an unbinding and threw me into a quagmire of terrors. My first dream of sense, of bodily immobility, showed my identification with Ruhi's feeling of being damned, of not being able to do anything. This sense evoked in me the urge to go closer to the father which was satisfied by becoming the "tomboy" of the second dream. It has been my struggle with Ruhi of bringing the father closer to her in a non-threatening way. Leaning on my *Balaji*—thinkers, supervisor and analyst—I began to realize that for the birth and nurture of the male-part, it was necessary that the distant father and the silent, hostile mother came together, erotically investing in the Self. I could make use of my intuitive sense when her *bhagat* consulted me and asked for my advice. I shared that Ruhi could benefit if both her parents could somehow be made part of her healing. Thereafter, he recommended that she should recite *Hanuman Chalisa* and *Hanumat Kavach* with her mother and visit the temple with her father every Saturday, where he was to circle some offerings around Ruhi's head seven times before offering them to *Balaji*. Now, the distant and punitive parents were part of healing enactments, investing in their daughter. Perhaps, through me, she had managed to get the parental couple together—facilitated by maternal warmth and the reflective paternal function I tried to bring in. In addition to this, both of us together framed a prayer for her to recite—*"Oh Almighty Balaji . . . please come into my heart, so we may together face this force . . . please transform all harmful forces in me into benevolent ones . . . "* In the stance of prayer, the notorious *samkat*-Ruhi could be her vulnerable self. The prayer was framed with the hope of resuscitating the image of strengthening the paternal element and "the transformative maternal" one (Bollas 1987). A week into praying—*" . . . after talking to you the last time I had made up my mind that I will try to be happy in all situations . . . I used to get scared and this let samkat dominate me. . . . I decided not to be afraid. . . . I will do what samkat stops me from doing. . . . I stepped out of the house also two-three times . . . and it has been a week that samkat has not possessed me. . . . I have told father to take me to temple everyday . . . it makes me feel relaxed. . . . Everything is fine, but whenever I sit down to pray, samkat flashes before me images of penis against the idols of deities. . . . "* She was coming close to the father-*Balaji,* sexually. At that time I could not think of anything to say to her and told her that I would speak to her later. As had happened on many occasions, her state worsened on not receiving the desired response from me. Her difficulty was an inability to imagine herself not invested by the other.

At this stage, another form of *samkat*, a heavy man, emerged, followed by Ruhi finding her voice and asserting herself for the first time with a customer who was not paying Ruhi her due for services she offered. Being assertive for the first time made her anxious and she repeatedly asked for my validation to the birth of this new part in her, leading to more openings in her–penis-images, images of naked men and women, pulsating sensations in the vagina spreading through and shaking her entire body. I received the surge of sexual content as her body was increasingly brought into the world of words. The in-dwelling of soma in psyche had begun to happen, depicted in the confidence with which she was planning her future, in dreaming, doing (the male does), and in admiring her beauty. More healing images emerged in her *duta* part, which, in stark contrast to selfish *bhuta*, came with empathy, concern, and a wish to guide and help other possessed individuals in the *Balaji* temple. There was greater ease in dynamics between Ruhi and her brother and he had become more supportive. Watching another possessed girl being beaten by her younger brothers led Ruhi to a realization—*"Didi, I was thinking that on one side is my family . . . my samkat has slapped Mummy, N (elder sister) and M (younger brother) . . . abused everyone, but they did not leave my side . . . they kept standing beside me. . . . It is true that ever since I have been to Balaji temple my eyes have opened. . . . I got a chance to see a lot about the world . . ."* She was now beginning to appreciate survival of her objects from her destruction. From fear of the penis (fear of establishing sexual intimacy in marriage) and the consequent reluctance to even entertain the idea of a love relationship, she was now treading toward an imagination of the right man for her. Interestingly, her Mr. Right had attributes which stood in stark contrast to her own father—open-mindedness and understanding toward her need for independence. She did not want to suffer like her mother. The wish was for a man who would not invade her inner space, but would embrace, love, and enhance her. A few days after following the healing ritual recommended by the *bhagat*—*". . . Early morning, after taking shower, cleaning the temple, the minute I began chanting Hanumat Kavach, Babaji removed all those images . . . and then I finished the prayer without any disturbance. . . . Now, every day, I worship Balaji, look into his eyes and share all tensions . . . and he listens . . . I feel very relaxed . . . I work the entire day without any trouble . . . "*

Today, *samkat* manifests itself only in the form of headaches. Both the father and the brother are encouraging Ruhi, helping her establish her salon, investing time, money, and energy in publicizing her work. However, the mother is yet to come alive to her needs. She still remains silent and distant. She has constituted her own perfect parental couple by worshipping *Balaji* and goddess *Kali*—recites *Hanuman Chalisa*, and *Durga Saptashati*. In her world I was experienced as the *"duta"* sent by *Balaji*. Ruhi said in a moment of gratitude—*" . . . you have explained me so many things . . . truly, you have really helped me . . . It is true, I now believe completely in Balaji, that he sends someone or the other . . . He sent you for me . . ."*

REFLECTIONS AND VISIONS

Terror emanated from being thrown in what Eigen (2010) calls the "Z-dimension." Owing to a lack of external and internal transformative function, Bion would say, no thought was possible and one "would go straight from an impulse to an action . . . into the body, or into the external world through action" (Symington and Symington 1996). The shadow of this terror fell on failure in psychic work, and was manifested in states of collapse and fainting spells or as Eigen said, it can also go "into the head as hyper-mentation, seeing devils or other spirits, often bad ones, or being trapped by an eye-mind rather than body-mind. The evacuated, still born sense of trauma can be hidden, imprisoned, trapped in the body, making some dimensions of the body itself a prison" (Eigen personal communication 2013). It is in the cultural category of *samkat* that terror, precipitating from *atripta* or unmetabolized states, gets organized. We owe it to Winnicott (1963) to enlighten us that an impinging environment leads to the constitution of a righteous and socially compliant false-self, split from the true-self, which preserves, among other things, hostility and sexuality. In possession, joy remained preserved with the true self in its incommunicado, and yet, disaster was averted as the true-self parts were found by the *samkat.* It is then placed at God's feet, who is believed to gather the scatter, like a *djinn* in a bottle, so fusion can be restored. *Balaji* fostered living of *atripta* (unlived) true-self parts by implicitly saying—*"You can be free with whatever desires you have . . . I am here . . ."*

As musical instruments are beaten, rhythmic chants envelop the possessed person, like the mother's hand rhythmically pressing against body, ushering one into a sleep-state, twisting beyond recognition; the body is thrown back to a state where it was only becoming, not-yet-embodied. The body-mind link is gradually established, in defiance, in breaking away from the collective, in giving body to *atripta* or unlived self-parts. Multiple chances are afforded in *peshi* where the body can move freely, making forms and poses, life flows through unclogging veins not known by the body in a suffocating household. Eigen (2011) wrote, "a ball player can make a great catch one moment and drop the ball the next. One moment, alpha body, the next a beta moment, one moment flowing, the next blocked, paralyzed" (p. 120). For Eigen, *spirit* or affective attitude, facilitates the transition from beta to alpha body. In possession, faith, music,[15] and *spirit* of impulses makes this transition possible. "Impulses, like *spirit,* link mind-body." The body, which collapsed when faced with demands to process emotional content, became a cauldron overflowing with emotional aliveness, in the frenzy of possession. Prayers like *Hanuman Chalisa* and *Durga Saptashati* request for strength, intelligence, and true knowledge as tools which can relieve one's pain. Each recitation of *Hanuman Chalisa* establishes him as a repository of learning, an ardent listener and understanding parent, whose bravery is unparalleled. He removes all pain and suffering, cures all diseases, grants all happiness, worldly and divine comforts, and, most importantly, alleviates all the fear that one's own destructive urges may evoke. Achreja's (2013) reflections on *Durga Saptashati* were very helpful in order to see the proximity of Bion's thinking to Indian philosophical notions concerning distress and its *nivaaran* (resolution). *Swami Satyananda Saraswati* of *Devi Mandir* in his acclaimed translation of *Chandi Patha* has recognized *asuras* (demons) as "thoughts"— thoughts that occlude sentient beings from perception and realization of their own inherent divinity. Truly, such psychic demons are enemies of our realization of godhead and, hence, they are enemies of *devas.* In a similar vein, *devas* may be understood as forces that combat thought-demons, that is, forces of clear perception. This prayer is to that part of the maternal which facilitates evacuation of unthinkable states, of "she who tears apart thought." It acknowledges the worshipper's slim capacities to process emotional states. Perhaps through its repeated recitation, Ruhi wishes to be granted a boon of reinstatement of family like the King in the prayer and knowledge for self-realization to liberate her from the grief associated with the unending cycle of death (destruction) and life (resurrection) that goes on in the internal object world and reach a capacity to forgive the object who brings death with its disappearance and appears again with sparks of life. Could it be that multiple recitations of these prayers cleared her perception and she came to appreciate her objects better? In my family, praying for every need was a common thing. The experience of praying before sleeping was of being gently enveloped by a safety net. *"Where mother could not be, God was."* Gradually I learned to use just the right words, to express, ask, connect with others, and even address disturbances in relationships. Use of prayer to help Ruhi was an attempt precisely to bring her in touch with her needy self, to help her ally with the tenacious father and transformative mother in God. However, as a psychodynamically inclined therapist, I am also inclined to think of parts of the self that are swept under the carpet, only to emerge later, grimacing, creeping into the territory of dreams, disrupting the psychic processes, and causing nightmares. Some psychological work is attempted, in the shift from terror to splitting. For the purpose of discussion here I would like to focus on splitting in "being" and "doing." The male element in its excess is a reckless doer, divorced from its relationship with the being or its need to know the being. This reckless male element evokes extreme thrill which cannot be inhabited by the body and thus catapults the body into great fear. It was the fear of the male element which cultural values reinforced, and which yet provided space in possession to be a male. It was this which sought to be diluted. Recurrent sexual images and fantasies latent in them were worked out in our dialogues. In becoming part of a containing process, I was required to take on the role of a mother who could ease the fear of penis and say—*You should live this experience . . . there is no danger in it . . . only ecstasy.*

FROM THE EYE/I OF THE "DOUBLE"

As therapists, the emphasis during our training is on articulation of psychic distress into words. Eigen (2011) calls the idea of putting one's feelings into words an "odd locution." He asks, "How does one do that? Can you picture it? Sometimes I think of drawing feelings from a well and pouring them, a little at a time, into buckets of words. Often we do the reverse. We try to fill the well with words. Instead of drawing from a deep and bottomless well, we pour words into it. We lower word buckets down, hoping to catch something, often coming up with more words. Some of these words are juicy enough, some dry. But we fear that what we pull up is what we put in, missing living water." Eigen invokes Winnicott's attention to wordlessness: "Some babies specialize in thinking, and reach out for words; others specialize in auditory, visual, or other sensuous experience, and in memories and creative imagination of a hallucinatory kind, and these latter may not reach out for words. There is no question of the one being normal and the other abnormal. Misunderstandings may occur in debate through the fact that one person talking belongs to the thinking and verbalizing kind, while another belongs to the kind that hallucinates in the visual and auditory field instead of experiencing the self in words. Somehow the word people tend to claim sanity, and those who see visions do not know how to defend their positions when accused of insanity. Logical argument really belongs to the verbaliser. Feeling or a feeling of certainty or truth or real belong to the other" (Winnicott 1992, p. 155) as quoted by Eigen 2011, p. 59–60).

Such training leaves out that aspect of experience which is not represented, which will not go into words because it will not go into thought. How are representations arrived at? In earliest infancy, the world is perceived through sensory experience. When the object disappears, the infant responds by a wishful hallucination that denies the object's absence and retains the feeling of pleasure. When this hallucinatory satisfaction fails, a word-presentation of the object may emerge, the object can now be thought about in its absence. "It is now possible to put into words what it means for the object to be there or not and to reflect on whatever multiple layers of significance for the person the object may have. An object-relationship can develop because the object has become internally representable" (Botella and Botella, 2005, p. xxii). The consistent and satisfactory presence of the object creates a link between impulse and meaning. However, if the object, in turn, fails to mirror or achieve a psychic representation of the baby, the traumatic effect may be that the baby cannot then achieve its own representation of itself. In mother, as infant's first "double," the infant may discover itself reflected in her gaze. "The infant will experience in her what he already potentially has in himself." In the clinical situation the analyst working as a double to the patient opens his or her own psyche to a regressive movement, from words to non-verbal experience and sensory, hallucinatory kind of perception that reflects the predicament of the patient's psyche. He picks up, at an unconscious level of awareness, the patient's experience of non-representation.

In my interactions with Ruhi, the body increasingly entered the world of words. Since I went through similar processes or was concurrently going through those processes, the unbinding happened first in me. The forcible coming apart of the subject and object in my mind is an equivalent of the terror of my nightmare. Being in the territory between dreaming and reality, I experienced the crippling fear of the unthinkable. *The fear of ghosts is indeed the fear of the unknown, not-represented and un-metabolized by the psyche which evokes horror.* The cultural category of *samkat* was not available to me. I had to learn to carry the tensions evoked in me and wait for the metabolizing maternal in Kakar, Botella and Botella, and Eigen to grant me some alpha moments. In telling myself *"to patiently wait for Balaji to unlock her buddhi,"* I took a stance of a devout *bhagat.* I had experienced sufficient internal letting go, to move from knowing to being. Psychic work was facilitated, through an unconscious to unconscious process, testified through states of nightmares in me, which were in line with disavowed parts of Ruhi, and resulted in creation of new images in her. Expansions in me, desire to facilitate comparable evolution in her within our close relationship, led to a stance of an analysand in her, doubting her motives.

Like the wolf for the Botellas, *Hanuman,* through my use of prayer and *bhagat's* use of the ritual, solicited psychic work (not to the degree aimed at in clinical work) while the "right not to communicate" is preserved. In looking at it as possession, although the distress is made culturally figurable, it was up to me to try and make it increasingly intelligible.

For Ruhi the part that remained non-represented and evoked terror was the male-part—the *Masan* which possessed her. The mother not only became unavailable but also was perceived as investing more in her son. What was unthinkable was the idea that "she was not-invested in by the parental couple, because she was a girl born in a culture which favored the boy." Her possession by spirit of a boy was as if saying—*"So here you want a boy, here it is, so this is the kind of boy I would become!"* Later on, in being a double for Ruhi, picking on the unthinkable part of her experience, when I eat up this boy, by first making him into a candy, a candy-selling boy, it is as if this allows or liberates Ruhi to envision him in the leftover *gandagi* that she would like to cleanse. The boy that I eat up parts of, and subsequently the boy that emerges in the images of Ruhi, became somewhat harmless. The candy part—the oral greed part, the threat that I would be thrown out of this village, they are all symbolized in this child, and have now gone inside. I wonder whether the child, divested of his dangers and toxins, has now gone to Ruhi through an unconscious to unconscious communication, allowing her to be assertive with the father, brother, and her customers, gradually embracing her beauty and her skills as a beautician. She now successfully manages a beauty salon at home, is finishing her graduation through correspondence, and from moment to moment invests in her beauty.

At first, I was anxious because I did not share Ruhi's language. I was worried that I may, knowingly or unknowingly, commit what Winnicott (1963) considered a "sin against the self," by penetrating a long way into her personality, and perhaps, threatening her "need to be secretly isolated." While remaining situated in the trenches between "culture and psyche" I learned that she was putting across her fear that if revealed, the world would exploit her. Drawing spirit from Eigen (2012), from my faithful father who serves God, and engaging with primitive states in myself and Ruhi, taught me, the hard way, that confrontation with such moments in the other calls for "an ethic of godliness"—to surrender being omniscient and omnipotent and shrink to make space for life that is struggling to be born, in the Self as in the other. Here an attempt has been to share a vision of a clinical model marked by cultural sensitivity, using elixirs of life from rich resources of culture found in myths, legends, and folklore. But, we must first begin asking ourselves how ready are we to be looked at as the *duta* sent by God who bows in front of life.

NOTES

1. This chapter is part of a doctoral research which aimed at understanding the phenomenon of spirit possesssion and exorcism among traditional healers and individuals possessed by spirits in churches of Delhi and the temple of Balaji, Rajasthan.
2. The grave site of Ganeshpuri, first and most charismatic priest and healer of Balaji temple, Rajasthan.
3. "Samkat" is a Hindi reference to possessing spirit.
4. An Indian sweet dish made of milk, rice, and nuts.
5. 3–5 years old.
6. Masan refers to a child-ghost which feeds on fetuses.
7. "Sardarni" refers to a Sikh woman, known, in Punjabi culture, to be able to use her body well to wrestle her way into making possible an intense sexual experience.
8. "Balaji Maharaj ki Jai" means "Hail the Almighty Balaji."
9. "Peshi" is a local reference to state of frenzy in which the possessing spirit manifests itself.
10. "Bal Brahmachari" is how the *celibate* Balaji or Hanuman is often addressed.
11. This song is from a Hindi film–"Raja aur Runk" (Pratyagatma, 1968). The lyrics translated in English are:

My name is Chameli (Jasmine), I am an indifferent gardener,
I have come alone from Bikaner,
Oh Policeman speak on, just open the door,
I am waiting here on your door from a long time

12. Hindi word meaning a local healer.
13. A "duta" is a messenger of God.
14. Hanuman is the Hindu monkey-god, also referred to as Bal Brahmachari/celibate Balaji, blessed with fearlessness and power over evil.
15. "Music creates experience but also plays a role in processing experience . . . Dance creates experience and catalyses body processing of it at the same time" (Eigen 2012).

REFERENCES

Achreja, V. "The Speaking Tree: Who Are The Demons That Devi Slays?," Delhi: *Times of India*. 2013.

Akhtar, S. *Comprehensive Dictionary of Psychoanalysis.* London: Karnac Books Ltd., 2009.

Bion, W. "A Theory of Thinking." In *International Journal of Psychoanalysis* 43(1962): 306–310.

Bollas, C. *The Shadow of the Object: Psychoanalysis of the Unthought Known.* New York: Columbia University Press, 1987.

Botella, C. and Botella, S. *The Work of Psychic Figurability: Mental States without Representation.* Hove and New York: Brunner-Routledge, Taylor and Francis Group, 2005.

Eigen, M. "The Area of Faith in Winnicott, Lacan, and Bion," In *The Electrified Tightrope.* NJ, USA: Jason Aronson Inc., 1993.

Eigen, M. Personal communication. November 20, 2013.

Eigen, M. *Contact with the Depths.* London: Karnac Books Ltd., 2011.

Eigen, M. *Eigen in Seoul: Madness and Murder.* London: Karnac Books Ltd., 2010.

Eigen, M. *Kabbalah and Psychoanalysis.* London: Karnac Books Ltd., 2012.

Eigen, M. *The Psychotic Core*. London: Karnac, 2004.

Freud, S. *Findings, Ideas, Problems.* S.E., 23. London: Hogarth, 1938 [1961].

Green, A. "The Intuition of the Negative in Playing and Reality." In *The Dead Mother: The Work of Andre Green.* New York: Routledge, 1999, p. 209.

Green, A. *On Private Madness.* London: The Hogarth Press Ltd., 1986.

Kakar S. *Shamans, Mystics and Doctors.* New York: Knoph, 1982.

Kakar S. *The Inner World,* Second Edition. Delhi: Oxford University Press, 1981.

Kristeva, J. *Powers of Horror: An Essay on Abjection.* New York: Columbia University Press, 1982.

Mitrani, J. *Ordinary People and Extraordinary Protections*. London: Brunner-Routledge. 2001.

Pratyagatma, K. *Raja Aur Runk.* India: Prasad Productions, 1968.

Symington J. and Symington N. *The Clinical Thinking of Wilfred Bion*. London: Routledge, 1996.
Winnicott, D. W. *Psychoanalytic Explorations*. Eds. C. Winnicott, Cambridge, Mass: Harvard University Press. 1992.
Winnicott. D. W. "Communicating and Not Communicating Leading to a Study of Certain Opposites." In *The Maturational Processes and The Facilitating Environment.* London: Hogarth Press Ltd., 1963[1965].
Winnicott. D. W. *Playing and Reality.* London: Tavistock Publications, 1971.

Woman with Birds
Image by Katharina Poggendorf-Kakar

Erotik
Image by Katharina Poggendorf-Kakar

Man and Woman with Birds
Image by Katharina Poggendorf-Kakar

Woman with Birds 2
Image by Katharina Poggendorf-Kakar

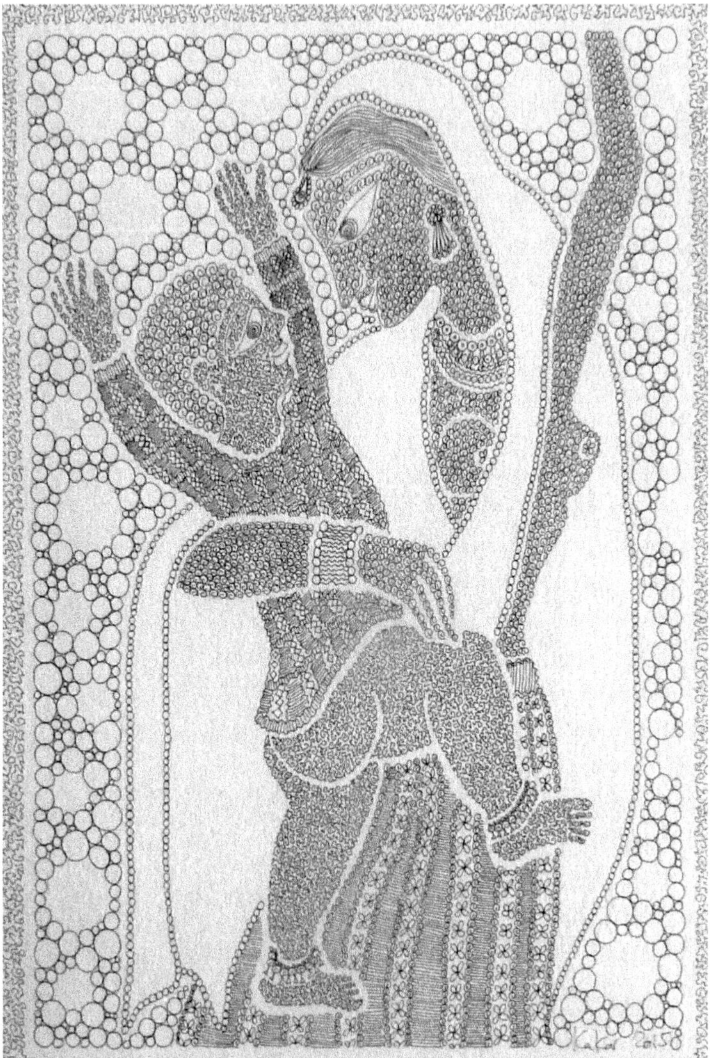

Mother and Child
Image by Katharina Poggendorf-Kakar

Erotik 2
Image by Katharina Poggendorf-Kakar

Man and Woman with Flower
Image by Katharina Poggendorf-Kakar

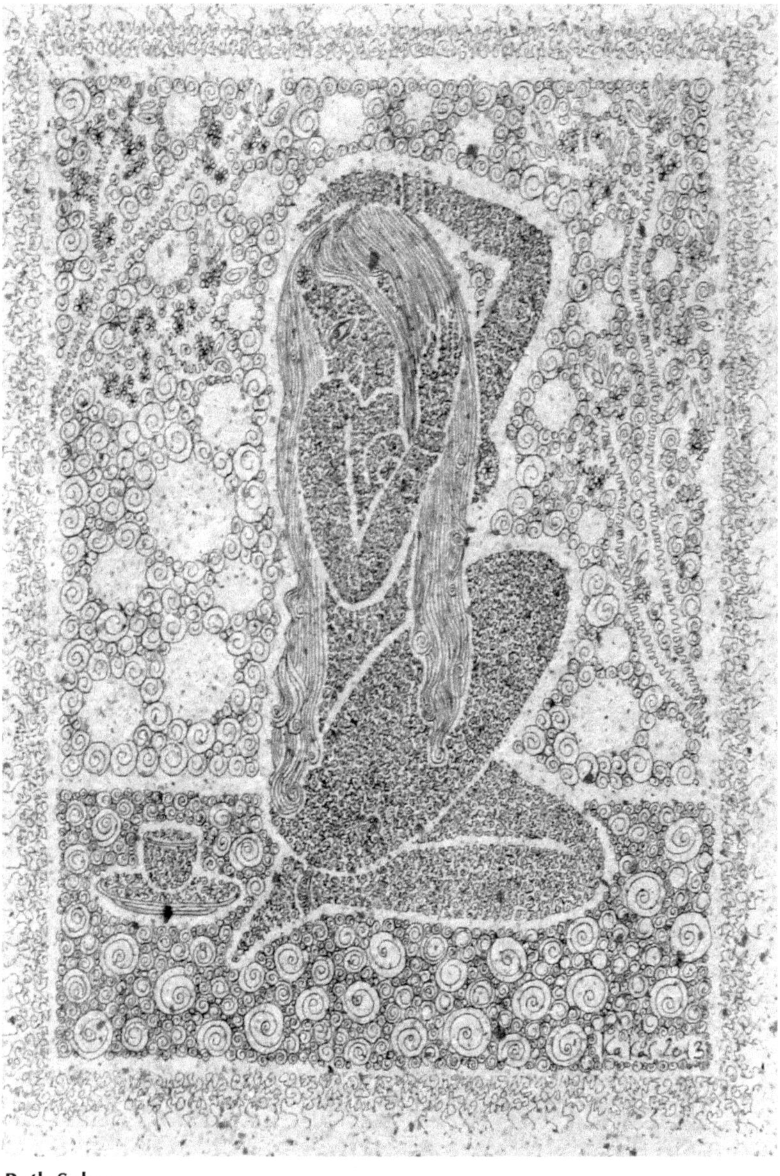

Bath Subar
Image by Katharina Poggendorf-Kakar

Women and Mirror
Image by Katharina Poggendorf-Kakar

Chapter Seven

Only Hindu, Also the Patient; Only Muslim, Also the Therapist

Recovering the Historical Other

Zehra Mehdi

The syncretic culture which *nurtured* both Hindus and Muslims within the broader cultural identity of "Indians" was ruptured by the Partition of the country in 1947, leaving them as predominantly Hindus and Muslims. They moved from the point of surviving with each other to not being able to survive each other (see Nandy 1983, 1987, 1990, 2002, 2013). Alan Roland (2014) finds the two communities suffering a shared history of silence, which continues across generations where both Hindus and Muslims born after the Partition become carriers of this history which functions like post memory.[1]

Indian professor of psychoanalysis Ashok Nagpal writes, "In a wounded town . . . people find it difficult to relate to each other . . . since they are beset with the articulation of pain and trauma . . . they recover each other in the clinic" (p. 168, 2006). His words remind one of Wilfred Bion's famous writing, "When two personalities meet, an emotional storm is created" (1979, p. 321). Bion's use of the word "personalities" opens psychoanalytic fantasies as to what constitutes an emotional storm (Eigen 2005, p. 29)[2] and thereby offers one of several conceptions of what happens inside the clinic. Simply put, *two people survive each other by surviving what happens to them when with each other*. By surviving with each other and through each other they come to what Nagpal calls "recovering in the clinic."

If these two generational "personalities" were to meet in the analytic space, what would they say to each other? What emotional storm—what psychoanalytic fantasies would a Hindu and Muslim bring for each other when they meet as a patient and a therapist? In the process, how will they survive and perhaps *recover* each other?

Partition did not just part the subcontinent into two nation states, but created "parts" of each other. Born out of a shared history of Partition what do Hindus and Muslims recover *of* each other in the analytical space?

Analyzing the *narrative truth* of psychosis in which a *Hindu* patient and a *Muslim* therapist meet each other in an analytic space—*not only as patient and therapist but also as patient and therapist and pursue a dialogue where they only talk as Hindu-Muslim but also talk as Hindu-Muslim.*[3]

This chapter distills the case to arrive at a few conjectures about this conversation and explores through it a place where history recovers "the Other" of, and for, the two communities.

MUSLIM IN THE MIND

From Idealization to Persecution

A 22-year-old female, Rupal, pursuing a postgraduate degree in English, came with symptoms of obsessive thoughts leading to compulsive rituals, distressing her for the last two years before she came for therapy. She had decided to go for therapy after a year and a half of being "unable to manage them on her own."[4] Our therapy lasted two years (November 2011-December 2013) where I saw her two times a week in face-to-face psychoanalytical psychotherapy.

For the past year, she said, she had experienced repetitive intrusive thoughts about sexuality and violence around her body, which distressed her immensely. Whenever she had felt she looked good she would "get thoughts" accusing her of being sexual and threatening her that, as a consequence, she would lose the parts of her body that she admired. Sometimes "they told her" she would die or be disabled because she was so sexual. She called them "negative thoughts." She felt scared by them and would engage in long hours of washing and scrubbing the admired body parts until she caused a rash. She felt she had created evidence through her blistered skin to answer back to the *negative thoughts* which accused her of being "sexual" every time she admired her body. However, she continued to be tormented. She did not relate to any affect and remained intellectual about the question of sexuality.

NEGATIVE THOUGHTS: PARANOIA

Exploring the nature of these negative thoughts and compulsive rituals revealed an underlying psychotic personality.[5] Her description of getting thoughts had obsessive traits that seemed to have a psychotic structure.

Though she said they were thoughts, she felt they would speak and experienced them as voices. These voices were neither outside nor did she experience them coming from within her. She simply said that "negative thoughts came to her as voices." Later, in therapy, she shared how she felt it was the voice of other women which was causing these negative thoughts. These other women found her admiration of self a sign of pride, implying sexual desire which they disapproved of, and cursed her through negative thoughts. She tried to show them how she was ugly by scarring her skin through repeatedly scraping it. However, they remained unconvinced. They would spare her for some time only to reappear, telling her that her experience of pleasure was filled with sexual suggestion, triggering the whole obsessive compulsive cycle again. Manifested in an obsessive pattern, where temporary relief was provided through compulsive rituals, her experience of negative thoughts as voices of other women cursing her was clearly psychotic. Her skin eruption was a direct manifestation of her delusion of persecution, which to me suggested a weak link with reality as she alienated herself from her own inflictions upon her body. It was the curse of other women which was causing her skin to peel and not her own compulsive rituals. She experienced her body only through the envy of the other women, to the extent that primary narcissism around the body was taken over by paranoid fears.

Nancy McWilliams (1994) writes how "paranoid states are bound by experiences of envy through shame" (p. 208). The paranoid states use denial such that their shame remains inaccessible and their envy projected. It was through this disavowed envy that Rupal recovered her body, but the shame around it continued to be denied. Her delusion of persecution can be explained by Freud's (1911) account of paranoia of a psychotic variety. The experience of her body as shameful was defended through reaction formation, making it a source of pride which could not be accepted and was thus projected onto the other woman as envy.[6]

"BEING SEEN": SHAME AND DOUBT

It was gradually revealed that shame around the body was especially related to her relationship with her mother, which was fraught with violence. In the clinic, she brought a long-standing history of a disturbed relationship with the mother, beginning with childhood.[7] She remembered being beaten as a child in public, sometimes with such viciousness that the neighbors had to intervene. It left her with a distinct feeling of "being seen." She did not remember what caused such a punishment, but recalled how her body turned blue after every incident of such physical abuse.[8] Erik Erikson writes how, when a sense of control over one's body cannot be experienced, the virtue of will—exercising free choice as well as self-restraint is replaced by experience of shame and doubt in infancy (1964, p. 119). Suspended autonomy compromised her ability to choose or let go—or have a distinction between outside and inside, beginning with her body. While she experienced shame with respect to her body, she was unable to determine if it was hers (inside), or belonged to someone else (outside). She was unable to determine if her "negative thoughts" were hers (inside), or were voices in her head (outside). Rupal recalled being told as a child how, if she did anything naughty, it would tell the world that her mother was horrible. Rupal's earliest childhood memories around the mother were dominated by her rage, bitterness, and a constant sense of distrust around people.

SEXUALITY

It became increasingly clear in the clinic that Rupal's views on sexuality were determined by her mother's views, which seemed rather distorted. On one hand, her mother incessantly elicited sexual details in conversations and described the woman's body as one that is consumed by sexual hunger. On the other hand, she would accuse Rupal of being perpetually sexual and would ask her to strip, scrutinize her body, and disapprove of her various body parts. Despite sharing such details of undergoing abuse at the hands of a psychotic mother she remained unconscious of its link with her afflictions.[9] As I tried to link her interactions with her mother with her current symptoms, I was met with strong resistance in which she accused me of calling her mother, and by (implication) her, crazy. I used this to illustrate how, in her experience, she and her mother were fused, where if either one were to be crazy, it would hold equally true for the other one. This interpretation was met with similar resistance.

A considerable way into the sessions, she said that she had been in a relationship for the past few years with a Muslim man. Upon probing why it was never mentioned in sessions before, she hesitantly admitted being unsure about my reaction to her dating a Muslim since I was one too. She believed that I would have envied her, hence she had to keep it a secret from me.[10] This was the first of many such moments in the clinic that intrigued, surprised, and, later, even shocked me.

That day, I was intrigued by her reference to my religion. Suddenly, I was reminded I was a Muslim.

Rupal's account of her relationship showed that it was largely one-sided. It wasn't a sexual relationship at all and appeared to be unconsummated. She thrived on it being superior in thought, categorically away from indulgent sexuality. On suggesting to her that intellect could have been a defense against sexuality, she got very angry and accused me of running down her relationship by "calling it sexual." She insisted that her love was "pure" and 'beyond sexuality.'

BAD MUSLIM: GOOD MUSLIM

In the second year of therapy, she began to develop paranoid ideas about me. She was convinced that I was a bad Muslim because I wore a *bindi*, did not cover my head, and wanted to speak about sexuality. It appeared as if she had ideas about what being a Muslim meant, while I had none. This thought discomforted me, making me wonder about the links between how she saw me as a therapist, and how she saw me as a Muslim. Until now, I had kept them separate.

I went on to explore her fantasies about Muslims, which were enumerated thus: Muslims were better people because of their faith in Allah who was the powerful, merciful and benevolent[11]; Muslim men were exceedingly aesthetic (reciting Urdu poetry; exhibited an etiquette in behavior (*adab*); and respected culture and tradition (by following *tameez* and *tehzeeb*). They loved their women dearly and treated them with politeness (by referring them to them as *aap*). They also protected them from the "evil, desirous" eyes of other men by keeping them in the veil. Muslim women were exceedingly beautiful primarily because they wore the veil. They were also generous because they did not fight over their husbands and shared them with other women (referencing Sharia allowing a Muslim man to have four wives).

There was something about her description of Muslims which felt odd. She spoke with a certainty around it which could not be questioned and, if challenged, was met with agitation. She reiterated that as I was a bad Muslim, I did not understand her. Her idealization of Muslims led her to believe in Islam as a faith where Allah was more powerful than gods of other religions. Asking her to elaborate this idea elicited a cryptic account of her paranoia. She claimed that Allah had told her, through signs and messages, how He would protect her if she was in a relationship with a Muslim man and if she believed in Islam. She did not elaborate further, saying how she didn't want to share it with a *kafir* (non-believer) like me who did not observe *Ramzaan*[12]

HISTORICAL PERSECUTION

Her idealization of Muslims was in absolute contrast to her mother, who despised Muslims. Her mother had shared with the stories *her* mother had told her about Partition. For Rupal's maternal grandmother Muslims were sexual, violent, dirty, and distrustful. They were responsible for the Partition and continued to instigate communal violence in the country. Her children were not allowed to speak to Muslims, and in case they did, they would be doomed to an eternity in Hell. Given this hate for Muslims, it was understandable why Rupal kept her relationship a secret.[13]

What was the relationship between Rupal's idealization of the Muslim and her mother's hatred of them? Was it mere coincidence that she had sought a therapist who was Muslim? If not, then how did it play out in her relationship with the Muslim therapist and what did it indicate about her relationship with her mother? Further, did it bring the Muslim therapist and the mother in a relationship with each other in the session?

Rupal explained her idealization of Islam in the face of her mother's hate for Muslims as an attempt to show her mother the goodness of Islam and tell her how she had been wrong about Muslims. It seemed, however, that Islam as religion and "Muslim," as a historical category, were used to primarily escape the mother's psychosis. This analysis enraged Rupal and she lashed out at me saying how I was insistent on proving her mother crazy and that her mother had been right about Muslims inciting violence.

Her accusation that I was a violence-inciting Muslim took her back to her mother. Following this altercation between us, she did not return for therapy for two weeks. She returned in the third week with accentuated symptoms of paranoia. Her apparent relationship with the Muslim man was over, leaving her scared about not being protected by Allah anymore, so much so, that she had become fearful of Muslims. In her fear, she identified with her mother's version of the Muslim, and found them violent, sexual, distrustful, and bearing hatred for her. All her ideas had turned completely around in about two weeks' time.

HATE AS THE HISTORICAL OTHER

While I was seen as a bad Muslim in relation to Islam, in relation to history, I was seen as the persecuting Muslim. She directed the wrath of her psychotic rage, in which she was convinced that I was "out there to get her." She accused me of hating her because she was a Hindu, and hence I was the one who had dared to take away "my man."[14] Her increased skin rashes were attributed to an idea that I had cursed her solely because she was a Hindu and thus she "could not be more beautiful than me." She accused me of being overly sexual and having caused her relationship to break by calling it sexual. On several occasions, she accused me of things which happened in the outside world such as the Batla House encounter, alleging how all Muslims were terrorists and I had helped them to kill the police officer who was Hindu. Anything I said to her in sessions was experienced by her as persecutory. On enquiring how she imagined any further clinical work with a therapist like me who was causing her harm, she said that I was the reason for her being sick so it was now my responsibility to witness her "breakdown" and to see what I had done to her "as a Muslim."

DEATH OF THE MOTHER; KILLING OF THE HISTORICAL OTHER

Ten months into our final year in therapy, which had been more or less filled with her psychotic rage around me, our therapeutic work was once again interrupted. She called me at five in the morning one day to say how she had lost her mother to cancer and she had wanted me to know. She was awfully calm and assured, in contrast to my emotional response to the news, by saying how she was fine and would be coming to see me after some weeks. I was deeply upset about her mother's death.

She resumed her sessions with a sense of calm. She spoke of how her mother had been suffering from cancer, a fact no one had known except her father.[15] Her mother had been in and out of hospitals, but that had been understood as usual medical afflictions. Although she had been at her mother's bedside when she died, Rupal couldn't believe that her mother was dead. While everyone wept in her family, she had been unable to shed a tear. It was in sessions that she had cried for the first time after her death; however she felt "nothing" after crying. On pointing out how it was not that she didn't feel, but perhaps that she felt too much, she quietened, saying how she "just couldn't feel so much," and announced her discontinuation of therapy. On asking her to take her time and reconsider later, she replied that I had killed the mother and, by continuing to come for therapy, she couldn't betray her mother anymore. That was our last session.

Her departure affected me immensely. I was distraught and felt miserable for a couple of weeks. I kept thinking she would return for therapy and wondered what I had done, for her to disrupt our clinical consultation. While presenting her case in a psychoanalytical group supervision, I found myself concluding how her departure had made me feel that she had been right about me killing her mother. Besides peer reflections about my identifying with the part of the patient that felt it had killed the mother, the clinical supervisor asked me *"Zehra . . . How do you feel you killed the mother?"* He didn't want me to answer, rather he wanted me to think about it. He initiated a process of reflection. My immediate thought was "hate"—I had killed the mother with hate. It sounded like I was identifying with projections of the patient on me as the persecutory Muslim. However, it did feel that the feeling of hate was my own. On keeping my supervisor's question in mind over several weeks I arrived at an odd thought. There was something about the way he said "Zehra" which made me feel how Muslim my name was! It struck me that my feeling that I had killed her with hate had something to do with my feeling of how Muslim I was. I realized how I was responding from a history of Hindu-Muslim relations, which was essentially psychotic.

HINDU-MUSLIM: A PSYCHOTIC RELATION

Hindu-Muslim relations in India are fossilized around the Partition of the country. Salman Akhtar (2005) explains how the British served as a common enemy for both Hindus and Muslims, whose removal after Partition plunged both communities into what he called "villain hunger." It is the primitive need to blame someone for one's hardships which takes one away from sadness such that one doesn't have to mourn one's losses. Hindus and Muslims, caught in an inability to mourn the unresolved grief of loss of land and relocation, sought each other as villains, attributing the fault of the Partition to each other's community. Sudhir Kakar (1996) writes how, in situations of communal violence, the two communities constructed each other as containers of what was unacceptable in themselves, and saw each other as possessing rampant sexuality and essaying fervor of violence. In *Shaman's Mystics and Doctors* (1982) Kakar presents a cultural study of shamanism in India and explains states of possession, where a Hindu possessed by a Muslim spirit (*a jin*) and a Muslim by a Hindu spirit (*devi)* live out states which earlier had been dismissed and projected onto the other. In states of trance, for example, a Hindu woman would crave meat while a Muslim woman would worship an idol. These behaviors are never identified as one's own, as one is out of trance and continued to belong to the other community.

Ashis Nandy comments on how Hindu-Muslim relations in India moved from splitting and projecting in Partition, to annihilation in the Gujarat riots, indicating how hate was not enough, and one needed to destroy what is hated in order to feel omnipotent. This relationship between Hindus and Muslims, operating through the primary defense of splitting and projection, is a reflection of one's own fear for the "safety of the psyche" (Frosh 1989, Rustin 1999, Elliot 1994, Clarke 2001) which ubiquitously translates as "safety of the community," rendering the other community as a threat to this endangered survival. This was seen in rumors collected in cities of Gujarat after communal violence in 2002, where Hindus and Muslims with their projections around sexuality and violence, were seen as threatening to each other's survival; Hindus feared being castrated and Muslims feared being converted.

Large group identities of Hindus and Muslims are maintained through "externalization of discrepancies within themselves onto the other," explains Vamik Volkan (1997), such that both groups' identities are bereft of similarity and premised on difference. A Hindu is what a Muslim is not. An antithetical polarization needs to be fueled, to continue to see each other as the enemy. It is only by destroying the enemy one can get past one's own fear of death.

Essentially located in phantasy, and expressed through paranoia, Hindus and Muslims enthrall each other in a psychotic relationship.

HISTORICAL TRUTH: MUSLIM AS THE OTHER

Constantly reflecting her idealization as well as persecution around Muslims to her internal world, I understood Rupal's response to me as a Muslim, as part of the transference dialogue. However, every time she made a reference to me being Muslim, looking at her like a Hindu, although with delusional content, I felt it was very close to the historical view of the Muslim and Hindu which was premised on paranoia as well. The awareness of this historical relation made me conscious in sessions about being Muslim. I felt my historical location interfered with my countertransference reactions, leaving me confused; was I responding like a therapist by being a Muslim in her head, or a Muslim sharing my historical truth with her?

Donald Spence, in his book *Narrative Truth and Historical Truth* (1982) explains that historical truth is different from narrative truth. Psychoanalysis in the sessions constructs a narrative which, even though it claims to be a reconstruction, goes on to assume complete power of the construction, such that one's narrative of one's life becomes true to an extent, that it replaces the possibility of an external objective reality. Narrative truth *becomes the* historical reality; the truth of history, which is the way things are, is considered neither true nor real in the session.

My confusion about responding from the historical position of being a Muslim was that it had no place in the psychoanalytical frame. It was a matter of history, if anything, but of no relevance to Rupal's narrative in sessions. It could be explored in my own analysis in relation to my inner world where it might have emerged as my historical reality (Abbasi 2008). However, in her inner world my historical location was neither real nor true. In sessions, I could only speak as the Muslim in her head, which was her reality. It was this conflict between her historical reality, in which she saw me as a persecutory Muslim, and my historical truth, where in the construction of the Hindu I was once, which made me unsure about my feelings for her.

This speculation was less dominant when she made references to my religious and cultural identity as a Muslim. Her idealization of Islam and her fascination for Muslims was not a source of conflict for me, primarily because I am less anxious around issues of religion and culture. My views around them emerged from personal experiences, and didn't carry a baggage of conformity which was predetermined. My adherence to Islam, and participating in the social and cultural imagination of being a Muslim, was a dialogue for my inner world that I engaged in my personal work. It was my historical identity as a Muslim, which was as if determined by Partition and was re-invoked in incidents of communal violence. As a historical Muslim, born from an identity of splits, I held myself in doubt with respect to the Hindu. *It was here that I believed I had indeed killed the mother.*

KILLING THE MOTHER IN HISTORICAL REALITY

I wondered about the psychoanalytical meaning of this killing and its relation with my historical identity. In the assessment of Islam, while her mother hated Muslims, Rupal tried to separate it from her fused identity with the mother. However, this idealization was also based on her fused identity with her boyfriend, who was Muslim. In all, she tried to replace one fused identity with the other, and when it didn't succeed, she regressed to the first fused identity with the mother and like her, hated the Muslim. While I was able to reflect upon her fusion with the mother, whom she didn't find abusive, her idealization of Islam and fascination with the Muslim was premised on fusion with a Muslim, I was unable to reflect upon her regression to her mother. In hindsight, I realize how it was her mother who had been my historical other. Being a first-generation Partition survivor, she was the first born to a psychotic Hindu-Muslim relation and perhaps was trapped in it as well. As a *second-born*, I had, perhaps through psychoanalysis, gone past it and yet continued to remain in its grip; under this influence I felt I had killed her as a Muslim, her historical other.

Though psychoanalytically developed, this killing of the Hindu as a Muslim is the historical truth that has not yet entered the "in" narrative and continues to lie outside the historical reality of the session. Unable to interpret her regressive fusion with the mother effectively, I had lost the opportunity to save the mother in Rupal's inner world. Her anger toward me was in fact her anger toward her mother. It wasn't that she saw me as the mother. Instead, she saw me as her mother's historical other; a Muslim in whose historical location she could evoke and justify her projections, never facing her anger toward her mother. Had I been able to interpret her persecution against my being Muslim using my historical location of the other; making her explore my possibility of hating her mother, my historical other—the Hindu, I might have created a space in session where her mother could be separated from her, could be hated, and hence have a chance of surviving internally. I felt I killed the mother outside the sessions because I had failed to kill her inside by consequence had been unable to save her in Rupal's inner world.

CONCLUSION: RECOVERING "EACH OTHER" IN HISTORY

Freud writes in *Constructions in Analysis* (1937) how delusions appear as equivalent to constructions which we build in the course of the analytic treatment—they are attempts at explanation, and cure, though under the conditions of psychosis, can do no more than replace the fragment of reality that is being disavowed in the present, by another fragment that had already been disavowed in the remote past. In the construction of analyzing the psychosis of the patient, the delusion of being hated by the Muslim, attempts to explain how the disavowed aspects of self are replaced by the disavowed aspects of a community. This delusion of being hated by the Muslim carries a kernel of truth, where it brings a return of the past—the historical truth of Muslim as the Historical Other. Inserted in place of a rejected inner psychic reality, a delusion of being persecuted by the Muslim recovers Hindu as the Historical Other.

The attempt of this chapter was to explore how Hindus and Muslims converse with each other given their historical relation in an analytical setting. Hindus and Muslims meet each other in the delusion of the patient. The Muslim exists in the historical conversation with the Hindu, forgotten through Partition and repeated in the mind. The chapter is about how the therapist "makes out" that which has been forgotten, in the conversation between Hindus and Muslims, is what is repeated in the mind. The work of the therapist is to allow the Muslim, as the Historical Other, to recover the Hindu as the Historical other, who speaks to the patient that keeps Hindu and Muslim in her mind.[16]

ENDING NOTE:

It has been two years since Rupal discontinued therapy and I have thought about her often. A few months ago, she messaged me saying how she had been miserable and wanted to resume therapy but was afraid of me hating her because of what the right-wing Prime Minister was doing to Muslims; she made references to arrests, communal remarks, beef bans, and love jihad. I wondered, every time she placed her delusion in the context of the politics of the country, about who was really psychotic? Though she continued to speak locked in the idiom of the historical relationship, wasn't she carrying on a crucial dialogue on the behalf of the two communities in her delusion?

As Jacqueline Rose posits "It's not who speaks in the unconscious but what speaks in it"—It is not a Hindu or a Muslim in one's unconscious but what becomes Hindu and Muslim in one's unconscious.

NOTES

1. Mariana Hirsch writes in *Generation of Post Memory: Writing and Visual Culture* (2012) about the notion of "post memory" which describes the relationship of the second generation to powerful, often traumatic, experiences that preceded their births but that were nevertheless transmitted to them so deeply as to seem to constitute memories in their own right.

2. Eigen in his book *Emotional Storm* (2005) departs from the Bionion notion of personality and quotes "people in its place"; "When two *people* meet an emotional storm is created." He understands emotional storm as crucial to human development and relatedness and including all aspects from longing to blind rage as critical for psychic growth.

3. The statement by the use of "only and also" concerns itself with the theme of inside and outside both being different and similar at the same time. It falls under the rubric of concepts such as "Me-not me" and "Subjective Objective" (Wininicott, 1945,1953) and is eloquently expressed by Botella's (2005) formula: "only inside; also outside."

4. She was referred to me by a colleague who had seen her for 10 sessions of psychotherapy, informed by analysis though not psychoanalytical. He had to terminate work with her as his consultation was increased according to the hospital policy, making it unaffordable for the patient. I had just started private clinical practice and was working with patients on a low fee. I began psychoanalytical psychotherapy with her twice a week face to face.

5. Nancy McWilliams (1994) explains how the essential nature of human being cannot be understood without the appreciation of two distinct interacting dimensions—developmental level of personality and the defensive styles within that level (p. 40). It relates to degree of pathology and the expression of that pathology. In the present case while the symptom of obsessive compulsive was an expression of pathology, sessions in the future determined the degree of pathology to be psychosis.

6. *I love you* is replaced by *I hate you* (reaction formation) where it becomes you hate (projected) in relation to the other (Screber's case details; Freud's psychic mechanism for Paranoia).

7. During a heated argument the mother had slapped her and ripped off her clothes in front of her father and brother demanding her to do openly what she was pursuing on the sly—seducing the men in the family. She had gone on to explain how it had

been a familiar scene since childhood following which she described her childhood experiences with the mother.

8. Her father was unable to stop the mother and explained to her instead how she must never make her mother unhappy or else be prepared to deserve such a fate. She realized now how her father was scared of her mother and avoided all possible communication with her especially in public spaces lest she said something embarrassing.

9. While the dynamic of the relation continued to be unconscious, the relationship with the mother came in sessions at the end of the first year following a physical assault at the hands of the former.

10. She shared how she felt understood by me and did not want to disrupt it by becoming the object of my envy.

11. It was the literal translation of *BisMillahIrRehman-ir-Raheem,* which is recited before any significant work is carried out.

12. It is the Islamic month of fasting, considered pious and integral to Muslims of all sects. She had seen me drink water in the month and concluded how I was a *kafir*. In reality I did not observe Ramzaan.

13. Her mother did eventually got to know of her relationship. Hell broke loose! She accused her of being his mistress, openly cursing Rupal saying how she was impure (*apavirta*) and was doomed to hell. She wanted to see where all she had been touched saying which she tore her clothes yelling how all her mothering had gone to waste, all she had told her for so many years about Muslims had been futile, and *the bastards had polluted her daughter*. She alleged her for conspiring against her by seducing her husband and her son. While the son and the father had been spectators to the violence her [whose?] sister had intervened dismissing Rupal's answer as a silly prank assuring her how it was impossible. She made Rupal apologize and since then her mother made it a point to humiliate Muslims, insisting Rupal affirmed it.

14. A reference to her previous boyfriend who was Muslim.

15. She had been in and out of hospitals but nothing was revealed of her illness. Rest of the family was under the impression of it being a regular medical checkup.

16. I express my gratitude to Shifa Haq for her comments on the first draft of the paper; Karuna Chandrashekhar and Sayandeb Chowdhury for their editorial recommendations.

REFERENCES

Abbasi, A. "Whose Side Are You On? Muslim Psychoanalysts treating Non-Muslim Patients." In *The Crescent and the Couch: Cross Currents between Islam and Psychoanalysis*, 335–50, edited by Salman Akhtar. Lanham, MD: Jason Aronson, 2008.

Akhtar, S. "Hindu-Muslim Relations in India: Past, Present and Future."In *Freud along the Ganges.* New York: Other Press, 2005.

Bion, W. R. (1979) "Making the best of a Bad Job. Bulletin British Psychoanalytic Society." February 1979. Reprinted in Clinical Seminars and Four Papers (1987). [Reprinted in Clinical Seminars and Other Works: London: Karnac Books, 1994].

Botella, S and Botella, C (2005) *The Work of Psychic Figurability: Mental States Without Representation*. New York: Routledge, 2005.

Clarke, M. (2001). "The Klenian Position: Phantasy, Splitting and the Language of Psychic Violence," *Journal for the Psychoanalysis of Culture and Society, 6*: 289–297.

Eigen, M. *Emotional Storm*. Middletown CT: Wesleyan University Press, 2005.

Elliot, A. *Psychoanalytic Theory: An Introduction*. Blackwell: Oxford, UK and Cambridge: M.A., 1994. Reprinted 1997.

Erikson, E. H. (1964). *Insight and Responsibility* New York. W.W. Norton & Company, Inc.

Freud, S. (1911) *Psycho-analytic Notes on an Autobiographical Account of a Case of Paranoia (Dementia Paranoides)*. Hogarth Press, London, S.E. 18 (1975), 221-232.

Freud, S. *Constructions in Analysis,* 258–9, (S.E. Vol. 23, 1937).

Frosh, S. *Psychoanalysis and Psychology*. London: Macmillan, 1989.

Hirsch. M. (2012) *The Generation of Post Memory: Writing and Visual Culture after the Holocaust*. New York: Columbia University Press, 2012.

Kakar, S. *Colors of Violence: Cultural Identities, Religion and Conflict*. Chicago: University of Chicago Press, 1996.

Kakar, S. *Shamans, Mystics Doctors: A Psychological Enquiry into India and its Healing Traditions*. New Delhi. Oxford University Press, 1982.

Lerman, A., H. Moore, S. Frosh, S. Chaudhuri, and A. Sen. *Conversations with Jacqueline Rose*. New York: Seagull Books, 2010.

McWilliams, N. *Psychoanalytic Diagnosis: Understanding the Personality Structure in the Clinical Process*. New York: The Guilford Press, 1994.

Nagpal, A. "Clinical Reflections on Forgiveness." In *Wounded History: Religion, Conflict, Psyche and Social Healing,* 165–172, edited by John Chathanatt and Manindra Thakur. (Delhi: Media house, 2006.

Nandy, A. *Intimate enemy: Loss and Recovery of Self under Colonialism* (Delhi. Oxford University Press, 1983.

Nandy, A. *Regimes of Narcissism and Regimes of Despair*. UK: Oxford University Press, 2013.

Nandy, A. *Time Wraps: Silent and Evasive Pasts in Indian Politics and Religion*. London: Hurst, 2002.

Nandy, A. "The Politics of Secularism and the Recovery of Religious Tolerance." In *Mirrors of Violence-Communities, Riots and Survivors in South Asia*, 69–93, edited by Veena Das. Delhi: Oxford University Press, 1990.

Nandy, A. *Traditions, Tyranny and Utopias: Essays in the Politics of Awareness*. Delhi: Oxford University Press, 1987.

Roland, A. *Journeys to Foreign Selves: Asians and Asian Americans in Global Era*. New Delhi: Oxford University Press, 2014.

Rustin, M. "Conclusions: A New Culture of Warfare." In *Welfare and Culture in Europe: Towards a New Paradigm in Social Policy,* pp 275-81, edited by Prue Chamberlayne, Andrew Cooper, Richard Freeman, and Michael Rustin. London: Jessica Kingsley Publishers, 1999.

Spence, D. P. *Narrative and Historical Truth: Meaning and Interpretation in Psychoanalysis*. New York: W.W. Norton, 1982.

Volkan, V.D. *Bloodlines: From Ethnic Pride to Ethnic Terrorism*. New York: Farrar, Straus, and Giroux, 1997.

Winnicott, D.W. "Primitive Emotional Development." *International Journal of Psychoanalysis* XXVI(1945):137–143.

Winnicott, D.W. "Transitional Objects and Transitional Phenomena—A Study of the First Not-Me Possession." *International Journal of Psychoanalysis* 34(1953):89–97.

Chapter Eight

Disaster Diaries

Riot-Affected Children in Ahmedabad and Hyderabad

Atreyee Sen and Manasi Kumar

DISASTER DIARIES: EXCERPTS FROM FIELDNOTES

Manasi Kumar

Akram is 12 years old, studies in class 7 in Ahmedabad city where he lives with his maternal family since his father was killed during the 2002 riots. His paternal grandmother threw them out of their house (mother, him, and his younger sister). He works part-time as a mechanic in a garage where he earns 3000 rupees which comes in handy for the running of the household. He describes himself as someone who laughs a lot and loves to visit different places with his sister. He loves to ride bikes and watch movies and really wants to sit in an airplane. He shared that his relationship with his mother was good and he always did what she asked him to do. He also says that he gives her money whenever there's a need. He gets worried about marrying off his sister now that his father is no more. Shortly after his father's death, his maternal grandparents died of shock (perhaps there was some illness too that was not known to him). He appeared like a very chirpy boy who got quite anxious and sullen when some of these troubling experiences were recalled. He shared that obeying his mother was important and he followed her advice carefully but that she became upset and distant when he did not listen to her.

Shera is 10 years old and has the most disturbing appearance, as she looks extremely unwell, thin, and morose. During our meeting, she rarely made eye contact; in fact she squatted on the bed with her face bent down, rarely looking up when I asked her anything. She stays with her mother and four siblings—one elder brother and sister, the others younger. Her father was shot dead in the riots. Her mother makes incense sticks. She described herself as someone who loves playing with her friends, especially hide & seek. She told me that her mother gives her money when needed and helps her with her studies. She and her siblings make "rakhis," Hindu armbands that girls tie to their brothers during a rakhi festival. The payment received for this laborious work is extremely low but she doesn't complain. She mentions that the family has had several misfortunes since the father's death. She herself suffers from a broken ribcage and Chikungunya (a viral infection), which makes her weak and inefficient at work both at school and home. Though she would like to be a teacher, she doesn't know if she can pursue her education, as the family income isn't enough.

Atreyee Sen

Arshed, 10, who lives with his parents in a Hyderabad slum, says:

> *In December 2003, riots broke out between Hindus and Muslims in the northern quarters of Hyderabad. Our slum area was particularly affected by the rising tensions. I was sent off for safe-keeping to my uncle's house in another part of the city. My brother, a six-year-old, remained behind as my parents were sure that a small child could be hidden in a box or a barrel if communal antagonisms escalated into violence. I returned to the slums after a few weeks and found my mother sitting at the doorstep of our small family shack; she had a glazed look and held her head in her hands. My father sat on a creaky bed, swaying from side to side and whispering "he is gone, he is gone (chala gaya, chala gaya)." My neighbour walked up to me, put his hand on my shoulder and said "come and say goodbye to your brother." He walked with me to the cemetery. He said my brother was struck on the head when trapped between rioters on the streets, and had finally died after two days. The neighbor pointed toward a freshly covered grave. When I bent over and touched the earth my hand were caught in the stringed net of flowers resting over the grave. My small brother was tugging at my arm. I couldn't save him. My uncle said, "You are all that your parents have right now, you will grow up and be their crutch." I said, "Let me grow up first." That evening, I was summoned by the local vigilante group. It constituted of other riot-affected slum boys. Everyone was angry, everyone was concerned about the survival of young children during violence. Without offering a word of consolation to my grieving parents I went off to meet them. In the dying light of the day, I was given a crude sword by one of the older boys, "for your self-protection" (tere suraksha ke liye). I realized I was officially a member of the local patrol, there was no looking back (peeche mudke na dekha).*

Alam, 10, who lives with his uncle in a Hyderabad slum says:

> *So many children die during the riots. One day you are playing with them, football, flying kites, running around, going to work together, going to school together. And then they are gone, poof, they turn into small graves. You walk*

past the cemetery every day and you cannot forget the riots. Or they don't have a leg and can't play football anymore. They don't have an arm, they can't hold a cricket bat anymore. You see them limping around on crutches, and they avoid making eye contact with you. One of their pajama legs is usually flapping in the wind; they become concerned whether it can be neatly folded and pinned to their waist so that it doesn't get trapped in their crutch or get dirty . . . . Conversations also change among the children you know. Everyone wants to talk about the violence. . . . We become scared at night that the ghosts of dead children will haunt us because we survived. I once stole some marbles from Mehr. He died during the riots; he was strangled. Now he knows I was the thief, what if he is thinking about revenge? My parents said "Think about revenge against the Hindus, forget about Mehr's revenge." But I think Mehr will come after me.

Trauma can be a subject of direct or indirect inquiry in any disaster research. This chapter will offer a critical interdisciplinary perspective on the narrativization of trauma among young children affected by Hindu-Muslim riots in two different communally sensitive urban areas in India. By drawing select strands from psychological and anthropological approaches, and relating it to the articulation of trauma among young children, the authors will attempt to review what trauma signifies among children, how attachment and trauma frameworks are useful reference points toward comprehending childhoods afflicted by brutal collective violence, and how complex memories and discourses of physical disability and social disconnection are developed and sustained by riot-affected children.

The theme of trauma symbolized the core of psychoanalytic theorization. The traumatized psyche was conceptualized as registering blows to the psyche outside the domain of ordinary awareness, with hypnotic methods working to provide release of repressed material by a cathartic method (Breuer & Freud 1895). The later psychoanalytic focus (from 1890 onwards) shifted to repressed memories of sexual trauma and how trauma was internalized (Leys 2000). By 1897, Freud disregarded his thesis of seduction trauma and focused attention on internal processes and unconscious metabolization of trauma. Laplanche (1999) drew attention to how Freud problematized the origins of trauma by pointing to the phenomena of "deferred action" (*nachtraglichkeit*) or "afterwardsness" as Laplanche terms it. The trauma, as constituted by a relationship between two events or experiences: a first event that was not thought to be traumatic (because it came too early in a child's maturation to be understood), and a second event that was not inherently traumatic but triggered memories of the first one and colored the memory with traumatic hues (van Haute & Geyskens 2004). Freud rejected a straightforward causal analysis of trauma in which assaults from outside affected the human being. Freud's thesis complicated the understanding of trauma as he highlighted the role played by traumatic memory and unconscious motivations where the memories become unstable by virtue of the presence of a vivacious fantasy life.

The study of traumatic neurosis for Freud became a theoretical problem demanding an exploration of repetition, processes of mourning, defenses of the ego and, above all conceptualization of his dual-drive theory life and death drives. Ferenczi can be credited with working on similar themes focusing on the transfer of trauma from adult to child and the differences in their languages and organization of trauma. Despite this turning toward mechanisms of defense and ego functioning, the problem of trauma kept coming up in the form of the role of external reality or impingement of the external environment on human instincts (Leys 2000). Henry Krystal (1978, 1985) on anxiety, affects, and trauma, Khan (1974) on cumulative trauma, Ilse Grubich-Simitus (1984) on "concretism of metaphors of traumatized," and Oliner (1996) on "psychotic like breakdown in trauma survivors," among others, provided some account of the internal ramifications of excessive impingements from outside.

However, World War I revived "shell shock" and combat trauma, and PTSD came into the picture. Trauma inflicted from outside was revived once again. The understanding of anxiety as both cause and cure of trauma (Leys 2000), in its ego-protective function and subsequent seeping into the human protective shield, provided opportunities to study various shades of anxiety. Trauma thus comes to be understood both as a breach in the protective shield or unbinding (Freud 1926) as well as a certain kind of mimetic identification (lack of memory of trauma as opposed to repression of it, resorting to mechanisms such as identification with the aggressor, where there is susceptibility and openness to all identifications).

The later work of Caruth (1995) and van der Kolk et al. (1996a) (later also with the work of Dori Laub (2005) and Shoshana Felman (1995), provided a bridge between empiricism and deconstructionism for trauma theory to argue that the "literal" speech and symptoms of the traumatized were the (literal) repetitions of the trauma (Leys 2000, pg. 229). It was argued that the memories emanating from trauma are not "explicit" or "declarative," but rather "implicit" and "procedural non-declarative," associated with different parts of the brain (and classically conditioned responses). Herman (1992) returned to flashbacks, dissociative states, intrusions, nightmares, etc., by arguing for their recollection and integration back into the inner world of her abused child subject's memories. However, with these developments, Frankel (1994, cited in Leys 2000, p. 243), raised an important concern: is the remembered trauma historically true or is the recall of historically true trauma necessary for healing? Even within psychoanalysis, analysts such as Andre Green (2000),

Roy Schafer (1980), and Donald Spence (1984) deliberated on the historical truth, hermeneutic interpretations of remembered events and memories, and their relevance to the practice of psychoanalysis in clinic and public/research domains. Van der Kolk et al. (1996b) evidence for structural deficit or a wound created by trauma, and the performative theory of traumatic theory of Caruth, undermined the radical nature of Freud's unconscious repression due to their stress on the literality of trauma. Political events such as the Vietnam War, and the radical feminist movement in the 1960s and 1970s, provided an immense playground for PTSD and literary examinations of trauma with the issue of culpability, testimony of violence and trauma (Das 1990; Butler 2003) drawing interest in understanding the consequences of these events in the public domain.

The science, and consequent poignant portrayal, of this "literality" of trauma provided a boost toward understanding passivity and the end of representation, but it also ran into an epistemological quandary of not finding sufficient ground to account for Freud's "perpetual recurrence of the same thing" (Leys 2000), since, by repeating trauma, one becomes a subject of it and not merely a passive victim (van Haute and Geyskens 2007).

Freud's idea of the death instinct emanating from traumatic neurosis continues to remain contested. However, his insistence on studying the problem of death instinct provided vital links between the origins of life, such that it is the original *hilflosigkeit* of early childhood. Since then, the *primacy of the child* became the hallmark of psychoanalytic thinking (Kristeva 2002). It is in this sense that Widlocher and Fairfield (2003), and van Haute and Geyskens (2007) pointed to the unresolved tension between primacy of trauma versus that of attachment within psychoanalysis as the old debate between life and death instincts, sexuality, and attachment got revived. While many analysts (e.g., Anna Freud, Winnicott, Klein to begin with) championed the ideas of security, transmission of external-internal threat, the critical importance of early mother-child relations, remained closest in terms of linking external traumatic influence on early development (see, Fonagy 2001, Gullestad 2003). Threatening to displace the primacy of sexuality, Bowlby's thesis of the centrality of attachment and primal helplessness provided a great impetus in rethinking the hierarchy and ontology of human needs. Those engaged in assembling the attachment-trauma puzzle posed by Bowlby point to its connection with earlier debates between Freud and Ferenczi, and later additions by Laplanche (1999) and others (particularly Stein 2003, Leys 2000, Widlocher and Fairfield 2003, Geyskens and Van Haute 2004, 2007).

Seen this way, the death instinct was reinterpreted in the form of the primacy of the child—of *hilflosigkeit*—and helplessness and dependency were understood to be the beginnings of all beginnings as well as at the heart of all traumatic neurosis and loss. It is to Melanie Klein that the desexualization of the child's trauma can be attributed, though she upheld the banner of universal primacy of the child and trauma in her writings (which Laplanche explained well by calling her work "ipsocentric"—otherness enters in an unexplained way in her theory). Van Haute and Geyskens (2007) argue that Klein reduced the child's need to the most basic—that of hunger and thirst. Both negative experiences were conceptualized as the driving force of the human baby. While Anna Freud, in her theorization, refused to see the needs of the child in isolation, Bowlby argued that the initial helplessness, need for love and safety were the bases of attachment (bringing in "positive" experience as drivers of self-sustenance and development). Attachment and loss belonged to the domain of normal development with the need for proximity to the mother and separation anxiety resulting in its absence or emanating from it. What Freud attributed to a secondary instinct or need was shown by Bowlby to be primal and immediate in its own right. Curiosity, a sense of mastery, aggression, and repetition of trauma were then phenomena explained by these early experiences with a significant other (this happened along with the impetus provided by other object relations theorists) (Laplanche 2001; Geyskens and van Haute 2004). Though Bowlby's view of temporality was rather linear, and the distinction between normality and pathology not as radical as Freud's, it was his contribution that "attachment became an original dimension in the life of the instinct" (van Haute and Geyskens 2007, p.108). Direct harm, abuse, and neglect of children, direct observational work and intervention with families and children brought out the debate of the real influences on the child's development vs. those psychic influences with which psychoanalytic practice was concerned. The study of how external events mapped on to the psychic reality have become, since then, areas of intensive research.

NATURE OF EXTERNAL REALITY: PSYCHIC VS. REAL

In reconciling the impact of traumatic events such as disasters and looking at their impact on a child's attachment, a key question is the nature of reality that will be studied. While attachment tools tried to elaborate dominant mental states and internal working models which sustained those states, the reality of the external environment is also a compelling factor that needs some accountability. In psychoanalysis, trauma has essentially been understood as a relation between the external event and a concomitant internal reverberation, provoking large-scale disturbance in the functioning of the individual. Freud (1921) and many of his followers visualize the trauma process by using the concept of "protective shield," a barrier between the outer and inner mental life that is perforated by psychic overload. This equation is indicative of a complex relationship marked by the temporal sequences in which trauma recurs and re-presents (disturbance in memory function) itself in painful ways (Freud 1921). Thus, it is as if the trauma did not occur a long time ago, but as if it is happening again and again every day. Winnicott (1971) suggested that there should be some grading of external environment in terms of the impingements it makes on the parent-child world. Freud and Burlingham (1943) were pioneers in calling attention to children's psychic experiences during the war and systematically studied environmental trauma and defenses used by children to endure it. In the late 1960s and 1970s Anna Freud turned her interest to the psychoanalytic categorization of childhood symptomatology and to the problems of technique in working with emotionally deprived and socially disadvantaged children including those with non-neurotic disturbances: various forms of developmental delay and deviation (Edgcumbe 1983). She advanced the idea that disturbances needed to be studied more in the nature of personality stunting or deformation acquired in the process of adapting to an inadequate or malignant environment.

Along with understanding the confusion of tongues between an adult and child, there is also a need to integrate the gaps in external and internal environments. By thinking that only psychic reality is the domain of unconscious motivations, repression, and all things deep, the exposition of a human mind would not be adequate. External reality which includes social conditions—both facilitating and adverse conditions—has have to be better understood (LeVine 2001, Altman 2005). Hence, anthropological enquiry into trauma pulls away from reviewing traumatic experience as a deep psychological process; anthropologists develop multiple perspectives on comprehending trauma as a cultural construct, which determines the ways in which both adults and children who have suffered from trauma reconnect with the family, community, and adopt various moral pathways of healing and reconciliation. Lester (2013), for example, while developing a critical anthropology of trauma prefers to use the language of "re-tethering" instead of attachment, and makes a case for local responses to traumatic events. She states:

> People find ways to go on living—not just by resolving deep psychological conflicts or by reorganizing their experience to meet existing categories, but through ongoing, iterative, continuous processes of meaning-making that emerge in relationship with others, across a variety of levels and contexts, and through time. (2013, pg. 754)

We also emphasize the suffering that people undergo when faced with sudden and brutal ruptures in everyday life, and yet our research highlights how actors continue to bridge the gap between their ontological isolation and wider practices of human relatedness, especially after surviving a disaster.

PSYCHOLOGICAL TERRAIN AND SOCIAL REALITY OF EVENTS UNDER INQUIRY

There are areas of overlap between natural and human-induced disasters. Sen (1999) argues that famines are usually caused by a lack of purchasing power or entitlements and are not necessarily caused by drought and consequent food shortage; in effect, famine is the result of human actions rather than entirely caused by a natural phenomenon. Natural disasters and complex emergencies can occur concurrently (Spiegel 2005). Similarly, violence unleashes complex and difficult life conditions. Survivors carry the impact of both the increasing persecution and violence and of threats such as mass killing or genocide, in extreme cases. Their basic needs for security, for feelings of effectiveness and control over important events in their lives, for positive identity, for positive connections to other people and communities, and for a comprehension of reality and of their own place in the world have all been deeply frustrated (Staub 1989, 2003a, 2003b, 2003c, 2006; Staub and Pearlman 2001, 2006). With the exception of anthropologist Veena Das' work (1990; also see Nussbaum 2007) on the Sikh community affected in the 1984 Delhi Hindu-Sikh riots, there are few contemporary scholarly studies on childhood adversities, child trauma, or social impact of collective/critical events on young children. The challenge before the authors, therefore, has been enormous in terms of finding new ways of conceptualizing the problem of complex disasters, their long-term effects on children, and post-disaster adversities. Thinking through the anthropological enterprise of participant observation as a way of understanding children and their struggles becomes the next concern.

FIELD WORK IN PSYCHOANALYTICALLY MINDED RESEARCH

The main hurdle after a golden period of interaction between psychoanalysis and anthropology, from Mead to Malinowski (1928-1950), came in the form of universalistic bias and an apathy toward cross-cultural sensitivity or exchange on childhood and child development issues. While the neo-Freudian influences used the field observations to criticize developmental formulations (e.g., Kurtz 1992, LeVine and Norman 2001), thorough and in-depth cultural explorations within psychoanalytic developmental theorization did not become popular. Obeyesekere (1990) points out that in both the disciplines of psychoanalysis and anthropology it is well recognized that some of our insights in fact come from our subjects/informants and this is a situation impossible in natural sciences (p. 238). Therefore an ethnography or anthropology of childhood is meant to be a descriptive account, based on field observations and one involving interviews of participants, of the lives, activities, and experiences of children in a particular place and time, and also involve the social, cultural, institutional, and economic contexts that make sense of their behavior there and then (Patel and Kleinman 2003). The fieldwork has to uphold the plasticity principle and human variability forms the main tenet of the research. The anthropology of childhood and psychoanalytic anthropology have suffered from the chronic instability of dominant theories concerning the child's psychological development during the twentieth century (Piaget's universalistic accounts came under attack from Shweder and LeVine [1984]; similarly, Kohlberg's cognitively based model of moral development [1984] was similarly criticized by Shweder and LeVine [1984]; Carol Gilligan's conception of gender differences in development was challenged by Miller [1994] and the Bowlby-Ainsworth attachment theory have also been criticized for their universalistic bias by LeVine & Norman [2001] and by Burman [2007]). It can be said that the relations between anthropology, developmental psychology, and psychoanalysis on issues of child development have been distant and sporadic.

In doing field work, the necessity of transcending those opposing perspectives was established very early; the field worker must remain open to native views while simultaneously seeking an academic understanding; a balance must be attained between description and explanation, between the idiographic and the nomothetic. And this entire discussion leads us to the question of our own fieldwork(s) which involved studying both the social and the psychological, sometimes barely managing to capture both.

STRANDS OF FIELDWORK IN COMMUNALLY SENSITIVE AHMEDABAD

The Gujarat riots that took place in February 2002 and continued untill March-April of that year were some of the worst riots in the history of social violence in India. Communal violence broke out in the capital city of Ahmedabad and in surrounding areas, over the gruesome burning of Hindu activists (travelling by train) in the town of Godhra (Gujarat) early in the morning of 27 February, 2002, and continued for the next four months. Over 2000 Muslims and 254 Hindus were killed; 20,000 Muslims and about 10,000 Hindus were displaced and property worth 5 million rupees was destroyed (Mehta, Vankar, and Patel 2005). International Human Rights Watch Report (2002) reported over 1000 cases of rape and mutilation of women and children.

> *Case 7: Deepak, 12, lives in Ahmedabad city, where he was interviewed in the SEWA's regional office inside the old city quarters. His father was killed in the riots and his mother remarried. Unfortunately, his mother was unable to keep him citing that he was aggressive and violent with her and often rejecting of his step-father. He lives with his paternal grandmother and uncle and aunty, both of whom Deepak said were a bit rough with him. He felt abandoned by his mother and his violent outbursts were about making some contact with her, which were met with cold rejection. During the interview Deepak was quite cheerful and talked about a number of things like running away from the hostel, the loving care his granny gave, and the harassment from mother, uncle, and aunty. He described himself as someone who played and shared with everyone and can be funny, often making his cousins laugh. He shared a lot about his life and when we started talking about the relationship with his mother and separation from her, he got up, crying incessantly, saying that his stomach was aching. I felt quite shocked and unable to comprehend initially, however later I could recognize how hurtful his mother's rejection of him was. I organized another meeting to understand what happened with him that day and to complete the interview. He shared how difficult it is to talk about his mother.*

For the riot-affected children, the actual loss was more palpable and responsibilities felt more from their end than forced on them by their parents. Despite the fact that more than five or six years had elapsed after the riots, when first contact was made with the children in the riots sample, several children and their families were still fighting for compensation for the lost parent, sibling, or other relatives and also for the physical damage to property. The missing people were not yet declared dead so there were children who spoke about their parent/relative or sibling as if they were alive and many were waiting for the parent to return, so clearly the fact that the loss was a permanent one had not yet sunk in. Since the riots became a matter of national debate and furor, as well as being a deep embarrassment for the State government (see National Human Rights Commission Report 2003–04, Patel and Kleinman 2003, many civil society organizations as well as the National Human Rights) Commission went back time and again to record testimonies of the survivors. The children spoke to the researcher about feeling very burnt out and disturbed about narrating their loss and experiences during riots time and again to different people.

Apart from this, the children in this sample were working for more than five to eight hours a day after attending their schools, to supplement their families' income. The researcher had to interview at least 18 children at their work place—typically a carpet factory on the outskirts of the city, or visit their homes or employer's home where they made *bidis* (local cigarettes), kites or *rakhis* (armbands used in a Hindu festival), or did embroidery work. The wage earned was just about 80 pence–1 pound (about 60–85 rupees) per week and it involved working strenuous hours in extremely dilapidated settings. The interview videos with some of these children are a witness to the kind of setting alluded to here.

In their descriptions of life after the riots, the children spoke and wrote (in the riots' trauma assessment questionnaire) about feeling an overwhelming sense of guilt of surviving the ordeal while their parent(s) or sibling(s) perished and a great moral sense of duty to serve the family. Young girls were found saying that they did not want to get married and wanted to stay with their parents, helping and serving them in their later life.

Listed below are a few factors that provide a roadmap toward understanding the long-term import of the two events under study:

Varied Degrees of Relational Deprivation

Both events, despite being different in origins, present a set of relational deprivations that are yet to be fully understood. As in the previous DMHR research, the violence presents greater vulnerabilities for children and families alike (Norris et al. 2006, Catani et al. 2008, 2009) than instances of natural disasters, though the rural context in many developing countries presents greater hardships and lack of resources in comparison to urban areas. In this research the earthquake-affected sample from the Kutch largely represents the rural, and the riots represent urban Gujarat. Therefore, social exclusion and lack of resources emanating from both events seem to have competing disadvantages.

Active and Passive Exclusion

The riots in Gujarat present active social exclusion where a deliberate attempt is made to exclude people from accessing resources, asserting their basic rights and freedom, and resulting in various transgressions and violations of their personal and social boundaries (Sen 2000, Butler 2003, Nussbaum 2006). On the other hand, in rural Gujarat in the aftermath of the severe earthquake, the more passive form of exclusion, in social conditions that foster deprivation, is demonstrated (Spodek 2001, Mehta 2001). The critical question in this research is then to see if children recognize and get differentially affected by the active seclusion in the context of riots or the more passive exclusion in case of earthquake.

THE HISTORY OF COMMUNAL VIOLENCE AND THE ROLE OF CHILDREN IN HYDERABAD

In the long history of communal discord in India, the voices and narratives of children being tortured, maimed, killed, or being orphaned has been largely missing. While their experiences have been enmeshed with the despair of their parents, siblings, and extended families, the children, especially, have been victims of violent conflict. Their agency, initiative, and independent aspirations to overcome and address their loss and anxieties through their own ideas and actions have remained marginalized in academic and policy-related analysis. My anthropological investigation into the lives of a group of Muslim slum children who have been affected by sporadic, yet ruthlessly violent, outbreaks of communal riots in Hyderabad revealed that young male slum children were far more dependent on each other for physical survival and emotional and economic sustenance than either on their families or on post-conflict NGO intervention. My ethnographic landscape was Sultanpur, a Muslim-dominated ghetto in the northern quarters of Hyderabad, where large sections of impoverished boys (aged between 9–14 years) conspired to form local child squads, and made violent attempts to claim and control peripheral, public spaces, for the safety and mobility of riot-affected children. The coordinated actions of these child squads, which preferred to align themselves with the terminology of "soldiering," brought forth the significance of Sultanpur as a complex urban turf that spawned and sustained a new culture of child belligerence.

Unlike Ahmedabad, Hyderabad is not a city which has been on the primary radar of communalist politics in India. Yet it has a legacy of prolonged enmity between Hindus and Muslims which has been traced far back to the period of Asaf Jahi dynastic/Nizami rule (between 1724 and 1948). Even though colonial heads of state had often admired the lack of conflict in the princely state, historians have shown how Hindus across caste beliefs and backgrounds organizsed resistances against Muslim domination in the city. The nature of inter-religious tensions came to a head at the beginning of the twentieth century, especially with the formation of a radical Muslim organization, Majlis-e-Ittehadul-Muslimeen in 1929. "Between 1937 and 1940, Hyderabad's much vaunted communal accord was irreparably shattered by a series of bloody riots and political demonstrations culminating in a nine-month campaign of civil disobedience by over 8,000 Hindus against the Darbar" (Copland 1988, pg. 784: 88). Majlis leaders spent the initial years trying to unify all classes and categories of Muslims on the same platform, but with a change in political leadership, the organization donned a brutal garb against minorities in the city. Through the 1940s, the paramilitary wing of the Majlis, the Razakars, spread a network of violence and terror in Hyderabad and its surrounding areas. The newly independent Indian Union, still in the process of negotiating the annexation of Hyderabad, expressed concern about the extreme chaos in the state. In September 1948, the Indian Army invaded the city and incorporated Hyderabad into the Telegana region in the southern part of India (later consolidated into the state of Andhra Pradesh). Besides setting a temporary ban on the Majlis, this invasion, also known as the "police action," had an enormous impact on the culture and configuration of the city. Several scholars highlighted the sudden marginalization of an important urban center within its surrounding rural, Dravidian society. For example, due to the domination of Telegu speakers in the region, Urdu, the primary language spoken and shared by affluent and underprivileged Hyderabadi Muslims, became increasingly insignificant. For several years, this form of symbolic and social assaults largely impacted young school-going Muslim children, especially when they were crudely taunted for speaking the official language of Pakistan. A decade of political, linguistic, and cultural battles led to the revival of the Majlis in 1957, and the new leaders gained a foothold in the rapidly expanding urban slums. The party developed a particularly strong base in the Charminar constituency of the old city (where I conducted my fieldwork), and eventually inspired the rise of other parallel radical organizations in Hyderabad (such as the Darsgah Jihad-O-Shahadath) which successfully mobilized large groups of slum children into their movement. Their most successful campaign carried an image of a small child in paramilitary uniform holding a poster saying "The Quran will be the constitution of Allah, and I will be the soldier of Allah."

The national level communal politics and the rise of Hindu nationalism deeply affected fragile religious relationships in Hyderabad. Communal polarizations in electoral politics became more acute when Hindu nationalist groups such as the Bharatiya Janata Party, (BJP), infiltrated into old city areas and pitched themselves against the local Majlis cells. The nature of rumormongering (Kakar 2005) and electioneering in these constituencies (Engineer 1991) hierarchized social and political practices in most of Hyderabad's housing colonies. Naidu's (1990) study of inflammatory communal relations and urban decay in the old city further suggests that the post-partition influx of Hindu refugee families coupled with rural-urban migration from Telugu-speaking areas significantly impacted inter-community relations. In addition, various political parties re-invented themselves as "anti-social elements," especially as the land mafia, resulting in high levels of crime in the old city. Corporations began to wonder about the impact of such communal tensions on younger children when several missionary schools, especially run by charitable groups for the poor, stopped offering admission to children from the old city as they could not attend classes during riots and curfews. Between 1978–84, Hyderabad saw a number of communal riots (sparked off by issues ranging from a Muslim woman being raped in a police station to conflict over the immersion of idols during Hindu festivals). In 1990, when Hindu nationalists made their first attempt to tear down the Babri Masjid in the temple town of Ayodhya (claiming that the historical mosque was the site for the birth of a mythological Hindu god, Ram), Hyderabad witnessed over a fortnight of crippling riots which left over a hundred people dead and many more critically injured. An NGO (COVA), which acted as a peace mediator during the riots, reported that stabbing became an important mob strategy, and knife edges were dipped in cyanide for more fatal attacks. Even though the communal element of the clashes was highlighted in the press and the media, most old city dwellers described the riots as a battle between Hindu and Muslim land sharks. "The BJP and the Majlis usually work together for land grabbing, often giving each other commissions. They probably had a fight over sharing profits which led to the communal battle," said Javed, a senior citizen and old city dweller. During the 1990 riots, however, mobs specifically attacked male children; boys were targeted, maimed, or killed with swords, spears, and stones, and hung from doorways to send a message to enemy communities (the police reports do not divulge information about the community backgrounds of these children). According to my child informants, however, it was poor Muslim boys ("we knew all about it") and this "trend" has continued over two decades into more recent times. Over the years, the slums got increasingly re-organized along communal lines and turned into what within urban anthropology has come to be understood as "hyperghettoes" (Wacquant 2010). Some of the public areas, especially the bazaars, once breathing spaces for inclusivity and sociality, came to be known as the Indo-Pakistan Line of Control. Flueckiger's (2006) ethnography of the life of a healer in Hyderabad showed how sections of urban Muslims retained nostalgia for the days before the "police action" when knowledge of other cultures was welcomed within most communities. Aroma, the chief protagonist in Flueckiger's account, remained worried that children growing up in segregated colonies encountered tensions and vulnerability, without any experience of inter-faith camaraderie that often characterized times of peace.

According to the inhabitants of Sultanpur, this ghetto, located close to the Charminar, one of the city's chief tourist attractions, housed approximately 10,000 Urdu-speaking, Muslim families (even though periodic surveys by NGOs, housing figures, and census operations by the local municipal corporation pegged the number closer to 30,000). The area was organized into a neatly structured mosaic of enclaves and shanties, and relatively well maintained lanes and by-lanes. For many generations, Sultanpur was the primary home and hub of craftsmen and traders who operated out of the nearby bangle, fabric, and pearl bazaars. Over four decades, Sultanpar saw robust, sporadic spurts of communal clashes with middle- and lower-class Hindus, usually living in residential neighborhoods around the Charminar. Sultanpur-*wallah*s described how these conflicts, at times sparked off by narrower issues such as slum-dwellers siphoning off water from Hindu-dominated housing estates, were resolved speedily by negotiations among community leaders. Over time, these quotidian clashes became more violent expressions of religious discontent, involving burning homes, looting shops, and physical attacks on small children, eventually driving a deeper wedge into local Hindu-Muslim relations. Also, the lack of state control over religious processions and the subsequent lifting of a ban on loudspeakers increased the scope for speeches, slogans, and communal incitement in public (Naidu 1990). Sultanpur also saw bouts of rioting in 1992 (when Hindu nationalists successfully tore down the controversial mosque in Ayodhya), and again in 2003 (when local Hindus tried to restrict Muslim residents from publicly marking the tenth anniversary of the destruction of the mosque). In 2007, a pipe-bomb blast near the Mecca Masjid and serial blasts near the Charminar killed several residents of Sultanpur, including children, and the ensuing blame game between the BJP and Majlis members brought the communal tensions in the area into the media limelight. Hence, the history of communal violence in Hyderabad remained deeply imbricated with the nature of physical and symbolic attacks against children from the minority community.

The local residents (and various concerned NGO workers active in the Sultanpur area) suggested to me that child soldiering was a consequence of escalating communal antagonisms. Unlike Bombay, where I saw the small birth and rapid development of child aggression in the year and a half that I spent in a Hindu-dominated slum (Sen 2007), when in Hyderabad, I was directed by local NGOs to Sultanpur where child hostilities had intensified as a problem. Hence, for me, urban spaces in India were rendered comparable through the trope of male child violence. When I arrived in Sultanpur on a sultry afternoon (uncomfortable in my Hindu identity), I was surprised to be warmly welcomed within the community. I discovered that the local slum dwellers were also eager to gain deeper insight into the troubled rationale of child vigilantism. Despite their encounters with unpredictability and violence, Sultanpur-*wallah*s felt "children used to be children" (*bacche to bacche the*). Within what appeared to be the dominant cultural understanding of an ideal male childhood in the slum, boys spent time with their mates, balanced their lives between work and studies, maintained a certain standard of hygiene and religiosity, and most importantly they respected elders (*baro ki izzat karna*). Further, the boys were admiring and afraid of their fathers, affectionate towards their mothers, playful with their older and younger siblings. "Who were the worst child offenders? The boys who smoked a *bidi* and we could pull their ears if we caught them," said Aiyaz, one of the slum dwellers I met in Sultanpur. This reminiscence of an idyllic, gentle childhood lost to communal violence remained the official parental discourse in the slums.

Dreading the Dead: The Turn toward Child Violence in Sultanpur

While conducting research in Sultanpur, I attempted to design a local, more intimate history of riot-affected boys through the voices of children themselves. My extended research on the violent expression of child vulnerability has been debated, discussed, and published over the years. For the purpose of this chapter I will remain focused on the experiences of children who turned toward collective violence mainly as a response to the trauma of being victimized during the clashes. While chatting with the boys about forming child protection squads, I discovered that their initial decisions to fight violence with violence were related to being faced with their own mortality, *maut ke mooh dekhne ke baad* (after seeing the face of death). A number of boys lost their friends in the riots. While only a small group of boys discussed having seen children being attacked or killed during the riots, most of them talked about being absent during the actual violence (hidden in a box, or running away, or being taken to the homes of relatives living elsewhere, or getting on a train to leave for their native villages) and then returned to see and experience the physical absence of their friends. They spoke of their memories of walking through the piles of burning debris from homes and shops, hearing the sounds of grief-stricken wailing, and peering through clouds of thick smoke in search of other familiar or friendly child faces. "Even though some of the children were not hurt or dead, they were often not coming back to Sultanpur for the fear of death," said Aslam, 10, one of my informants. Thus, some of the choices made by slum children to turn toward organized violence, centered around the direct experiences of riots (mobs targeting male children, children seeing the funerals of their friends and families, "touching fresh graves and imagining what it felt to lie under it," hearing about the death of children in past riots, etc). Most of the children also suffered forms of displacement (children being sent back to the villages for safe-keeping, taken out of school, having their mobility restricted and kept at home, etc). At times, what the children identified as trauma and scarring was related to lack of answers to their questions about loss: such as wondering in vain about the whereabouts of missing best friends (not identified as dead) as after the riots most parents became increasingly suspicious, and secretive about children who were kept away from Sultanpur.

This constant state of fear and flux, especially while negotiating communally tense public places, also made the boys acutely aware of diminishing numbers of male children in the slums. The loss of friends through death, displacement, or disability, and dread of the dead, preoccupied the male children. Significantly, my informants showed less fear of being haunted by angry adult ghosts and far greater anxiety about the malevolent spirits of dead children rising from the dead. The fear of vengeful child ghosts was quite common as the children often shared guilt of survival, and talked quite incessantly about their resentful friends who didn't get a chance to simply enjoy play, toys, and jokes; "the latter could never cross over as their lives were cut short too early" said Aziz, 12. Thus, the children were touched by various experiences of violence even if they did not see rioting masses or were not subjected to physical assaults. To contest these various experiences of trauma and rupture, the children decided to "take matters into their own hands," and a few of them initiated a system of armed night and day patrols in the slums. The boys felt safer in groups, collected crude knives and swords as their weapons, showed plenty of internal bonhomie, and used persuasive tactics of recruitment of other children. The fact that these strategies eventually attracted more child troops into everyday vigilantism underlined the collective experience of child trauma and its collective response in Sultanpur. While the child retribution squads were considered morally reprehensible by adults, amongst the children, the act of saving their own lives and the lives of other children was a form of attachment to the act of living itself, and was tethered to their constant aspiration to survive the fragility of childhoods in violent poverty and grow into the adult world with physical security and emotional integrity. At the same time, the reiteration of trauma, scarring, loss, and fear in child discussions and child conversations, whether it was about the absence of friends or the fear of haunting, was also an attachment to a past when the child world was less vulnerable to violent threats from the incomprehensible politics and religious debates in the adult world.

Some Concluding Comments: Social Vulnerabilities and Childhood Studies in India

The focus on children in the context of everyday life under conditions of vulnerability holds great promise for enriching our understanding of how disputations over culture and forms of belongingness are enacted repeatedly and undramatically: culture becomes a breathing, living form rather than a fixed one (Das and Reynolds 2003). Most states in low-income and middle-income countries simply do not have the resources to craft comprehensive welfare policies for the poor. Thus, the impact of chronic poverty on the survival of children presents extremely pressing problems in these countries (Scheper-Hughes 1992). Cohen (2001), in a cross-national survey of child's labor in

India, Canada, and Norway concludes that there is a continuum—from children who appear not to contribute to the domestic economy to children whose contribution is so substantial that the household survival depends on their earnings. Challenging the dominant conception of children as passive and dependent, proponents of a new sociology of childhood have massed careful data to demonstrate the variations in children's contribution to domestic work and care, to family earnings (Das and Reynolds 2003), and to other forms of market-mediated work activities (Burman 2005). In low-income communities, children's work is equally important for sustaining the household as well as for providing access to new opportunities through schooling (Cohen 2001).

The deterministic theories that postulate a single trajectory of children's moral development have been challenged in the field of child psychology (Kakar 2001). For instance, Erik Erikson (1964) looking at the development occurring over the lifespan and Carol Gilligan's (1982) work on gender identity. There are several debates arguing that truth about suffering should be recorded and made public (Butler 2003). Hence, it becomes important to determine which standards of descriptions should be employed in recounting events of this nature (Das 1995). In the current study, the child attachment interviews are put to multiple uses: ranging from interviews as the testimonies of children of their everyday life struggle to an elaboration of their parental and familial attachment networks.

What is important is how and whether the real and felt negative effects can be overcome over a lifecourse and/or between generations, and if not, what is it that prevents outcomes (Harper, Marcus, and Moore 2003, pg. 4). The Capabilities approach developed by economist Amartya Sen insists that we should focus on the real freedoms that people have for leading a valuable life (Robeyns 2003, pg. 61). The approach refuses normative judgments made exclusively on income, commodities, or material resources. Capabilities are people's potential functionings. Functionings are beings and doings (Sen 1982). And thus, as a means of enhancing the well-being of its people, a society also needs to focus on the freedom to achieve the intrinsic capabilities of individuals. Attachment can be seen as a function of a child's capabilities that are intergenerationally nurtured and passed on. Psychologists think children are endowed to look for secure attachments, though, at the end of the day, it is also the mother, father, family, and our social milieu and culture that instill and reinforce secure attachment. So there exists a dual process of initiation of the capability for secure attachment—one which a human being is programmed to strive toward (like love, trust, empathy, etc.) and on the other hand it is also to be harnessed and developed in the course of one's life through socialization. It is in this domain that these young girls and boys are contesting their struggle for survival, identity, and freedom to achieve what they desire. Achieved functioning is also an index of deprivation capabilities and helps us access which capabilities are marred or not allowed to develop.

In the context of the fieldwork conducted by both authors, disability and its relationship with trauma is a flexible and contested subject. Not only is it intimately linked to physical suffering and mobility, it also reinvigorates the category of social disability. The latter remains consistently related to the fear among riot-affected children about their inadequacy as complete human beings, and their incapacity to return to social and familial "normalcy" in the aftermath of riots. Physical disability not only causes trauma to the children who have been impaired or deformed during the outbreak of violence, it also has a severe impact on children who have witnessed attacks on their family members and friends which have led to disability. Young boys and girls become increasingly aware that their friends are lost to them as active children, they suffer from guilt and anxiety of possession and hauntings as physically undamaged survivors of violence, and through the presence of disabled children within the community they are reminded of their own physical and sexual vulnerability during future outbreak of riots.

REFERENCES

Altman, N. "Psychoanalysis and Social Criticism: Reply to Commentaries." *Psychoanalytic Dialogues, 15*(2005): 405–408.

Breuer, J. and Freud, S. *Studies on Hysteria.* Standard Edition of the Complete Psychological Works of Sigmund Freud, Vol. 2, Hogarth Press: London, 1895.

Burman, E. "Engendering Development: Some Methodological Perspectives on Child Labour [41 paragraphs]." *Forum Qualitative Sozialforschung/Forum: Qualitative Social Research, 7*(2005), Art 1, http://nbn-resolving.de/urn:nbn:de:0114-fqs060120

Burman, E. *Deconstructing Developmental Psychology, Second edition.* Hove, Sussex: Routledge, 2007.

Butler, J. "Violence, Mourning and Politics." *Studies in Gender and Society, 4*(2003): 9–37.

Caruth, C. 2001. "An interview with Jean Laplanche." *Postmodern Culture 11*(2001).

Caruth, C. *Trauma: Explorations in Memory.* Baltimore: Johns Hopkins University Press, 1995.

Catani, C., Schauer, E., Elbert, T., Missmahl, I., Bette, J.-P., & Neuner F. "War Trauma, Child Labor and Family Violence: Life Adversities and PTSD in a Sample of School Children in Kabul." *Journal of Traumatic Stress 22*(2009):163–171.

Catani, C., Jacob N., Schauer, E., Kohila, M., & Neuner, F. "Family Violence, War, and Natural Disasters: Effect of Extreme Stress on Children's Mental Health in Sri Lanka." *BMC Psychiatry 8*(2008): 33

Cohen, R. "Children's Contribution to Household Labour in Three Sociocultural Contexts: A Southern Indian Village, a Norwegian Town and a Canadian City." *Comparative Sociology 42*(2001): 353–367.

Copland, Ian. "'Communalism' in Princely India: The Case of Hyderabad, 1930–1940,' *Modern Asian Studies 22*(1988): 783–814.

Das, V. *Mirrors of Violence: Communities, Riots and Survivors in South Asia.* Delhi: Oxford University Press, 1990.

Das, V. and Reynolds, P. *The Child on the Wing: Children Negotiating the Everyday in the Geography of Violence*. Department of Anthropology, Johns Hopkins University, 2003. Available at: http://anthropology.jhu.edu/child_on_the_wing/index.html.

Das, V. *Critical Events: An Anthropological Perspective on Contemporary India.* Delhi: Oxford University Press, 1995.

Dori, L. "Traumatic Shutdown of Narrative and Symbolization: A Death Instinct Derivative." *Contemporary Psychoanalysis, 41*(2005): 307–326.

Edgcumbe, R. "Anna Freud—Child Analyst." *Int. J. Psycho-Anal.* 64(1983): 427–433.

Engineer, A. A. "Hyderabad Riots: An Analytical Report." In *Communal Riots in Post-Independence India*, edited by Asghar Ali Engineer. Delhi: Sangam Books, 1991.

Erikson, E. *Insight and Responsibility.* New York: Norton, 1964.

Felman, S. "Education and Crisis." In *Trauma: Explorations in Memory*, edited and introduced by Cathy Caruth. Baltimore: The Johns Hopkins University Press, 1995.

Flueckiger, J. B. *In Amma's Healing Room: Gender & Vernacular Islam in South India.* Indiana: Indiana University Press, 2006.

Fonagy, P. *Attachment Theory and Psychoanalysis.* New York: Other Press, 2001.

Frankel, F. H. "The Concept of Flashbacks in Historical Perspective." *International Journal of Clinical and Experimental Hypnosis 42*(1994): 321–36.

Freud, A, and Burlingham, D.T. *War and Children.* New York: Medical War Books, 1943.

Freud, S. "Inhibitions, Symptoms and Anxiety." *Collected Works of Sigmund Freud,* Standard Edition, *20*(1926): 77–175.

Freud, S. "Group Psychology and the Analysis of the Ego." *Collected Works of Sigmund Freud,* Standard edition, 18, pp. 65–143. International Psychoanalytic and Hogarth Press, 1921.

Geyskens, T., Van Haute, P. (2007). *From death instinct to attachment theory. The primacy of child in Freud, Klein and Hermann*. New York: Other Press: US.

Geyskens, T. Van Haute, P. (2004). *Confusion of Tongues: The Primacy of Sexuality in Freud, Ferenczi, and Laplanche*. New York: Other Press: US.

Gilligan, C. *In a Different Voice: Psychological Theory and Women's Development.* Library of Congress Cataloguing, 1982.

Green, A. *The Chains of Eros: The Sexual in Psychoanalysis.* London: Karnac Books, 2000.

Grubrich-Simitis, I. "From Concretism to Metaphor—Thoughts on Some Theoretical and Technical Aspects of the Psychoanalytic Work with Children of Holocaust Survivors." *Psychoanal. St. Child 39*(1984): 301–319.

Gullestad, S.E. "One Depression or Many?," *Scandinavian Psychoanalytic Review, 26*(2003): 123–130.

Harper, C., Marcus, R., and Moore, K. "Enduring Poverty and the Conditions of Childhood: Lifecourse and Intergenerational Poverty Transmissions." *World Development 31*(2003): 535–554.

Herman, Judith Lewis. *Trauma and Recovery: The Aftermath of Violence from Domestic Abuse to Political Terror.* New York: Basic Books, 1997[1992].

Human Rights Watch. "We have no orders to save you: State participation and complicity in communal violence in Gujarat." 2002. Available at: www.hrw.org/reports/2002/india/gujarat.pdf.

Kakar, S. "Rumors and Religious Riots." In *Rumor Mills: The Social Impact of Rumor and Legend*, 53–60, edited by G.A. Fine, V. Campion-Vincent, and C. Heath. New York: Aldine, 2005.

Kakar, S. *The Essential Writings of Sudhir Kakar.* New Delhi: Oxford University Press, 2001.

Khan, M.R. "The Concept of Cumulative Trauma." *Psychoanalytic Study of the Child, 18*(1963): 286–306.

Khan, M.R. *The Privacy of the Self.* New York: International Universities Press, 1974.

Kohlberg, L. *Essays on Moral Development: Vol. 2, The Psychology of Moral Development.* San Francisco: Harper and Row, 1984.

Kristeva, J. *Intimate Revolt: The Power and Limits of Psychoanalysis.* New York: Columbia University Press, 2002.

Krystal H. "Trauma and The Stimulus Barrier." *Psychoanalytic Inquiry* 5(1985):131–161.

Krystal, H. "Trauma and Affects." *Psychoanalytic Study of the Child* 33(1978):81–116

Kurtz, SA. *All the Mothers are One: Hindu India and the Cultural Reshaping of Psychoanalysis.* New York: Columbia University Press, 1992.

Laplanche, J. *Essays on Otherness*. London: Routledge, 1999.

Lester, R. "Back From the Edge of Existence: A Critical Anthropology of Trauma." *Transcultural Psychiatry 50*(2013): 753.

LeVine, R. & Norman, K. "Attachment in Anthropological Perspective." In *Anthropology and Child Development: A Cross-cultural Reader*, edited by R. Levine. Oxford: Blackwell, 2001.

Leys, R. (2000). *Trauma: A Geneology*. Chicago: The University of Chicago Press.

Mehta, K., Vankar, G., and Patel, V. "Validity of the Construct of Posttraumatic Stress Disorder in a Low-income Country. Interview Study of Women in Gujarat, India." *Br J Psychiatry, 187*(2005): 585–586.

Mehta, L. "Reflections on Kutch Earthquake." *Economic and Political Weekly 36*(2001): 2931–2936.

Miller, D. *Women Who Hurt Themselves: A Book of Hope and Understanding.* New York: Basic Books, 1994.

Naidu, R.K. "Academic Self-respect vs. Pseudo Universalism: The Travails of an Indian Psychology Teacher." *Indian Journal of Social Science, 3*(1990): 569–575.

National Human Rights Commission. *Annual Report 2003–2004.* Faridkot House, Copernicus Marg, New Delhi 110 001, India.

Norris, F.H., Galea, S., Friedman, M.J., and Watson, P.J., eds. *Methods for Disaster Mental Health Research.* New York: The Guildford Press, 2006.

Nussbaum, M. *Frontiers of Justice: Disability, Nationality, Species Membership.* Cambridge, Massachusetts: The Belknap Press Harvard University Press, 2006.

Nussbaum, M. *The Clash Within Democracy, Religious Violence, and India's Future.* Cambridge, Massachusetts: Belknap Press of Harvard University Press, 2007.

Obeyesekere, G. *The Work of Culture: Symbolic Transformation In Psychoanalysis and Anthropology.* Chicago: The University of Chicago Press, 1990.

Oliner, M.M. "External Reality: The Elusive Dimension of Psychoanalysis." *Psychoanal Q., 65*(1996):267–300.

Patel, V. & Kleinman, A. "Poverty and Common Mental Disorder in Developing Countries." *Bulletin of the World Health Organisation 81*(2003): 609–615.

Robeyns, I. "Sen's Capability Approach and Gender Inequality." *Feminist Economics, 9*(2003): 61–92.

Schafer, R. "Narration in Psychoanalysis." *Critical Inquiry 7*(1980): 29–53.

Scheper-Hughes, N. *Death Without Weeping: The Violence of Everyday Life in Brazil.* Berkeley: University of California Press, 1992.

Sen, A. *Development as Freedom.* New York: Oxford University Press, 1999.

Sen, A. *Freedom, Rationality, and Social Choice: The Arrow Lectures and Other Essays.* Oxford: Oxford University Press, 2000.

Sen, A. *Imperial Illusions.* Washington D.C. / Online: The New Republic, 2007.

Sen, A. *Poverty and Famines: An Essay on Entitlement and Deprivation.* Oxford New York: Clarendon Press, Oxford University Press, 1982.

Shweder, R. A. and LeVine, R. A., eds. *Culture Theory: Essays on Mind, Self, and Emotion,* 137–157. Cambridge, UK: Cambridge University Press, 1984.

Spence, D. *Narrative Truth and Historical Truth: Meaning and Interpretation in Psychoanalysis.* New York: W. W. Norton & Company, 1984.

Spiegel, A. "The Dictionary of Disorder." *The New Yorker,* January 3, 2005.

Spodek, H. "Crises and Response: Ahmedabad 2000." *Economic and Political Weekly, 36*(2001): 1627–1638.

Staub, E. "Notes on Cultures of Violence, Cultures of Caring and Peace, and the Fulfillment of Basic Human Needs." *Political Psychology 24*(2003a): 1–21.

Staub, E. "Notes on Terrorism: Origins and Prevention." *Peace and Conflict: Journal of Peace Psychology, 8*(2003b): 207–214.

Staub, E. *The Psychology of Good and Evil: Why Children, Adults and Groups Help and Harm Others.* New York: Cambridge University Press, 2003c.

Staub, E. "Reconciliation after Genocide, Mass Killing, or Intractable Conflict: Understanding the Roots of Violence, Psychological Recovery, and Steps toward a General Theory." *Political Psychology, 27*(2006): 867–894.

Staub, E. *The Roots of Evil: The Origins of Genocide and Other Group Violence.* New York: Cambridge University Press, 1989.

Staub, E., & Pearlman, L.A. "Advancing Healing and Reconciliation." In *Psychological Interventions in Times of Crisis,* 213–243, edited by R. Sternberg and L. Barbanel. New York: Springer Publishing Co., Inc., 2006.

Staub, E., and Pearlman, L.A. "Healing, Reconciliation, and Forgiving after Genocide and Other Collective Violence." In *Forgiveness and Reconciliation: Religion, Public Policy, and Conflict Transformation,* 195–217, edited by S.J. Helmick, G. Raymond, and R.L. Petersen. Radnor, PA: Templeton Foundation Press, 2001.

Stein, R. "Vertical Mystical Homoeros: An Altered Form of Desire in Fundamentalism." *Studies in Gender and Sexuality 4*(2003): 38–58.

van der Kolk, B.A., McFarlane, A.C., and van der Hart, O. "A General Approach to Treatment of Posttraumatic Stress Disorder." In *Traumatic Stress: The Effects of Overwhelming Experience on Mind, Body, and Society,* 417–440, edited by B.A. Van der Kolk, A.C. McFarlane, and L. Weisaeth. New York: Guilford Press, 1996a.

van der Kolk, B.A., McFarlane, A.C., and Weisaeth, L., eds. *Traumatic Stress: The Effects of Overwhelming Experience on Mind, Body, and Society,* 559–575. New York: Guilford Press, 1996b.

van Haute, P. and Geyskens, T. *A Confusion of Tongues: The Primacy of Sexuality in Freud, Ferenczi and Laplanche.* New York: Other Press, 2004.

van Haute, P. and Geyskens, T. *From Death Instinct to Attachment Theory: The Primacy of the Child in Freud, Klein, and Hermann.* New York: Other Press, 2007.

Veena Das' work (1990) in (2007) Nussbaum, M. *The Clash Within Democracy, Religious Violence, and India's Future.* Cambridge, Massachusetts: Belknap Press of Harvard University Press, 2007.

Wacquant, L. "Urban Desolation and Symbolic Denigration in the Hyperghetto," *Social Psychology Quarterly, 73*(2010): 215–219.

Widlocher, D. & Fairfield S. *Infantile Sexuality and Attachment.* London: Karnac Books, 2003.

Winnicott, D. W. *Playing and Reality.* London: Tavistock Publications Ltd, 1971.

Part III

CULTURAL IDENTITY AND INDIAN IMAGINATION

Chapter Nine

Two Cultures? Frontiers of Faith in Yoga and Psychoanalysis

Ajeet N. Mathur

INTRODUCTION

Psychoanalysis and yoga have a lot in common.[1] They are both practices that enable you to experience yourself from another point of view and to value outcomes for human well-being brought about through increased self-awareness. They both accept the notion that lived reality involves multiple layers/planes of consciousness; that the body and the mind affect each other; that emotions and affective states involve unconscious processes which impact conscious thoughts, feelings, and actions; that sleep and dreams have important restorative functions; that dreams contribute to our understanding about ourselves; and that a person's identity provides the continuity acknowledged by others. Yet, despite the precession of yoga in the Indian terroir, and the subsequent emergence and import of psychoanalysis from the West, the two traditions stand apart as if they are untouchables for each other.

This is intriguing because they both value human well-being through increased self-awareness, both have been confirmed as worthwhile and are well subscribed—often, by even the same persons! Yoga and psychoanalysis are distinguishable by differences in the beliefs, norms, values, and attitudes surrounding their practices because they have evolved from assumptions and methodologies unique to their evolutionary trajectories. Each, in its various hues, has been impregnated with social rituals, customs, and traditions akin to those in religious systems. Their communities of practice come across as flag-bearers of two distinct cultures. Yet, neither would be possible without some modicum of faith in humanity and in the capacity of self to function as an instrument and interlocutory container for emotional, psychological, and spiritual processes. This paper focuses on the correspondences, differences, convergences, and divergences at the frontiers of faith in Yoga and

Psychoanalysis, both of which hold out extraordinary promise of experiential insights and self-learning for human well-being. Such an endeavor by its very nature invites inaccuracy because it is impossible to take out elements from the two traditions without attention to their distinct trajectories.

As practices, psychoanalysis and yoga are both enactments of faith in the sense that knowledge and experience about them is not enough for their practice. They draw on four common values: empathy, compassion, tolerance, and human dignity. At the frontiers of faith is a common core belief in both that minds are like parachutes—they function best when they are open! Any journey involving experiential learning can be of value only by participating in it. Questions of coping with anxieties and defending against anxieties arise throughout life. Life without some trust and faith would be an unbearable burden marked by extreme anxiety and unease. Faith can thus get easily distorted from its essence as a spiritual attitude—signifying endeavor toward adherence to the trappings of systems including religious systems as defense against thanatos anxiety. Spirituality is about purpose, place, meaning, inspiration, and wisdom and not about religion. In this sense, it may be said that spirituality begins where religion ends and reality is experienced when spirituality is also transcended.

Kakar (2009) notes that any engagement with the spiritual in psychoanalysis has been regarded with considerable suspicion. This is despite considerable evidence from many non-western societies that spiritual notions of intimate connections between self and not-self are at odds with the supposedly rational insistence on an enduring separation between the two instead of working at integrating spirit and psyche. Might spirituality enhance a psychoanalyst's capacity for empathy? Do spiritual mentors actively fostering idealization with their disciples breed unhealthy dependency, or do they inculcate a healthy alliance for facilitating self-awareness? Kakar raises intriguing questions. Ghoshal (2013) raises a concern that the *guru-shishya parampara* may hinder expression of the negative transference, while conceding that there is no evidence that the course of psychoanalysis in the Indian terroir has hindered transference per se. This leaves us wondering how many shades of attachment there might be that Bowlby (1988) missed. If the attachment system is regarded as having a function to provide proximity to a caregiver, its functions in affect regulation involve interfaces with fear systems and exploratory systems too. Ogden (2009) maintains that psychological work with live emotional experience may be unconscious, preconscious (as in a patient's free associations and an analyst's reverie), or conscious. Thus, Winnicottian space, Bionian containment, and Loewaldian eye on the patient/disciple's well-being each have their own value.

The core fabric of the existential puzzle contained in the question "*Who am I?*" (Laing 1960) was answered by Laing as "*I am what I make myself to be*" but the answer was reached through phenomenological methods. Any psychological method (psychoanalysis or psychotherapy) involves taking care of the mind. Hoch (1993), after practizing psychiatry and psychoanalysis in India, ceased distinguishing between taking care of the "soul/spirit" and taking care of the mind, and regarded psychoanalysis and psychotherapy as spiritual endeavors. According to her, what is important is the source of distress such as *bhaya* (separation anxiety/fear of a cosmic kind, rather than the Freudian notion of separation from mother) or *shok* (sorrow) arising out of *karma, moh (attachment)*, delusions, or ignorance. Vaidyanathan and Kripal (2002) have also drawn attention to the connections between psychoanalytic thinking and Indian traditions. Freud's desk was littered with archaeological artefacts from many cultures. Freud admitted that he drew inspiration from these as muses because he believed his work was like archaeology, plumbing the depths of the human mind and the stirrings of the human spirit.

There are elements comparable to the analyst-analysand relationship in a yoga shikshak-abhyasi relationship or Guru-chela relationship (Neki 1973). There are also differences. Yogic practices such as Trataka, Pranayams, Mudras, and Yoganidra have been distinguished from hypnotic states because in these consciousness is maintained in a waking state under control of the self. They are also different from pychoanalytic cathexis. So, while there are overlaps, there are also practices unique to yoga and unique to psychoanalysis. The connections between body and mind are worth mentioning. The effects of yoga have been scientifically studied to demonstrate changes in metabolism, hormonal secretions, transcriptional gene regulations, endocrine activity, intracellular DNA and RNA, and on the sympathetic and parasympathetic nervous systems (Mangaltheertham 2013). One cannot do meditation any more than one can do "transference." Meditation is a state that is reached through *dhyana* after withdrawing the senses into oneself. Transference is an outcome when a therapeutic relationship is established. Both are processes, both are journeys, and neither has an assured cause-effect timeline for measurable outcomes.

The Indian taxonomy of emotions, the *bhava* system, distinguishes feelings of envy and hatred that trigger projections and transferences as a separate category called *sanchar bhava* (transference). This first known attempt by humanity at understanding processes of projections and introjections formed the core of notions around which concepts such as *vyabhichari bhava* (transitional anxiety states of being, numbering 33 according to Bharat Muni and 52 according to Buddhists), *rasa* (essence/chemical juices tasted in the body aroused from chemical changes in the body following an emotion or *jouissance*), and *mudra* (poses and gestures correlated with cultivation of specific *bhavas* or emotion-states) were introduced. This distinction was missing in the Aristotelian taxonomy of emotions built around the dichotomous notion of pain or pleasure supplemented by the reality principle in psychoanalysis. The theories formulated and the practices derived for the performing arts, notably music, drama, and dance, documented in the Natyashastra, were an early acknowledgement of what was much later termed as "emotional labor" (Hochschild 1983).

Language has always been important in psychoanalysis and there continues to be considerable resistance in psychoanalysis to expanding the notions connected with the unconscious to include implications arising from new knowledge of neurological and neuropharmacological insights, bodily resonances, and yoga. Yogic traditions always regarded the body, mind, and spirit to be a holistic unit and conceptualize vortices of energy that connect transmissible impulses and manifest in myriad ways. At the risk of some oversimplification, there is a difference between believing "I am in the body and have a mind and body" versus the notion that "the body is in me." The significance of sound on a physical plane was discovered by the influence of sound vibrations in healing. The Rafai Sufis found that the resonance of sound at a certain pitch of vibrations makes the body invulnerable to cuts and burns (Khan 1988, p. 108). Vocal musical sounds for healing are used in many traditions around the world ranging from ragas to Gregorian chants to hymns.

The distinction between consciousness while awake (*jagrata*) and while dreaming (*swapna*) led to recognition of the unconscious (*sushupti)* state. Consciousness and mindfulness interested those who valued reflecting and learning from experiences. The notion of *vitarka* (assumptions or suppositions) as preparatory to clear vision about phenomenan was termed *vichara.* This has etymologically diffused to other Indo-European and Ugric language traditions, where the tradition of dwelling on the day's experiences at sunset in reflective contemplation (and meditations for cleansing residual impressions of the day) is known as *vecher, vespers, vespera*, and *viisaus.* The capacity to forget, eschew desires, and not hanker after understanding (dwelling in not-knowing) are common to both traditions, yoga and psychoanalysis.

THE EVOLUTIONARY TRAJECTORIES OF YOGA AND PSYCHOANALYSIS

Natural phenomena as understood require assimilation in a culture to engage in practices even when they concern libidinous energies and polyvalent drives. To wonder is to inquire into what sustains life, the significance of breathing, what is inside the mind, what is behind the senses, and whether we all share some common sensations and perceptions as part of inalienable dignity. To quote Kakar and Kakar (2007, p. 75): "The Kamasutra's most valuable insight is that pleasure needs to be cultivated, that (even) in the realm of sex, nature requires culture" (parentheses mine). The way in which people reinforce norms, values, beliefs, and attitudes in a given context is what provides a common outlook or culture for inter-generational recipes. This culture of what is understood of nature requires to be encased in a living tradition, to be experientially verified by every contemporary generation. Without that, any insight would become ossified as an artefact, historically endowed with fixed, discrete, and outdated meaning. Inter-generational continuities of lived traditions involve both continuity and change. Herein lies the genesis of the difference between yoga and psychoanalysis in their evolutionary trajectories. The trajectory of yoga was characterized by discontinuities whereas psychoanalysis, once established, was never lost despite its myriad variants of practice.

From trying to observe, mimic, and understand nature arose the first experimentations of working with postures and breathing. This enabled getting in touch with the nature of choices and lived authority vesting in human nature, as part of larger nature. Thus arose the traditions of working with *prana* (life force) in *Tantra* and *Yoga*. The *Tantrikas* (those who followed *Tantra*) contributed to the thinking about what made the universe tick. Experiential Learning developed their thinking that humans are part of nature and the rest of nature is not something antagonistic to be subdued. They conceptualized universal forces as manifesting in two complementary divisions, *prakriti*, the feminine aspect, and *purusha*, the masculine aspect. Psychoanalysis developed similar notions about *anima* and *animus*. But *tantra* and *yoga* went further to develop a postulate that when *purusha* and *prakriti* come together in an act of cosmological creation at the macrocosmic level, and biological procreation at the procreative microcosmic level, in both instances they are joined by *prana*. Conception occurs when a space is created for *prana* to enter at the time when a sperm (*shuklam*) and an ovum (*shonitam*) come together and unite igniting yoga, the joining. There was no religious claptrap to clothe these beliefs until after the *Manusmriti* cast aspersions on the status of women.

The concepts of "immanent dualities and dyadic encounters" were further developed through y*oga* (Chattopadhyaya and Mathur 2012). Inquiring minds create and discover inquiry frames as an eternal feature of relating to the world (Mathur 2004). In their quest for good health and longer life, the potential *tantrika yogis* (*yoga* practitioners) explored their experience of nature by observing thunder, lightning, rain, snow, animals, trees, wind, soil, water, and fire. They noticed that tall palm trees of the *Palmyra* family withstood gale force winds when other trees fell. They saw seeds sprout and grow to great heights and cope with cyclones. Imitating this in practices and exercises gave rise to the *tadasana* (the palm tree posture) and the *tiryaka tadasana* (the dynamic or sideways moving palm tree posture). They noticed how eagles fly, how cats remain supple, and how snakes raise themselves by straightening their backbones. These experiences were applied in creating the *garuda asana* (eagle posture), *marjari asana* (the cat posture), and the *bhujanga asana* (the snake/cobra posture), respectively. Anthropologists noted this but could not explain the logic of how practices were evolving (Ingold 1994). The notion of unifiable life forces and mobilizable psychic forces in nature meant that every living entity was somehow a microcosm that contained the macrocosm in it. This was also the germinating idea underlying transference in psychoanalysis later on. The word psychoanalysis itself was coined by Freud to draw an analogy for the chemical analysis of elements for the study of psychic phenomena.

Many millennia after the origins of yoga, convergence in praxis, the core traditions, relevant insights, and useful recipes were noted in verses composed with astronomical markers to signify their chronology (Kak 2000). These passed on inter-generationally as the early verses of the *Rig Veda* (*smriti*) through chanting (from which the significance of bodily resonance of sounds was discovered) and listening by the ear (*shruti*) what the *rishis* ("seers," those who had experienced enlightenment) spoke. The fixity of Panini's Sanskrit grammar, perfected three millennia ago, has remained unimproved to our times (something unparalleled in any other language tradition). This enabled *shruti* to be transmitted without distortion. Patanjali's yoga sutras have been inter-generationally communicated and verified with the contemporary experiences of practice in every generation since then. While commentaries on the yoga sutras have continued to proliferate, the yoga sutras themselves have had no additions or modifications or revised editions!

The word *veda* signifies an approach toward comprehending the knowable infinite which cannot be bound. Everything inter-generationally passed on was supposed to be tested for relevance through what was experienced by, thought about, and revealed for each living generation before being further passed on, after suitable modifications. In this sense, *Veda* is the continuous process of inquiry into all kinds of phenomena and the reduction of any aspect of the inquiry to a fixed discrete form is no more than a text describing intermediate outcomes or routines or procedures noted or committed to memory at a discrete point in time. To fix it in form, and consider the form sacrosanct in meaning, would be antithetical for the spirit of inquiry. In an exploration into the Spencerian question, "What knowledge is of most worth?," it was noted that this quest had been part of the *Vedic* traditions, and was elaborated upon for curricular design implications in education systems from this perspective (Mathur 2000). In working with transference, psychoanalysts constantly ask themselves what kind of knowing is juxtaposed with not-knowing; in other words, that which needs to be discovered and unravelled. Grotstein's "beam of intense darkness" also draws attention to the virtuous imperative of dwelling in ambiguity and uncertainty that Bion valued (Grotstein 2007).

Very little is known about the living traditions of experiential learning through which yoga was transmitted from about the fifth century AD to the sixteenth century AD (until the time of the poet-philosopher Kabir), except for the fact that Sufis were also among its adherents (Khan 1988). Both the *Tantrika* and the *Vedic* traditions went underground. These started resurfacing in a limited way in the late nineteenth century and more openly in the twentieth century. Kaivalyadham in Lonavala, Sivananda Ashram in Rishikesh, followed by the Bihar School of Yoga in Munger, were among the earliest institutions to be established in yoga, whereas the Girindrashekhar Clinic and the Indian Psychoanalytic Society were the first institutions in India for psychoanalysis. The Girindrashekhar-Freud correspondence and the Romain Rolland-Freud correspondence bear testimony to the encounter of psychoanalysis with Indian mysticism and its concept of five sheaths of human existence which are realizable. Despite Freud's rejection of the "oceanic state," there is now considerable agreement among psychoanalysts that self-explorations of identity can enable people to identify with the cosmos inside of themselves (Saarinen 2012).

The indigenous ideas and the methodologies were known as *darshan,* referring to that which has been seen or experienced. This is precisely what Rolland claimed and also what yogis have been attesting all along in the narratives of attainable states of self-awareness, when the me and not-me divide vanishes. During the medieval and colonial periods of Indian history, the invaders needed to see their own reflections in a space that had a different culture. Inter-group distrust has a tendency to manifest in defenses to obliterate the other as a means of protecting one's identity (Mathur 2007). The Freud-Einstein correspondence on the inevitability of war arising from the need to demarcate the other, as part of identifying who "we" are from who is "them," brought this out very clearly. As in the case of many other Sanskrit words, *darshan* was incorrectly translated by Max Mueller as "philosophy," thereby stripping it of its basis in experiential learning. The word *darshan* was only occasionally used to connote philosophy as received wisdom, and the equivalent word for philosophy was *shastra*. Unfortunately, *shastra* was translated into English as "scripture," or more specifically "Hindu scripture."

This mirrored the European tradition (as in the *Oxford English Dictionary*) to portray "scripture" as "Bible"! Neither the brahmins nor the animists had any scripture. There was no ideology tracing its behavioral or spiritual norms to prescriptions or proscriptions from an unapproachable supreme being.

During the later *Vedic* period, experiential learning traditions, through which yoga was transmitted, are recorded in dialogues of the *Upanishads.* Many of these dialogues were not conversations of interaction that occurred in a single conversation on a particular day. Rather, they represented engagement with inquiry by seekers over long periods of time. In *gurukulas* (educational communities of habitat organized around renowned scholars known as *acharyas* and *gurus*), students/disciples in the age group of eight to eighteen were helped over long periods of time to learn by experiencing the living methodology. They learnt various skills and concepts through actual experience. It has been estimated that there were over 130 *Upanishads*. Only thirty-five *Upanishads* are available now. The practice of experiential learning methodologies is mentioned in the *Taittiria Upanishad* (Gambhirananda 1989). The idea that a hermeneutic endeavor can be structured as a normative primary task can be traced to these experiential learning traditions where the *gurukula* was an institution emphasizing experiential learning rather than rote learning or instruction. This stance also informed apprenticeship for advancing learning in arts and crafts and performing arts and other vocational streams. From this also arose notions of what belonged to the commons, what could be privately appropriated as property or endowment, and the nature of multiple belonging, affiliations, rights, and obligations.

An important aspect of experiential learning was in understanding nature, including human nature and universal forces. In the twentieth century, quantum mechanics has revealed that "all things in the universe that we see" are different configurations of elementary particles. Yet, we are not capable of actually seeing these dynamic configurations forming and dissolving because of perceptual limitations (Bohm and Basil 1933). The idea of transience is conveyed by the word *maya* for reality, not for illusion. Maya is the abbreviated form of the expression "*Mati Iti ma, Yati iti ya*" to describe the measurable reality that is passing away or disappearing even as it is measured, because it is transitory.[2] The Bhagwat Geeta explains Maya in Chapter 18 by using metaphors.

The concept of *anu-bhava* (the Sanskrit word for a unit of experience) contains the idea that miniscule impressions constitute emotional, aesthetic, and psychological crystallizations of experiences. The process of experiencing (*anu-bhava)* produces transitory emotional impressions (*vyabhichari bhavas*) recognized in the Indian system of *bhava* (sentiment), which coagulate into durable states of primary emotions (the nine *rasas* of the *Rasa Siddhanta*). These undergo transformations in group dynamics to manifest psychologically as Bionian basic assumption groups (Mathur 2009). It is noteworthy that the Tavistock Institute that pioneered the study of group relations based on Bionian basic assumptions using a psychoanalytic approach has lately added a yoga event (from the Indian terroir of group relations work) in its group relations conferences in recognition of the correspondence between yoga and psychoanalytic frames.

The search for experiencing the cosmic force through yoga revolved around the idea that consciousness occurs in five planes or sheaths of human existence. One of the paths was through some of the branches of *yoga* known as *kriya yoga, kundalini yoga,* etc. Those who undertake to practice these branches of *yoga* are told that they would never get anywhere near experiencing their identity with the cosmic force unless they gave up, entirely, the desire to experience it and memory of attachments that controlled their behavior which resided in bodily responses. Instead, they were encouraged to experience and reflect on the eight dimensions of the yogic experience to reach complete self-awareness without preconceptions and without the hankering to merely reach higher awareness levels for sensory gratifications or sharper sensory perceptions (*siddhis*). This is reminiscent of Bion's idea of "without desire and without memory." The Bhagwat Geeta can also be regarded as an account of how Arjuna's neurosis was treated when he, as the analysand, underwent analysis with Krishna, and the dialogue that constitutes the Bhagwat Geeta is a record of Arjuna's transference to Krishna and its resolution (Chattopadhyay 1997).

METACULTURE OF INDIAN EXPERIENTIAL LEARNING TRADITIONS

The hallmark of Indian experiential learning traditions has been the emphasis on revelation through experience, and not on a politics of salvation. The Buddha never claimed that he could take anyone to self-awareness, only that, like himself, others too could practice and attain self-realization. The revelation was about experiencing identity with the all-pervading cosmic force. This meant, at a metacultural level, some idea, however vague, of non-difference between not only human beings, but also between human beings and all other kinds of things in the universe. The emphasis on empathy and non-violence arose from this notion of non-difference. There is a general belief, in India and abroad, that spirituality is to be found within various cultures of India. This sense of spirituality manifests through cultural traditions like hospitality to strangers, welcoming guests as divine (*atithi devo bhava*), sense of neighborliness outside the metropolises, with villages reflecting a feeling of being self-contained (as containers of ethos), and the spirit of the joint or extended family system extending to communities, even the entire world community in the dictum "*vasudhaiva kutumbakam.*"

These values and notions got distorted in the later eras and transformed into politics of salvation for relief from *thanatos* instincts. Many charlatans have set themselves up as gurus in various locations in India (and abroad) and changed the mode of spiritual quest, from revelation through experience to salvation through following the guru's leadership for their hordes of foreign followers and a sprinkling of gullible Indians (Mehta 1993). The idea of a Supreme Being to be worshipped as *Bhagwan* by followers of the so-called Hindu religion was invented and taught in line with the Judeo-Christian notion of a Supreme Being. In Sanskrit texts, *Bhagwan* is anyone who has certain characteristics. These are integrity, courage, beauty, wealth, etc., together with the capacity to remain non-attached to all of these. Krishna has been referred to as *Bhagwan* in the Bhagwat Geeta, not because he represented a plenitude of divinity, "but because he was a great yoga master who possessed characteristics necessary to be known as Bhagwan" (Chattopadhyay 1997).

The Bhagwat Geeta has been translated into English as the Song of God or Divine Song (Huxley 1946). However, it is really a song of non-attachment which explains *maya,* and that *prana* is indestructible which can neither be pierced nor burnt, and that it is only the transitory body that perishes. As noted by Chattopadhyay and Mathur (2012), when Christian missionaries arrived in India, Hinduism began to be regarded not as a way of life but as as a religion to convert "Hindus" to Christianity. In the nineteenth century, the British introduced a new education system and good jobs in British India became available only to those Indians who were educated in the new system taught through the English language. The loss of the experience-based education, and of the opportunity to realize through it one's identity with the all-pervading cosmic force left a deep void. While, in the past, the struggle had been to reach out to as many people as possible to develop self-awareness and skills to live harmoniously with respect for nature, the worship of Mammon ushered in an era of envy, competition, religious divides, and subservience to feudal and governmental authority.

WHAT REMAINS IN INDIA OF THE EXPERIENTIAL LEARNING TRADITIONS?

The earliest subcontinental philosophies of praxis and methodologies that survived by going underground for many millennia re-emerged only in the early 1960s (i.e., about a decade and a half after the last of the colonizers left). These are *Vipasana, Tantra, and Yoga.* In Indian metaculture, the notion of reciprocity in inter-generational relations has been strongly present. By itself, this has kept the living traditions alive to the extent that *sadhakas* (seekers) and advanced practitioners of experiential learning (self-realized persons) have reason to value both *connaissance* and *savoir*, and the capacity to establish temporary or permanent learning institutions that cherish experiential learning.

The human life-span in Indian culture is regarded as comprising four stages (Zimmer 1951, p.106): *brahmacharya,* the stage when *jijnyasa* (curiosity) is to be cultivated through education and socialization (nought to twenty-five); the *grahasta* stage of adult working and family life (twenty-five to fifty) in which *vivek* (discrimination, conscience) is to be exercised; *vairagya stage (*fifty to seventy-five*)* non-attachment to fruits of effort through one's working life; followed by *vanaprastha* stage of disengaging from worldly responsibilities, cultivating dispassion, and an end to all formal roles, and practicing *sanyam* (self-control from which the word *sanyas* arises) focusing on spiritual growth. This does not mean that normatively predominant activities of different stages are binding. They are indicative of the understanding of what is considered more important in the different stages of human life. Implicit in this framework is the notion that family and society can support such trajectories.

Succession in experiential learning traditions (both yoga and psychoanalysis) involves the transfer of tacit skills through development of capabilities. The *guru-chela* (teacher and disciple) tradition in India can be viewed as an enabling proactive paradigm and also as a reactive constraining one when differences in roles are seen through the prism of hierarchy. The word *guru* consists of two syllables: *gu* meaning darkness, ignorance; and *ru*, annihilation of darkness by insight or illumination. This is reminiscent of Grotstein (2007) and his attention to negative capability waiting for something to emerge. The word *guru*, although loosely used worldwide to connote "teachers with great knowledge or glamour power," is a *sui generis* concept, with emphasis on learning through practice of reflection, introspection, meditation, questioning, dialogue, and enactment, rather than through instruction. The *guru* is not a coach or trainer. For this reason, unless a *guru* has attained self-awareness and resolved inner conflicts within himself to extinguish or limit desires, he can only be an *adhyapak* (teacher), *pundit* (scholar), or *acharya* (professor). Recovery and reparation involve a journey toward the depressive position without being consumed by the sadness. The psychogenesis of the intersubjective relationships is an essential feature of civilizational evolution in both yoga and psychoanalysis.

Neki (1973) examined *guru-chela* relationships and developed a typology by connecting the sentient experience to role models in Indian mythology.

He identified seven forms of *guru-chela* relationships. Neki concluded that the *guru-chela* relationship enables succession only when unequals end up as co-equals. None of the relationships he examined could achieve co-equality except one—that between enemies—such as Rama and Ravana and that too only after Ravana had been mortally wounded. This is why successions in India are seldom accomplished smoothly.

Scholars have noted that Indian experiential learning traditions of knowing were almost extinguished in the nineteenth century by getting the natives to identify with the invader by embracing a different system of education (Mishra 1999). It is never easy for a suppressed tradition to resurface and thrive without an abiding commitment to institutional or organizational forms from motivations supported by power bases. When yoga re-surfaced in India in the twentieth century as a byproduct of nationalism, and decades after political independence, by the time it was recognized as a holistic system for health and well-being in 2005 under AYUSH, the sentiments surrounding its values had been layered over in diverse traditions. These included naturopathy, "Hindutva" revivalists, shaivite monk-sanyasins, vaishnavite sadhus, spiritual ashrams, religious sects such as natha sampradaya, yoga schools of Ashtanga yoga, Hatha yoga, Kriya yoga, Satyananda yoga, Bikram yoga, Iyengar yoga, Art of Living, Sahaj Marg, Ayurveda, Unani, Siddha, homeopathy, reflexology, acupressure and the esoteric practices of tantriks, eclectic pranahuti traditions of whirling dervishes and N*akshbandi* sufis, mindfulness and vipassana traditions among Buddhists, shatkarmas of Jains, and meditations and spiritual exercises of Franciscan Catholics and Jesuits. This potpourri of conduits and carriers renders it very difficult to separate the core of yoga from the paraphernalia and trappings surrounding it in its various lineages. Some of the traditions themselves have ossified into arrogant fortresses that have closed all doors and windows to thinking from anywhere outside of themselves. But it is important to attempt that to be able to grasp at their essential nature and the scope of offering that partially overlaps in notable ways the benefits available through psychoanalysis.

In contrast, psychoanalysis spread far and wide from its origins in Europe, taking root in many countries. Exchanging neurotic suffering for ordinary unhappiness (as Freud put it) acquired appeal. Elder (1994) notes that the real significance of Freudian psychoanalysis was the articulation of an entirely new form of psychological discourse of introspective consciousness. Its early professionalization in 1910 as an international system in a mutually recognized fraternity, organized by a peer group, carrying on conversations in a journal, enabled a certain homogeneity, and convergence of norms and standards (Loewenberg and Thompson 2010). This did not inhibit the application of psychoanalytic insights to other arenas such as psychoanalytic psychotherapy, the study of organizations, group relations, mass observation, and for understanding whole societies. And it kept psychoanalysis shorn of religious discourses and conflicts because there was no requirement in its methods to advance any particular religious persuasion, political agenda, ethnic preference, or linguistic exclusions. But it mainly catered to a particular affluent elite class of society, and faith in the efficacy of the method spread through word of mouth. Besides the competitive comparisons of the variants (Freudian, Jungian, Laingian, Kleinian, etc.) subscribed to by its practitioners, in certain circles, it has become almost a fashion statement to have an analyst to go to. It also provides a non-medical alternative devoid of the side-effects of medication for some, whereas for others it offers a "cure" concurrent with, but beyond, mere psychiatric treatment with drugs.

The Indian Psychoanalytic Society was founded in 1921, almost a decade after Girindrashekhar Bose began using psychoanalytic concepts and methods in his clinical practice in 1910. Nandy (1995) describes how Girindrashekhar Bose blended his initial fascination for yoga with emerging ideas in psychoanalysis.

PSYCHOANALYSIS AT THE MARGINS OF SOCIETY

Curiously, just as yoga was all but marginalized in India until its resurgence in the twentieth century, psychoanalysis now faces a similar specter of marginalization despite growth in the number of psychoanalysts worldwide. Eisold (2010) describes the collapse of the profession of psychoanalysis in the United States, pointing out that the interest in studying forces beyond our awareness has not diminished and that many new professions are embracing the unconscious. Meanwhile, psychoanalysis has been reduced to a service that has to compete like a commodity in the marketplace alongside other therapeutic alternatives. Eisold argues that collapse of trust in traditional authority, time pressures and budgets are just three of many reasons underlying the collapse of psychoanalysis in the United States. There are others. Researchers have been able to work with many layers of the unconscious, beginning with the autonomic nervous system and going on to the cognitive unconscious (which works by perceptual categorization including transference schemata). In contrast, psychoanalysts have become dogmatic, arrogant, and complacent about short therapies and psychopharmacological approaches. Lack of attention to unconscious self-esteem, emotional responses involving the cerebral cortex and the amygdala, role of metaphor grounded in embodied experience are also mentioned by Eisold. Eisold argues that the individual unconscious is best understood in the context of the social unconscious and organizational and societal forces that have caused fractures in communal structures.

There is also an interplay of four forces that I consider worth mentioning. Firstly, there is a large number of people who are more aware of the importance of personal psychological and emotional well-being than ever before. There is no corresponding supply of trained psychoanalysts available, and not even the entire pool of psychoanalysts taken together could attend to even a miniscule fraction of the people even if they worked day and night, if everyone were to want psychoanalysis as the preferred means for enhanced self-awareness and well-being. For this reason alone, psychoanalysis cannot be mainstreamed and remains marginal in its scope and impact.

Secondly, the availability of alternatives to psychoanalysis, such as other therapies or yoga, are less costly and less demanding from the perspective of time duration. Yoga can be learnt in one week (basic) to three weeks (advanced) from an instructor and a person can continue its practice for life. In India, it is available free in many institutions and at an affordable cost by other providers all over the country. Scientific studies have been conducted worldwide to demonstrate what benefits different practices of asanas, pranayams, mudras, and bandhs can bring. Its popularity and appeal has spread across the world. The World Yoga Convention 2013 witnessed the participation of more than 24,000 participants from 57 countries—a far greater number than any conference on psychoanalysis. France has introduced yoga into the school curriculum for schools supported by the Ministry of Education. The UN General Assembly has adopted June 21 as World Yoga Day since 2014.

Psychoanalysis is mainly sought out by those persons who wish to enter the therapeutic professions as analysts, therapists, counselors, etc., and need to understand themselves as analysands with an analyst, acquire basic skills in working with transference, and who would need the stamp of recognition to professionally establish their clinical therapeutic practices. But only if they have time and money to go to an analyst four times a week for about four years! And then do another training analysis under supervision.

Thirdly, healthcare systems and healthcare insurance practices have incentivized short therapies, and psychoanalysis is being increasingly regarded as a luxury, privately affordable only by a few affluent people among elite classes. The requirement that an ICD-10 or DSM-V diagnosis must precede treatment subsidy, and that subventions would be made available only for approvable standardized short therapeutic interventions justifiable on essential criteria, has loaded the dice against psychoanalysis. In contrast, therapies such as Intensive Short Term Dynamic Psychotherapy (ISTDP) have gained prominence and are spreading at a rapid pace.

Fourthly, Chakraborty (2010) has argued that "there is not much to repress in permissive societies" and that the "superego lost its sting" quite some time ago. This calls into question the very viability of the method in certain contexts. This can be contested by arguing that the nature of taboos may undergo change but to expect repression to be eradicated may be overstating the case. Yet, Eisold (2010) seems to agree with Chakrobarty by pointing to cataclysmic changes that have caused ruptures in the social and communal fabric and sparked irreversible traverse. That the boundaries of the internal and external worlds of individuals may be shifting is another explanation (Hämäläinen 2009).

To quote Rumi:

I've heard it said, there's a window
That opens from one mind to another
But if there's no wall, there's no need
For fitting the window or the latch.

BLENDING YOGA AND PSYCHOANALYTIC INSIGHTS IN EDUCATION SYSTEMS

Yoga, in its limited appeal as an alternative to physical training, has been traditionally regarded as a means to good health and personal well-being. In this form, it has remained an extra-curricular activity on the periphery of education in schools in post-independent India. As the full scope of yoga gets known to more people, it faces the same challenges that psychoanalysis faced in trying to find roots in academia, that is, universities designed for knowledge creation. The significance of mindful dialogue processes as internal conversations and as potential external interactions extending open system boundaries by postulating a new boundary of "understanding" arose from a doctoral dissertation spanning empirical work in India and Finland (Mattila 2008). Mattila has introduced mindfulness dialogues blending yogic methods and traditions with psychoanalytic insights in Turku, Finland, and for students at Nirma University, Ahmedabad, IIM Ahmedabad, and IIM Bangalore to prospect wisdom and knowing in organizations.

Both yoga and psychoanalysis are at the cusp of change and continuity. Let me mention five ways yoga has been brought into the educational curriculum at IIM Ahmedabad alongside psychoanalytic insights for the study of organizations:

- The introduction of yoga through asanas, pranayams, and mudras in the Working Conference on "Authority, Organisation, Strategies and Politics

of Relatedness" preparatory to dream work in a "harmony sensing matrix" alongside experiential learning through transference work in small and large groups.
- The exercise of Yoga Nidra in Corporate Retreats for Strategy and Organisation Development alongside dream work for visioning, discovering and interpreting strategies using psychoanalytic frames for the study of organization behavior.
- The adoption of yoga and pranayams for de-stressing after exercises such as mass observation and action research praxis using listening posts in the analytic tradition.
- The development of a new Course "Mysteries in Management" in the flagship MBA (PGP) program emphasizing consciousness and mindfulness to nurture curiosity for cultivating wonder.
- Yoga capsules (including pranayams and yoga nidra) as part of work with dyads, couples, and families, at the Centre for Gender Equity, Diversity, Inclusivity.

The shift in focus from looking at outward phenomena, without a location inside of oneself, toward mindful self-awareness of the whole body with attention to one's breath creates fields of harmony inside and outside. The range of participants involved with experiential learning through the mainstreaming of yoga in educational and developmental initiatives is already vast. Besides corporations across every sector of activity, there have been requests for programs from such diverse institutions as Kendriya Vidyalaya Sanghathan, Antarnad Foundation, and Border Security Force Academy. Yet, only the surface has been scratched so far.

This is not something alien to psychoanalytic traditions. The International Society for the Psychoanalytic Study of Organisations provides space for blending psychoanalytic insights with yoga in its explorations for understanding toxicity in organizations. It is noteworthy that Bion's concept of reverie also finds parallels in Buddhist meditation. Reverie is comparable to the state of mind of equanimity. Bion acknowledged that thought can be subordinate to the senses and the pleasure principle. While Freud considered emotions as close to their instinctual source, Bion recognized emotions as an integral part of mental life and its development. The alpha function is a mental digestive system for learning from experience. The capacity to think is then a pain-modifying apparatus and the absent goodness is initially experienced as a present evil. Mindfulness (a synonym for attention) in both yoga and psychoanalysis involves awakening and letting go "by observing of this penetrating through that" without interfering with the occurrence. (Pelled 2007).

CONCLUSION

These are early days in the mainstreaming of yoga, around questions of what knowledge is of most worth (Mathur 2000, 2003) and for bringing closer the underlying essence in the traditions of yoga and psychoanalysis. Attention to spirituality can help the analyst exercise more empathy and compassion whereas attention to the unconscious through psychoanalytic insights can expand the horizons of yoga to understand and use the psychic force of "*prana*" in many new ways. There are plenty of parallels between psychoanalysis and yoga for correspondences in emotional, psychological, and aesthetic traditions (Mathur 2009, Mathur 2013). But there are also significant differences. The high dependency in Indian culture, the lifelong obligations to family members, the preponderence of passive aggression over open defiance, attribution of stigma to identities, and the tolerance for high proliferation of boundary leakages, call for an enormous leap of faith for psychoanalysis to succeed in the Indian context. The frontiers of faith in yoga make no such demand. Yet, the frontiers of faith in yoga are not without their own set of demands. The practice of *dharma*, as what Kakar and Kakar regard as a "pivotal ethical concept" modulated by a "thou canst but try" ethos, coexists alongside the concept of *karma* that draws upon the notion of innate dispositions, with a relational orientation and with non-attachment regarded as a virtue.

It has been claimed by Brar (1970), and commented upon by Chakraborty (1970), that yoga transcends the limitations of psychoanalysis by recognizing a spiritual plane of existence. However, this is so only to the extent that spirituality really begins where the pull of religion ends and it is only by transcending spirituality that reality may be grasped. The syntax and grammar of the unconscious that has been discovered provided the foundations of psychoanalysis (Elder 1994). This is similar to the quest for identifying with the subtle body (*sookshma shareer*) rather than the gross body (*sthool shareer*). This further needs distinguishing between aiming to self-actualize versus theological or cosmological liberation. Yoga does not claim that a self-realized person has become liberated in the sense that liberation theologians would claim. A good night's sleep is regarded as an important restorative in both yoga and psychoanalysis because it puts us in touch with the unconscious (Vivekananda 2013). Dreams have their place in both yoga and psychoanalysis. The stage of *samadhi* postulated in yoga and demonstrated by yogis is further evidence that although frontiers of faith in yoga may have been pushed more than in psychoanalysis, the essential nature of both seeks to experience unplumbed depths of human consciousness. The foundations of the earliest traditions of thinking that have been inter-generationally passed on and revalidated in every generation cannot be considered primitive (Hallpike 1980). Ancient is not the same as primitive or obsolete. If a hundred years makes something ancient, western psychoanalysis is also now ancient, having been around for more than a century (Loewenberg and Thompson 2010). In this sense, the frontiers of yoga and psychoanalysis converge and raise hopes for possibilities of bringing the two cultures closer together as part of the same kind of human endeavor involving physical, intellectual, emotional, mental, and spiritual processes.

NOTES

1. This is a revised version of the paper presented at the First Annual Psychoanalytic conference: *"Psychoanalysis, Culture and Religion"* at Fortis Memorial Research Institute, Gurgaon, December 19–20, 2013. The author thanks Sudhir Kakar, Sari Mattila, Niloufer Kaul, Manasi Kumar, and an anonymous reviewer for suggestions and comments on a previous version of the paper. © 2015

2. For this insight, I am grateful to T.V. Raghu Anantnarayanan, the Master-Choreographer of the Sumedhas Learning Theatre.

REFERENCES

Bohm, David and Basil Hiley. *The Undivided Universe: An Ontological Interpretation of Quantum Theory*, published in the Taylor & Francis e-library 2009. first edition, London: Routledge, 1933.

Bowlby, J. *A Secure Base: Parent-Child Attachment and Healthy Human Development.* New York: Basic Books, 1988.

Brar, H.S. "Yoga and Psychoanalysis." *British Journal of Psychiatry*, 116 (1970): 201–206.

Burnet, J. *Of the Origin and Progress of Language* (*Volume I*), 234–239. Edinburgh: J. Bell. 1773.

Chakraborty, A. "Yoga and Psychoanalysis." *British Journal of Psychiatry* 117 (1970): 478.

Chakraborty, A. *My Life as a Psychiatrist*. (Kolkata: Stree, 2010.

Chattopadhyay, G.P. *Bhagavat Geeta: A Treatise on Managing Critical Decisions*. Kolkata: Eureka Publishers, 1997.

Chattopadhyay, Gouranga P. and Ajeet N. Mathur. "Experiential Learning: The Indian Experience from the Proto-historic Period to the Present." Chapter two, in *Group Relations Conferences: Tradition, Creativity and Succession in the Global Group Relations Network Volume, III,* 23–40, edited by Eliat Aram, Robert Baxter, and Avi Nutkevitch., London: Karnac, 2012.

Eisold, K. *What You Don't Know You Know: Our Hidden Motives in Life, Business and Everything Else.* New York: Other Press, 2010.

Elder, C.E. *The Grammar of the Unconscious: The Conceptual Foundations of Psychoanalysis.* Pennsylvania: State University Press, 1994.

Gambhirananda, Swami. ed. *Eight Upanisads, with the Commentary of Sankaracharya.* Kolkata: Advaita Ashrama, 1989.

Ghoshal, Arup. "Psychoanalysis today in India from the perspective of the socio-cultural matrix." Panel paper of the International Psychoanalytic Association Conference, 2013.

Grotstein, J.S. *A Beam of Intense Darkness.* London: Karnac, 2007.

Hallpike, C.R. *The Foundations of Primitive Thought.* Oxford: Clarendon Press, 1980.

Hämäläinen, O. "The Relationship of the Inner and the Outer in Psychoanalysis." *The International Journal of Psychoanalysis* 90(2009): 1277–1297.

Hoch, Erna. *Sources and Resources: A Western Psychiatrist's Search for Meaning in the Ancient Indian Sculptures.* Delhi: Book Faith, 1993.

Hochschild, A.R. *The Managed Heart.* Berkeley: University of California, 1983.

Huxley, A. "Introduction." In *Bhagavad Gita, Song of God,* edited by Swami Prabhavananda and C. Isherwood. California: Vedanta Press, 1946.

Ingold, T. "Humanity and Animality." In *Companion Encyclopaedia of Anthropology,* 15–16. New York: Routledge, 1994.

Kak, S. *The Astronomical Code of the Rig Veda.* New Delhi: Munshiram Manoharlal, 2000.

Kakar, S. and Kakar, K. *The Indians: Portrait of a People.* New Delhi: Penguin, 2007.

Kakar, S. *Mad and Divine: Spirit and Psyche in the Modern World.* Chicago: University of Chicago Press, 2009.

Khan, Hazrat I. *The Sufi Message Volume II.* Delhi: Motilal Banarsidas, 1988.

Laing, P. *The Divided Self.* London: Tavistock, 1960.

Loewenberg, P, and Thompson, N.L. *100 Years of the IPA.* London: Karnac, 2010.

Mangalthreertham, Swami. *Can Gene Activity be Altered Consciously*? Munger: World Yoga Convention Proceedings, 2013.

Mathur, A.N. *What Knowledge is of Most Worth?* Tampere: Tampere University, 2000. Abridged version published in *Internationalization of Curriculum Studies,* 137–177, edited by W. Pinar, D. Trueit, W. Doll & H. Wang. New York: Peter Lang, 2003.

Mathur, A.N. "Who Owns Traditional Knowledge?" *Economic and Political Weekly XXXVIII* (2003): 4471–4481.

Mathur, A.N. "Inquiring Minds and Inquiry Frames." In *Indigeneity and Universality,* 171–186, edited by P. N. Mukherjee and C. Sengupta. Thousand Oaks, CA: Sage, 2004.

Mathur, A. N. "Dare to Think the Unthought Known?" In *Dare to Think the Unthought Known? A Festschrift in Honour of Gouranga Chattopadhyay,* 1–32, edited by A. N. Mathur, (Tampere:Aivoairut Oy., 2006.

Mathur, A.N. 'Why does inter-group distrust turn violent?' In*Creative Thinking: Designing Future Possibilities,* 240–248, edited by S. Dingli, Malta: University of Malta Press, 2007.

Mathur, A.N. (2009). "The Good, Bad and Ugly: Distinguishing Management Pathologies from Organisational Evil." In *Conference Proceedings,* 13th APROS Conference, Monterrey, Mexico, 2009.

Mathur, A.N. "Emotional Submergence of Protest—A Triumph of Strategy or Catastrophic Risk Magnification?" 29th EGOS Colloquium July 4–6, 2013, Montreal, Canada, 2013.

Mattila, S. *Multi-Content Revelation through Dialogue Processes: A Study in Understanding the Hermeneutic Primary Task of Small Groups in the Context of Finland and India* (Publication 738). Tampere: Tampere University of Technology, 2008.

Mehta, Gita. *Karma Cola.* New Delhi: Penguin Books, 1993.

Mishra, R. *Before the Beginning and After the End.* New Delhi: Rupa, 1999.

Nandy, A. *The Savage Freud.* Delhi: Oxford University Press, 1995.

Neki, J.S. "Yoga and Psychoanalysis." *Comprehensive Psychiatry*, 8(1967): 160–167.

Neki, J.S. "Guru-Chela Relationship: The Possibility of a Therapeutic Paradigm." *American Journal of Orthopsychiatry, 43*(1973): 755–766.

Ogden, T.H. *Rediscovering Psychoanalysis: Thinking and Dreaming, Learning and Forgetting.* London: Routledge, 2009.

Pelled, E. "Learning from Experience: Bion's Concept of Reverie and Buddhist Meditation." *The International Journal of Psychoanalysis*, 88(2007): 1507–26.

Saarinen, J.A. "The Oceanic State: A Conceptual Elucidation in Terms of Modal Contact." *The International Journal of Psychoanalysis*, 93(2012): 939–961.

Vaidyanathan, T.G. and Kripal, Jeffrey. *Vishnu on Freud's desk: A Reader in Psychoanalysis and Hinduism.* Cachan: Lavoisier, 2002.

Vivekananda, R. *How to Get A Good Night's Sleep.* Munger: World Yoga Convention, 2013.

Zimmer, H. "Citing the 'Manusmriti.'' In *Philosophies of India,* p.106, edited by J. Campbell. Princeton, NJ: Bollinger Series, 1951.

Chapter Ten

Psychoanalysis, Culture, and the Cultural Unconscious

Sudhir Kakar

Most of our knowledge on how human beings feel, think, act, is derived from a small subset of the human population which the psychologists Joseph Henrich and his colleagues (2010, p.61) call what the psychologist Jonathan Haidt (2012, p.) calls WEIRD, the acronym standing for western, educated, industrialized, rich, and democratic. Psychologists, sociologists, psychotherapists, philosophers are as WEIRD as the subjects of their studies, ministrations, or speculations. It is this small group of statistical outliers that provides us with both the producers and subjects of our contemporary psychoanalytic knowledge we have then blithely proceeded to generalize to the rest of humankind.[1]

The psychologist Jonathan Haidt (2012) demonstrates the chasm between the WEIRD and others in a study of morality where he interviewed twelve groups of different social classes in different countries. He tells each interviewee different stories and then asks if there is something wrong in how someone acts in the story and, if so, why is it wrong. One of the stories goes:

> A man goes to the supermarket once a week and buys a chicken. But before cooking the chicken, he has sexual intercourse with it. Then he cooks it and eats it.

One of his groups was from students of the University of Pennsylvania, a liberal, Ivy League college in the United States and certainly the most WEIRD among the selected groups. This was the only group out of the twelve where a majority (73 percent) tolerated the chicken story, finding it OK. "It's his chicken, it's dead, nobody is getting hurt and it's being done in private.' (p.96)

Or to take Anurag Mishra's (2012) analogy of psychoanalysis and wine, the terroir of a wine is a specific place with its particular soil and climate where the wine is made and thus different terroirs, although made with the same sort of grape, have different wines. The terroir of human beings—historical, geographic, cultural, social, political, religious—too, varies and will produce different psychoanalytic wines. The terroir of psychoanalysis, for more than a century, has been and continues to be Western. It contains many Western cultural ideas and ideals that permeate psychotherapeutic theories and practice. Shared by analyst and patient alike, pervading the analytic space in which the two are functioning, fundamental ideas about human relationships, family, marriage, male and female, and so on, which are essentially cultural in origin, often remain unexamined, and are regarded as universally valid. As has been said, if a fish were a scientist, the last discovery it would make would be of water. Let me illustrate this by taking examples from India.

> My own interest in the role of culture in psychoanalytic psychotherapy and becoming an Indian *vigneron* of psychoanalytic wine did not begin as an abstract intellectual exercise but as a matter of vital personal import. Without my quite realizing it at the time, it began with my beginnings as an analyst, more than forty years ago, when I entered a five-day-a-week training analysis with a German analyst at the Sigmund-Freud Institut in Frankfurt. At first, I registered the role of culture in my analysis as a series of niggling feelings of discomfort whose source remained incomprehensible for many months. Indeed, many years were to pass before I began to comprehend the cultural landscape of the mind in more than a rudimentary fashion and make some sense of my experiences, both as an analysand and as an analyst, in cross-cultural therapeutic dyads (Kakar 1982, 1987, 1989, 1994, 1997).

I earned very little at the time and, in spite of my frequent complaints about my poverty from the couch, I was disappointed when my analyst was prompt in presenting his bill at the end of the month and did not offer to reduce his fees. Without ever asking him directly, I let fall enough hints that he could be helpful in getting me a better-paying job—for instance, as his assistant in the Institute where he held an important administrative position.

I did not have any problems in coming to my sessions on time but was resentful that my analyst was equally punctual in ending a session after exactly fifty minutes, sometimes when I had just got going and felt his involvement in my story had been equal to my own. After some months, I realized that my recurrent feelings of estrangement were not due to our cultural differences in forms of politeness, manners of speech, attitudes toward time, or even differences in our aesthetic sensibilities (to me, at that time, Beethoven was just so much noise while I doubt if he even knew of the existence of Hindustani classical music which so moved me). The estrangement involved much deeper cultural layers of the self, which were an irreducible part of my subjectivity as, I suppose, they were a part of his. In other words, if during a session we sometimes suddenly became strangers to each other, it was because each of us found himself locked into a specific cultural unconscious, consisting of a more or less closed system of cultural representations that were not easily accessible to conscious awareness. Glimmers of these deeper cultural layers became visible, although I did not fully recognize them till many years after the analysis ended.

To begin with the specific relationship: in the universe of teacher-healers, I had slotted my analyst into a place normally reserved for a personal guru. From the beginning of the training analysis, it seems, I had pre-consciously envisioned our relationship in terms of a guru-disciple bond, a much more intimate affair than the contractual doctor-patient relationship governing my analyst's professional orientation. In *my* cultural model, he was the personification of the wise old sage, benevolently directing a sincere and hardworking disciple who had abdicated the responsibility for his own welfare to the guru. My guru model also demanded that my analyst demonstrate his compassion, interest, warmth, and responsiveness much more openly than is usual or even possible in the psychoanalytic model guiding his therapeutic interventions. A handshake with a "Guten Morgen, Herr Kakar" at the beginning of the session and a handshake with an "Auf Wiedersehen, Herr Kakar" at the end of the session, even if accompanied by the beginnings of a smile, were not even starvation rations for someone who had adopted the analyst as his guru. Not that I was uncomfortable with long silences during a session, only that the silence needed to be embedded in other forms of communication. In an earlier paper, I have mentioned that the emphasis on speech and words in analytic communication is counter to the dominant Indian idiom in which words are only a small part of a vast store of signs and semiotics (Kakar 1985). In psychoanalytic therapy, speech reigns supreme. As Freud (1916, p.17) remarked, "Words were originally magic and to this day, words have retained much of their ancient magical power. By words one person can make another blissfully happy or drive him to despair, by words the teacher conveys his knowledge to his pupils, by words the orator carries his audience with him and determines their judgements and decisions. Words provoke affects and are in general the means of mutual influence among men. Words have a magical power. They can bring either the greatest happiness or deepest despair; they can transfer knowledge from teacher to student; words enable the orator to sway his audience and dictate its decisions. Words are capable of arousing the strongest emotions and prompting all men's actions." Of course, Freud's privileging of words is embedded in a profounder cultural difference on the relationship between speech and truth. Language in the Hindu, and especially in the Buddhist, world is inherently unfit to express what is real. It signifies distance between things and ourselves and thus misleads. Moreover, it inevitably generates illusions and ignorance. To speak is to be drawn into a network of mirages. Truth is unspoken, only silence is true.

In this vision of the relationship between speech and silence, the cultural expectation of the healer-teacher (in words of the sixteenth-century Indian saint Dabu) is that:

> The guru speaks first with the mind
> Then with the glance of the eye
> If the disciple fails to understand
> He instructs him at last by word of mouth
> He that understands the spoken word is a common man
> He that interprets the gesture is an initiate
> He that reads the thought of the mind
> Unsearchable, unfathomable, is a god. (Steinmann 1986, p.235)

I wonder how many of us realize that the rhythms of our spoken interpretations and silences are not only governed by the course of analysis, by what is happening in the analytic interaction, but are also culturally constituted? That the interpretations of silence, the analyst's of the patient and the patient's of the analyst, also contain cultural signifiers of which both may be unaware?

Our cultural orientations also attached varying importance to different family relationships. For instance, in my childhood, I had spent long periods of my young life in the extended families of my parents. Various uncles, aunts, and cousins had constituted a vital part of my growing-up experience. To pay them desultory attention or to reduce them to parental figures in the analytic interpretations felt like a serious impoverishment of my inner world.

This almost exclusive emphasis on the parental couple in psychoanalysis, I realized, has also to do with the modern Western conception of the family, which has the husband-wife couple as its fulcrum. In the traditional Indian view, which still exerts a powerful influence on how even most modern Indians view marriage, parent-sons and filial bonds among the sons override the importance of the couple as the foundation of the family. Cultural ideals demand that the universal dream of love, that constitutes and seeks to find its culmination in the couple, be muted. They enjoin the family to remain vigilant lest the couple becomes a fortress that shuts out all other relationships within the extended family.

On a general level, I realized later, our diverging conceptions of the "true" nature of human relationships were a consequence of a more fundamental divide in our cultural view of the person. In contrast to the modern West, the Indian experience of the self is not that of a bounded, unique individuality. The Indian person is not a self-contained center of awareness interacting with other, similar such individuals. Instead, the traditional Indian, in the dominant image of his culture, and in much of his personal experience of the self, is *constituted* of relationships. He is not a monad but derives his personal nature interpersonally. All affects, needs, and motives are relational and his distresses are disorders of relationships—not only with his human but also with his natural and cosmic orders.

This emphasis on the "dividual" (rather than the individual), transpersonal nature of man is not limited to traditional, rural India. Even with the urbanized and highly literate persons who form the bulk of patients for psychotherapy, the "relational" orientation is still the "natural" way of viewing the self and the world.

In practice, a frequent problem arose when I thought the psychotherapy was going well and the client was well on the road to a modicum of psychological autonomy, and then family members would come to me and complain, "What are you doing to my son/daughter? S/he is becoming independent of us. S/he wants to make her/his own choices now, thinks s/he knows what is best for her/him and doesn't listen to us." I vividly remember the patriarch of a large, extended business family, clad in suit and tie, but with the traditional turban as his headgear, walking into my office one day to discuss the progress in the therapy of his 21-year-old granddaughter who had become clinically depressed as the date for her arranged marriage with the scion of another rich family approached. Sitting across my desk with both his palms resting on the silver handle of a walking stick, he could barely hide his disappointment in me, "She may be better, doctor, but we are much worse." The families were baffled that the psychoanalytic ideal is to increase the individual's range of choices and not her integration with the family. Transference reactions in a patient may suppress this cultural view during and, for a while, but it returns as a nagging separation guilt, of having abandoned the family.

The yearning for relationships, for the confirming presence of loved persons and the distress aroused by their unavailability or unresponsiveness in time of need is thus a dominant cultural motif in Indian social relations. The motif is expressed variously but consistently. It is expressed in a person's feelings of helplessness when family members are absent, or in his or her difficulty in making decisions alone. In short, Indians tend to characteristically rely on the support of others to go through life and to deal with the exigencies imposed by the outside world (Kakar 1978).

Could it be that my analyst was like some other Western psychoanalysts, who I was reading at the time, who would choose to interpret this as a "weakness" in the Indian personality? An evaluation that invariably carries with it the general value implication that independence and initiative are "better" than mutual dependence and community? But it depends, of course, on a culture's vision of a "good society" and "individual merit" whether a person's behavior in relationships is nearer the isolation pole of the fusion-isolation continuum, as postulated by the dominant cultural tradition in the contemporary West, or the fusion pole advocated by traditional Indian culture. To borrow from Schoepenhauer's imagery, the basic problem of human relationships resembles that of hedgehogs on a cold night. They creep closer to each other for warmth, are pricked by quills and move away, but then get cold again and try to come nearer. This movement to and fro is repeated until an optimum position is reached in which the body temperature is above the freezing point and yet the pain inflicted by the quills (the nearness of the other) is still bearable. Independent of the positions our individual life histories had moved us to select on this continuum, in my Indian culture, in contrast to my analyst's German *Kultur*, the optimum position entailed the acceptance of more pain in order to get greater warmth.

Let me add that I am not advancing any simplified dichotomy between my analyst's Western cultural image of an individual, autonomous self and a relational, transpersonal self of my own Hindu culture. Both visions of human experience are present in all the major cultures, though a particular culture may, over a length of time, highlight and emphasize one at the expense of the other. What the advent of Enlightenment in the West has pushed to the background for the last couple of hundred years is still the dominant value of Indian identity; namely that the greatest source of human strength lies in a harmonious integration with the family and the group. This widespread consensus about what I have called the ideology of "familism" asserts that belonging to a community is the fundamental need of people. Only if a person truly belongs to such a community, naturally and unselfconsciously, can he or she enter the river of life and lead a full, creative and spontaneous life.

In practice, of course—and this is what makes psychoanalytic psychotherapy in non-Western societies possible—the cultural orientations of patients coming for psychoanalytic therapy are not diametrically opposite to those of the analyst. Most non-Western patients seen by analysts in North America and Europe are "assimilated" to the dominant culture of their host country to varying degrees, the contest between their original and new cultures not yet decisively tilted in the favor of one or the other. Similarly, in non-Western countries, the clients for psychoanalytic therapy—like their analysts—are westernized to varying degrees. In India, for instance, Indian analysts practice in the enclaves of Western modernity in Delhi, Mumbai, Kolkata, and Bangalore. Here, among the upper and middle classes, there are enough patients, Westernized to various degrees, who are attracted by a Freudian model of a person and the causes of his or her suffering, and look toward an analyst as their best ally in the realization of their full individuality.

What could my analyst have done? Did he need to acquire knowledge of my culture and, if so, what kind of knowledge? Would an anthropological, historical, or philosophical grounding in Hindu culture have made him understand me better? Or was it a *psychoanalytical* knowledge of my culture that would have been more helpful? Psychoanalytical knowledge of a culture is not equivalent to its anthropological knowledge, although there may be some overlap between the two. Psychoanalytic knowledge is primarily the knowledge of the culture's *imagination*, of its fantasy as encoded in its symbolic products—its myths and folktales, its popular art, literature, and cinema.

Besides asking about the kind of knowledge, we also need to ask the question "Which culture?" Would a psychoanalytic knowledge of Hindu culture have been sufficient in my case? Yes, I am a Hindu but I am also a Punjabi Khatri by birth. That is, my overarching Hindu culture has been mediated by my strong regional culture as a Punjabi and further by my Khatri caste. This Hindu Punjabi Khatri culture has been further modified by an agnostic father and a more traditional, believing mother, both of whom were also westernized to varying degrees. Is it not too much to expect any analyst to acquire this kind of prior cultural knowledge about his patients? On the other hand, is it OK for the analyst not to have *any* knowledge of his patient's cultural background? Or does the truth, as it often does, lie somewhere in the middle?

But, now comes the surprise. My analyst was very good—sensitive, insightful, patient. And, I discovered, as my analysis progressed, that my feelings of estrangement, which had given rise to all these questions, became fewer and fewer. What was happening? Was the cultural part of my self becoming less salient as the analysis touched ever-deeper layers of the self, as many psychoanalysts have claimed?

Most analysts have followed George Devereux's (1953) lead in maintaining that all those who seek help from a psychoanalyst have in common many fundamental and universal components in their personality structure. Together with the universality of the psychoanalytic method, these common factors sufficiently equip the analyst to understand and help his or her patient, irrespective of the patient's cultural background, a view reiterated by a panel of the American Psychoanalytic on the role of culture in psychoanalysis more than forty-five years ago (Jackson 1968). There are certainly difficulties, such as the ones enumerated by Ticho (1971), in treating patients of a different culture: a temporary impairment of the analyst's technical skills, empathy for the patient, diagnostic acumen, the stability of self and object representations, and the stirring up of counter-transference manifestations, which may not be easily distinguishable from stereotypical reactions to the foreign culture. Generally, though, given the analyst's empathetic stance and the rules of analytic procedure, these difficulties are temporary and do not require a change in analytic technique. It is useful but not essential for the analyst to understand the patient's cultural heritage.

I believe that these conclusions on the role of culture in psychoanalytic therapy, which would seem to apply to my own experience, are superficially true but deeply mistaken. For what I did, and what I believe most patients do, was to enthusiastically, if unconsciously, acculturate to the analyst's culture, in my case, both to his broader Western, north-European culture and to his particular Freudian psychoanalytic culture. The latter, we know, is informed by a vision of human experience that emphasizes man's individuality and his self-contained psyche. In the psychoanalytic vision, in Kenneth Kenniston's words (Adams 1979), each of us lives in our own subjective world, pursuing pleasures and private fantasies, constructing a life and a fate which will vanish when our time is over. It emphasizes the desirability of reflective awareness of one's inner states, insistence that our psyches harbor deeper secrets than we care to confess, the existence of an objective reality that can be known, and an essential complexity and tragedy of life where many wishes are fated to remain unfulfilled. I was, then, moving away from my own Hindu cultural heritage that sees life not as tragic but as a romantic quest that can extend over many births, with the goal and possibility of apprehending another, "higher" level of reality beyond the shared, verifiable, empirical reality of our world, our bodies and our emotions.

Now, we know that every form of therapy is also an enculturation. As Fancher (1993) remarks: "By the questions we ask, the things we empathize with, the themes we pick for our comment, the ways we conduct ourselves toward the patient, the language we use—by all these and a host of other ways, we communicate to the patient our notions{Freudian, Jungian, Kleinian, Lacanian, etc.} of what is 'normal' and normative. Our interpretations {Freudian, Jungian, Kleinian, Lacanian, etc.} of the origins of a patient's issues reveal in pure form our assumptions of what causes what, what is problematic about life, where the patient did not get what s/he needed, what should have been otherwise" (pp. 89–90).

As a patient in the throes of transference love, I was exquisitely attuned to the cues, to my analyst's values, beliefs, and vision of the fulfilled life, which even the most non-intrusive of analysts cannot help but scatter during the therapeutic process. I was quick to pick up the cues that unconsciously shaped my reactions and responses accordingly, with their overriding goal to please and be pleasing in the eyes of the beloved analyst. My intense need to be "understood" by the analyst, a need I shared with every patient, gave birth to an unconscious force that made me underplay those cultural parts of my self which I believed would be too foreign to the analyst's experience. In the transference-love, what I sought was closeness to the analyst, including the sharing of his culturally shaped interests, attitudes, and beliefs. This intense need to be close and to be understood, paradoxically by removing parts of the self from the analytic arena of understanding, was epitomized by the fact that I soon started dreaming in German, the language of my analyst, something I have not done before or after my analysis.

This tendency to excise a cultural part of the self is accelerated when the analysis is conducted in a language other than the mother tongue, wherein much of one's native culture is encoded. One's mother tongue, the language of one's childhood, is intimately linked with emotionally colored sensory-motor experiences. Psychoanalysis in a language that is not the patient's own is often in danger of leading to "operational thinking," that is, verbal expressions lacking associational links with feelings, symbols, and memories (Basch-Kahre 1984). However grammatically correct and rich in its vocabulary, the alien language suffers from emotional poverty, certainly as far as early memories are concerned.

The emotional poverty of language that is acquired much later has been dramatically demonstrated by an experiment in which subjects are asked the following question: A train is approaching at high speed. If you can push one individual on the track, stopping the train, it will save the lives of six others standing a little distance down the track. Will you push that individual in front of the train? Asked and answered in the mother tongue, most people show signs of an emotional dilemma and would not push the person to his death. The same question in the acquired language evokes much greater calculated rationality and the readiness to push one person in order to save the lives of six.

> How should a psychoanalyst, then, approach the issue of cultural difference of a client in his or her practice? The ideal situation would be that this difference exists only minimally, in the sense that the analyst has obtained a psychoanalytic knowledge of the patient's culture through a long immersion in its daily life and its myths, its folklore and literature, its language and its music—an absorption not through the bones, as in case of the patient, but through the head, and the heart. Anything less than this maximalist position has the danger of the analyst succumbing to the lure of cultural stereotyping in dealing with the particularities of the patient's experience. In cross-cultural therapeutic dyads, a little knowledge is indeed a dangerous thing, collapsing important differences, assuming sameness when only similarities exist. What the analyst needs is not a detailed knowledge of the patient's culture but a serious questioning and awareness of the assumptions underlying his own, i.e., the culture he was born into and the culture in which he has been professionally socialized as a psychoanalyst. In other words, what I am suggesting is that in the absence of the possibility of obtaining a deep psychoanalytic knowledge of the patient's culture, the analyst needs to strive for a state of affairs where the patient's feelings of estrangement, because of cultural differences from the analyst, are minimized and the

> patient does not cut off, or only minimally cuts off, the cultural part of the self from the therapeutic situation. This is possible only if the analyst can convey a cultural openness which comes from becoming aware of one's own culture's fundamental propositions about human nature, human experience, the fulfilled human life, and then to acknowledge their relativity by seeing them as cultural products, embedded in a particular place and time. The analyst needs to become sensitive to the hidden existence of what Kohut (1979, p.12) called "health and maturity moralities" of his or her particular analytical school. He needs to root out cultural judgments about what constitutes psychological maturity, gender-appropriate behaviors, "positive" or "negative" resolutions of developmental conflicts and complexes, that often appear in the garb of universally valid truths.

Given that ethnocentrism, the tendency to view alien cultures in terms of our own, and unresolved cultural chauvinism, are the patrimony of all human beings, including that of psychoanalysts, the acquisition of cultural openness is not an easy task. Cultural biases can lurk in the most unlikely places. For instance, to judge from the number of articles in psychoanalytic journals and books, psychoanalysis has traditionally accorded a high place to artistic creativity. To paint, sculpt, engage in literary and musical pursuits have not always and everywhere enjoyed the high prestige they do in modern Western societies. In other historical periods, many civilizations, including mine to this day, placed religious creativity at the top of their scale of desirable human endeavors. Psychoanalysts need to imagine that in such cultural settings, the following conclusion to a case report could be an example of a successful therapeutic outcome: "The patient's visions increased markedly in quantity and quality and the devotional mood took hold of her for longer and longer periods of time."

I would suggest that for optimal psychotherapy with patients from different cultures, what a psychoanalytical therapist needs is not an exhaustive knowledge of the patient's culture, but a reflective openness to and interrogation of his or her own cultural origins. A therapist can evaluate progress toward this openness by the increase in the feelings of curiosity and wonder in countertransference when the cultural parts of the patient's self find their voice in therapy, when the temptation to pathologize the cultural part of the patient's behavior decreases, when the analyst's own values no longer appear as normal and virtuous and when the analyst's wish to instruct the patient in these values diminishes markedly.

In the end, I hope I have not only provoked you to rethink your views about how the unconscious reveals itself but even how the unconscious is structured. That is, to challenge the traditional analytic notion that culture is built on top of an unconscious structure. Culture, as a fundamental way of viewing ourselves and the world we live in is not a later substrate in the formation of the psyche but is present from the beginning of life. Alfred Margulies (2014), in an earlier discussion of this chapter, pointed out that on deep levels culture and unconscious co-create each other; that their relationship is not like that of archeological layers but yin-yang, each shaping the other. Another way to think about the interaction between the individual and the cultural unconscious could be the well-known topological object: the Möebius strip. It`s a surface with only one side and one boundary and "If an ant were to crawl along the length of this strip, it would return to its starting point having traversed the entire length of the strip (on both sides of the original paper) without ever crossing an edge" (Horenstein 2015).

We know that this kind of relationship between the dynamic and cultural unconscious is even true neurobiologically.

Take the example of the Muller-Lyer illusion, where lines of equal length give impressions of different length, an illusion, created by the orientation of the arrow caps placed at their ends. This illusion is a consequence of our depth perspective shaped by the rectangular cues of buildings we live in. Children who grow up in round huts rarely experience the Muller-Lyer arrows as an illusion.

In other words, Marguiles goes on to say, "our cultural environment in its everyday structures, practices and aesthetics shapes the way our brains process visual information. And, if this is true for neurobiological non-conscious visual processing, it seems almost certain it would be true for psychoanalytically relevant unconscious processes and the impact of culture." (p.5)

For me, it has then become important to constantly remain aware of the Indian cultural context in clinical work and in my writings, but without sinking into traditionalism and becoming an apologist of tradition. On the other hand, because of the presence of many western cultural assumptions in psychoanalysis, as indeed they are in most social sciences, I also needed to critically look at psychoanalytic concepts without junking a discipline which has considerable explanatory power, not to speak of its individual and social emancipatory potential. Even as I question much of psychoanalytic superstructure, I continue to stand on its foundations and subscribe to its basic assumptions: the importance of the unconscious part of the mind in our thought and actions, the vital significance of early childhood experiences for later life, the importance of Eros in human motivation, the dynamic interplay, including conflict, between the conscious and unconscious parts of the mind, and the vital import of transference and counter-transference in the therapist and patient relationship. All the rest is up for grabs and just as we have begun to talk of modernity in the plural, of different modernities, perhaps we will soon be talking of Japanese, French, Chinese, Argentinian, and Indian psychoanalyses.

My own project of "translation" in the last forty years of work with Indian and Western patients has thus been guided by a view of the psyche wherein the individual, dynamic unconscious and the cultural unconscious are inextricably intertwined, each enriching, constraining, and shaping the other as they jointly evolve through life. The unconscious exists only when it is expressed through culture. In other words, to keep constantly in mind that the translation of psychoanalysis in a non-Western culture must give equal value to both the languages, of psychoanalysis and of the culture in which psychoanalysis is being received.

NOTE

1. Revised version of a talk sponsored by Division of Psychoanalysis (39) of the American Psychological Association, Boston Psychoanalytic Society and Institute, Massachusetts Institute for Psychoanalysis, New England Foundation for Psychoanalysis, and PINE Psychoanalytic Center, Boston, April, 19, 2014.

REFERENCES

Adams, V. "Freud's Work Thrives as Theory, Not Therapy." *The New York Times*, 14. August. (1979).

Basch-Kahre, E. "On difficulties arising in transference and countertransference when analyst and analysand have different socio-cultural backgrounds." *Int.R. Psychoanal.* 11(1984):61–67.

Devereux, G. "Cultural factors in psychoanalytic therapy." *J. Amer.Psychoanal. Assn* 1(1953): 629–655.

Fancher, R.T. "Psychoanalysis as culture." *Issues in Psychoanalytic Psychology*, 15(1993): 81–93.

Freud, S. *Introductory Lectures on Psycho-Analysis. S. E.*, 1916:16.

Haidt, J. *The Righteous Mind: Why Good People are Divided by Politics and Religion.* New York: Pantheon, 2012.

Henrich, J. , S.J. Heine and Norenzayan, A. "The weirdest people in the world?" *Behavioral and Brain Sciences* 33(2010): 61–83.

Horenstein, M. Personal communication. 2015.

Jackson, S. "Panel on aspects of culture in psychoanalytic theory and practice." *J. Amer. Psychoanal. Assn.* 16(1968):651–670.

Kakar, S. "Clinical work and cultural imagination." *Psychoanal. Q. 64*(994): 265–281.

Kakar, S. "Psychoanalysis and non-western cultures." *Int. R Psychoanal.* 12(1987):441–448.

Kakar, S. "Psychoanalysis and Non-Western Cultures." *Int. R. Psycho-Anal.*, 12(1985):441–448.

Kakar, S. "The maternal-feminine in Indian psychoanalysis." *Int. R. Psychoanal.* 16(1989): 355–362.

Kakar, S. *Culture and Psyche.* Delhi: Oxford Uuniversity Press, 1997.

Kakar, S. *Shamans, Mystics and Doctors.* New York: Knopf, 1982.

Kakar, S. *The Inner World: Childhood and Society in India.* Delhi and New York: Oxford Universiy Press, 1978.

Kohut, H. "The two analyses of Mr. Z." *Int. J. Psychoanal.* 60(1979):3–27.

Margulies, A. "Imagining the real: Discussion of Sudhir Kakar's 'Culture and Psychoanalysis,' Boston, April 19, 2014.

Mishra, A. "Sudhir Kakar—Psychoanalytic Wine from Indian Terroir: Towards a Compassionate Psychoanalysis." Unpublished Talk, Int. Psychol. Congress, Capetown, July, 2012.

Steinman, R.M. *Guru-Sisya-Sambandha: Das Meister-SchülerVerhältnisimtraditionellen und modernen Hinduismus.* Stuttgart: Steiner.1986.

Ticho, G. "Cultural aspects of transference and countertransference." *Bull. Meninger Clinic*, 35 (1971): 313–326.

Chapter Eleven

Imagining the Real

An Essay on Sudhir Kakar's "Culture and Psyche: A Personal Journey"

Alfred Margulies

Our colleague Sudhir Kakar (2014) began his presentation "Culture and Psychoanalysis" with the weird—and weirdness, I submit, is a perfect place for me to begin, too. Because the rest of this essay depends heavily on Kakar's to make sense, I now quote the beginning of his talk at some length:[1]

> Most of our knowledge on how human beings feel, think, act, is derived from a small subset of the human population which the psychologist Jonathan Haidt (2012) calls WEIRD, the acronym standing for western, educated, industrialized, rich and democratic. Psychologists, sociologists, psychotherapists, philosophers, are as WEIRD as the subjects of their studies, ministrations or speculations. It is this small group of statistical outliers that provides us with both the producers and subjects of our contemporary psychoanalytic knowledge we have then blithely proceeded to generalize to the rest of humankind.
>
> Haidt demonstrates the chasm between the WEIRD and others in his study of morality where he interviewed twelve groups of different social classes in different countries. He tells each interviewee different stories and then asks if there is something wrong in how someone acts in the story and, if so, why is it wrong. One of the stories goes:
>
> A man goes to the supermarket once a week and buys a chicken. But before cooking the chicken, he has sexual intercourse with it. Then he cooks it and eats it (p.3–4).
>
> One of his groups was from students of the University of Pennsylvania, a liberal, Ivy League college in the United States and certainly the most WEIRD among the selected groups. This was the only group out of the twelve where a majority (73 percent) tolerated the chicken story, finding it OK. "It's his chicken, it's dead, nobody is getting hurt and it's being done in private' . . . (p. 96).
>
> Or to take Anurag Mishra's . . . analogy of psychoanalysis and wine, the terroir of a wine is a specific place with its particular soil and climate where

> the wine is made and thus different terroirs, although made with the same sort of grape, have different wines. The terroir of human beings—historical, geographic, cultural, social, political, religious—too, varies and will produce different psychoanalytic wines. The terroir of psychoanalysis for more than a century has been and continues to be Western. Modern psychotherapy thus contains many Western cultural ideas and ideals that permeate psychotherapeutic theories and practice. Fundamental ideas about human relationships, family, marriage, male and female and so on which are essentially cultural in origin often remain unexamined and are regarded as universal by many Western therapists treating patients from different cultures.

With his opening story Kakar deftly—that is both gently and sharply—turns the tables on Western liberals. For me, Kakar's surprising paper evoked two reveries about cultural weirdness and unconscious structure that took me in surprisingly different directions: The first to Freud and Heidegger's conception of the uncanny. And my second association took me to my colleague Edward Hundert's (1995) book *Lessons from an Optical Illusion* and the implications for the intertwining of culture and neurobiology. These two paths (the weird and lessons from an optical illusion) come back together again and offer a third path that follows Kakar's vision of cultural imagination. So let's now go down each of these paths in turn.

AUTHENTIC WEIRDNESS

Astute students of the strangeness within, both Freud and Heidegger explored the weirdness of *Unheimlichkeit*, literally "not-at-home-ness," which translates as the uncanny. Freud (1919) of course aimed toward the dynamic unconscious: the uncanny signaled the return of the repressed. Heidegger (1962), taking a different path, thought the uncanny heralded those potentially authentic existential moments when being apprehends its own being; that is, moments when being-as-being jumps out at us, pulling us from our everyday absorption in the world and into a heightened state of awareness. And here we fall into a place of strangeness: we feel anxiety or dread.

At the margins of what (after Heidegger) I call "worlding," this existential strangeness sometimes offers the "authentic" clarity of surprising perspectives (Margulies 2000, 2015). And here we might find ourselves, as the poet Wallace Stevens (1972) put it, "more truly and more strange" (p. 55). The existential uncanny then emerges at the margins of being-in-the-world, at those liminal places on the edges of birth and death where we fall into and out of the world. And so witness our Western cultural struggles to define who is already alive (for example, when does inception begin?) and who is already dead (for example, when do we pull the plug?)—at these profoundly unsettling places we find what mortality means to us, places that evoke our deepest spiritual longings and conflicts about the meaning and sanctity of life.

CULTURAL ILLUSIONS

Kakar challenges not only our usual notions of how the unconscious reveals itself, but indeed our conceptions of how the unconscious gets structured. A more traditional notion of the unconscious posits that culture is built on top of a foundational unconscious structure, not unlike how we used to think of genes: a gene might express itself as varied phenotypes emerging differently within different environments. That is, genetic material achieves its varied expression within its environmental matrix. Individual people are actually secondary to the genotype, sort of like flowers sprouting from an extensive root system: the root system is primary and underground, the flowers a manifestation.

Another image might be of grapes expressing themselves in wine, which reflects their *terroir*. The environment works on the basic genetic structure of the grape to produce a distinctive wine specific to its soil, climate, sunlight, water, etc. But the grape—like the noble grapes Chardonnay, Pinot Noir, Cabernet—are primordial, the overlay is the essential environment. Hence, Bordeaux or Napa. And so, by analogy, we have universal unconscious structuring potentials, not unlike Jung's notions of archetypes, or from a more classical Freudian perspective: the Oedipal structures, libidinal stages, and so on.

Kakar, though, is suggesting a different path, one profound and hard to visualize: On deep levels culture and the unconscious co-create one another; that is, they are co-primordial. It is not that the unconscious is anterior, and it is not quite that culture is anterior; it is more like a yin-yang, each shaping, each bootstrapping, the other. The socio-cultural environment gets under our skin into the unconscious, and then the unconscious gets under the skin of our environment. Kakar is proposing a very strange, spiraling meta-conception—and one that we know to be true neurobiologically! Let me explain.

One might think that neurobiology is a straightforward primordial substrate from which visual experience is constructed. That is, neurobiology, the physical structure of our central nervous system, is fundamentally anterior to environmental experience. In this vein, neurobiology seems the necessary first step in a series in lock-step order: neurobiology (or brain), to individual, to culture. Indeed, this is the sequence of Western medical school curricula, with culture either not considered or added as a humanistic after-thought. But is neurobiology the primordial first mover in the creation of behavior? Well, yes and no.

Consider cross-cultural studies of optical illusions, I am here indebted to my colleague Edward Hundert's book (1995), *Lessons from an Optical Illusion.* For example, the famous images known as the Muller-Lyer Illusion, where lines of equal length give impressions of different length, an illusion, created by the orientation of the arrow caps placed on their ends (see Hundert 1995, p. 209). Richard Gregory (1966), a pioneer of artificial intelligence, proposed that these illusions were a consequence of how our visual system processes and makes sense of lines as information about depth perspective and size constancy scaling within the world that we actually live with its ubiquitous rectilinear shapes of buildings and box edges and so on.

But, a seeming paradox emerges. To quote Hundert (1995):

> It is tempting to call this phenomenon [the Muller-Lyer arrows illusion] of the accommodation of our plastic visual input analyzers to the realities of depth perspective and size constancy in our world a "natural phenomenon"—except for the simple fact that such rectilinear lines do not exist in nature! One may therefore ask what becomes of the visual input system in the brains of children who are raised in caves, or in round huts with no rectangular cues for depth perspective? . . . These people rarely experience the Muller-Lyer arrows as an illusion . . . (p. 211)

That is, our cultural environment in its everyday structures, practices, and aesthetics shapes the ways our brains process visual information. Just think of it: Culture shapes neurobiology! Where now is the first cause in our causal chain of perception? And, if this circular complexity of experience and structure is true for neurobiological non-conscious visual processing, it seems almost certain it would be true for psychoanalytically relevant unconscious processes and the impact of culture.

How heartening this circularity is for those of us who talk to and care deeply about actual individuals rather than aggregated statistical norms! That is, if this non-linear, recursive complexity is mind-boggling, it is also deeply reassuring: experience does indeed shape biology on a deep, deep level, which then shapes experience on a deep, deep level, in a spiral of uniqueness that flowers not only into wines, but into each individual. And this nonlinear, recursive complexity is precisely where clinical psychoanalysts live, from culture, to neurobiology, to individuals, circling back to culture, all shaping one another in this extraordinary richness of spiraling interaction. This evokes for me Freud's conception of *Nachtraglichkeit* (Freud 1918; and see Laplanche and Pontalis 1973, for a fuller history), translated as "deferred action," for the recursive spiraling of memory and significance, only here this iterative process stretches across cultures and evolution within the unconscious worlding of a people.

Which brings us back to the W.E.I.R.D. psychological studies Kakar cites at the beginning of his paper, that is, western "science" assumes universal significance—and this, too, is a cultural illusion as robust as the Muller-Lyer example. In short, the W.E.I.R.D. studies of western research are themselves exceedingly weird. And so we now conclude that understanding the essences of a culture's unconscious is of special importance to understand the essences of an individual's unconscious processes, that is, her complex worlding. But what, we now ask, are the implications for clinicians? And, most importantly, what is the path into understanding another's culture psychoanalytically?

"FACTIONS": OR, KAKAR'S IMAGINING THE REAL

Here Kakar (2014) asks a brilliant psychoanalytic question that points to a third path: Just how does a culture imagine itself? Reversing the vectors of causality, and psychoanalytic to its core, this question goes to fantasy, desire, history, and to the stories we tell ourselves from one generation to another. And these stories often come with shared multi-generational rituals, communal gatherings of all ages: the great array of religious stories, of historical origins, the world-wide oral traditions back before Homer's *The Iliad* and *The Odyssey*, the songs that sang us into being . . .

Kakar's novel approach offers a different Olympian view outside of ourselves: How does our culture imagine its origins and its dreams of the right way to live? How does it dream of lives in and out of balance? How does a culture sing of meaning and of one's place in the universe and tell the story of individual and collective purpose and the hazards along the way? How does a culture go to the liminal edge of meaning that unsettles, perplexes, and demands answers to that which will always be beyond us? What are our primal signifiers, our collective store of symbols, expressed in mythic structuring stories?

IN THIS VEIN I NOW ASK MYSELF: HOW DO WE DREAM OURSELVES?

An Example: Cultural Symbols, Up Close and Personal; A Message in a Dream

Over 40 years ago I awoke from this dream:

My mother and I are walking. I trip and stumble. She catches me, picks me up, and then she holds me in her lap. But this is so odd in so many ways:

I am a grown man, that is, a young man in my early 20s, and yet cradled by my mother.

So strange and moving to me: I am a layering of selves from different ages coming together in a powerful image. On waking, I immediately got both the image and the unconscious message. The image: Straight from Michelangelo's sculpture, "*The Pieta*," Mary holding the broken body of Jesus. The message: Though I am far away in Boston, I knew then with clarity that my mother was about to die of her cancer. She and everyone around her, though, had denied this imminent event—and in my dream it broke through with certainty. A message from my unconscious awareness of what was being denied: I knew that she was on the threshold.

And, surprising to me, though dreaming of the Pieta, I was a Southern Jew, raised kosher. Now Kakar (2014) speaks of the highly specific subcultures within his Indian culture, as in:

> Yes, I am a Hindu but also a Punjabi Khatri by birth. That is, my overarching Hindu culture has been mediated by my strong regional culture as a Punjabi and further by my Khatri caste. This Hindu Punjabi Khatri culture has been further modified by an agnostic father and a more traditional, believing mother, both . . . also westernized to varying degrees.

Like nested Russian dolls, all of these cultures are contained within cultures within more cultures. And so when I say I was a Southern Jew, raised kosher, that only hints at my cultural specificity and nuance. This to say, I was Southern, Virginian, Jewish, raised kosher, but not orthodox, with a more traditional believing mother, a father who ate "chow mein" with pork, but who told me the red thingies were "water-chestnuts," both parents strongly assimilated to the Southern culture within the American melting pot. And my American, patchwork unconscious lifted an iconic cultural image straight from Michelangelo's sculpture "*The Pieta*" in the Vatican! I had only seen photographs, but here is a powerful, archetypal Christian image. Surely grandiose for me to be so identified, but more, I think, universal and primal, that is, the image crystallized death, life, the earliest human connections and sorrow throughout all time, human suffering precisely because we are only human and long for something bigger. Mortal, we lose those we love; we know that we live on a horizon of time. That is, Madonna is the universal mother and Christ is a universal son, connected throughout all time. A mother's death became my stumble, my death—a part of my world dies.

My unconscious appropriated the Pieta from the great art of my culture to bring me the message I didn't want to see, but needed to experience. The artist, a seer, summons the imagination of the culture; artists dream the culture to its depths. Let us not forget that Freud's initial approach to dreams was as a model for neurotic symptom formation. And, yes, in this sense, I submit the artist imagines and instantiates the over-determined symptom and sign, both the dis-ease and flowering, of a culture itself.

Many years later I finally saw the actual Pieta in the Vatican, and uncannily, I felt as if the sculpture had been commissioned for me, personally. Face to face, I observed it closely: Michelangelo carved the marble so thin that the Madonna's cloak glowed in translucence, like lace, like life itself, tough and fragile. And here I noted: This perfect image was surreal, not real at all.

The proportions of the Madonna were unearthly, not of our experience in the real world—which, ironically, makes them so perfect! Like the Parthenon, an image of perfection, though each column is actually slightly askew, off by fractions of degrees to give the illusion of perfect Platonic linearity. That is, perfection is something we live abstractly, something we experience that never was, like Pythagorean perfect lines and points in space. Perfection, then, is created, co-created, through artistry. The artist imagines the reality she is trying to capture.

Or, more to the point, these creative illusions are like the taken-for-granted optical illusions of our Western world I described earlier. The sense of perspective is embedded in a culture's collective imagination, which gets wired into its neurobiology. And so my socio-cultural perception and imagination will be quite specific to my time, place, historical moment, that is my being-in-the-world which is nested within my culture's being-in-the-world, our "worlding."

Perspective then does not mean Cartesian truth, a gift to us Westerners from the Renaissance, but rather, it is relative to, an angle of vision. Or, as Kakar puts it in his wonderful paper, "Seduction and the Saint" (2003, p. 206): some primal fantasies are "a play, a dramatic enactment of a compelling fact-fiction ("faction") which might have been but was never real." A "Faction": how wonderful! A compelling fact-fiction emerges like Martin Buber's (1957) "imagining the real of the other," the bold empathic swing into another's life, into another's fantasies and imagination (see Margulies 1989; 2014).

FULL CIRCLE: SET ONESELF FREE

I think Heisenberg (though there is uncertainty here) once said the world is not only stranger than we think—it is stranger than we can think! And so let me paraphrase and bring these threads together: the world, that is, we ourselves in our-being-in-the-world, are always-already interconnected, top to bottom, conscious to unconscious, bottom to top. That is, we are not only weirder than we think, but we are weirder than we *can* think. To this impossible challenge, along with Sudhir Kakar, we must dream into the other's culture, we must imagine. . . .

NOTE

1. This chapter began as a discussion of Sudhir Kakar's talk "Culture and Psyche: A Personal Journey," presented in Cambridge, MA, on April 19, 2014, at Lesley College for a conference on "Culture and Psychoanalysis." For intelligibility, I have adapted my discussion to fit into this volume, primarily by more extensive quotations from Kakar's presented chapter.

REFERENCES

Buber, M. "Elements of the interhuman." *Psychiatry* 20(1957): 105–113.

Freud, S. "From the history of an infantile neurosis." *Standard Edition*, (New York: Norton) 1955, 17(1918): 3–122.

Freud, S. "The "Uncanny,"' *Standard Edition.* (New York: Norton), 1955, 17(1919): 217–252.

Gregory, R. *Eye and Brain: The Psychology of Seeing.* London: Weidenfeld and Nicolson, 1966.

Haidt, J. *The Righteous Mind: Why Good People are Divided by Politics and Religion.* New York: Pantheon, 2012.

Heidegger, M. *Being and Time*, trans. J. Macquarrie & E. Robinson. New York: Harper Collins, 1962.

Hundert, E. *Lessons from an Optical Illusion: On Nature and Nurture, Knowledge and Values.* Cambridge: Harvard Univ Press, 1995.

Kakar, S. "Culture and Psyche: A Personal Journey." unpublished manuscript. Talk presented in Cambridge, Massachusetts: Committee on International Relations for Psychoanalytic Psychology, Division of Psychoanalysis (39) of the American Psychological Association; Co-Sponsors: Boston Psychoanalytic Society and Institute; Massachusetts Institute for Psychoanalysis; Psychology and the Other Institute at Lesley University; The Paul G. Ecker, M.D. Center for Interdisciplinary Studies, New England Foundation for Psychoanalysis, and PINE Psychoanalytic Center. Apr. 19, 2014.

Kakar, S. "Seduction and the Saint: Desire and the Spiritual Quest." *Ann. Psychoanal* 31(2003):197–209.

Laplanche, J. & Pontalis, J.B. *The Language of Psycho–Analysis* (D. Nicholson–Smith, Trans.). New York: W. W. Norton & Co, 1973.

Margulies, A. "Falling Out of the World: Shock, Strangeness—and Afterwards." Unpublished manuscript, for the conference, "The Therapeutic Action of Psychodynamic Psychotherapy: Current Concepts of Cure," Boston. March 22, 2015.

Margulies, A. "After the Storm: Living and Dying in Psychoanalysis. With Discussants Shelly Orgel and Warren Poland." *Journal of the American Psychoanalytic Association* 62(2014): 863–905.
Margulies, A. "The Place of Strangeness, a review of Warren Poland's 'The Analyst's Witnessing and Otherness." *Journal of the American Psychoanalytic Association.* 48(2000): 72–79.
Margulies, A. *The Empathic Imagination.* (New York, Norton, 1989.
Stevens, W. *The Palm at the End of the Mind: Selected Poems, edited by* H. Stevens. NY: Vintage Books, 1972.

Chapter Twelve

As Psychoanalysis Travels

Manasi Kumar, Anup Dhar, and Anurag Mishra in Conversation with Sudhir Kakar

Manasi Kumar, Anup Dhar, Anurag Mishra
and Sudhir Kakar

Even people who are well-inclined toward psychoanalysis are often skeptical whether psychoanalysis is at all possible in a non-Western society such as India, with its different family system, religious beliefs, and cultural values from those of bourgeois Europe in which psychoanalysis had its origins.

Freud himself had hinted at some of the cultural difficulties a Western import like psychoanalysis may have in the Indian setting. In response to a letter from Romain Rolland who had sought Freud's views on the mystical experience, "the oceanic feeling," Freud (1930) stated his attitude toward India and things Indian when he wrote: "I shall now try with your guidance to penetrate into the Indian jungle from which until now an uncertain blending of Hellenic love of proportion, Jewish sobriety, and Philistine timidity have kept me away." (p. 392)

I do not give the easy answer to my skeptical friends that Indian analysts practice in the enclaves of Western modernity in Delhi, Mumbai, Kolkata ,and Bangalore. Here, among the upper and upper-middle classes, there are enough patients, Westernized to various degree, who are attracted by the Freudian model of the human and the causes of his or her suffering and look toward an analyst as their best ally in the realization of their full individuality. I know that the questioners—Manasi, Anup, and Anurag—are seeking an answer to the relevance of psychoanalysis for the majority of Indians who are still firmly rooted in their civilization. My answer is that, yes, traditional India is indeed very different. There is an emphasis on extended rather than a nuclear family, mother goddesses are vastly more important than a father-god, the nature of a person is not viewed as individual and instinctual but as inter- and transpersonal. Further, there are fundamental differences on the nature of human experience and the fulfilled human life. Psychoanalysis, we know, is informed by a vision of human experience that emphasizes man's individuality and his self-contained psyche. In the psychoanalytic vision, each of us lives in our own subjective world, pursuing pleasures and private fantasies, constructing a life and a fate that will vanish when our time is over. This view emphasizes the essential complexity and tragedy of life whereby many wishes are fated to remain unfulfilled. The psychoanalytic vision is in contrast to the Indian, specifically Hindu cultural heritage, which sees life not as tragic but as a romantic quest that can extend over many births, with the goal and possibility of apprehending another, "higher" level of reality beyond the shared, verifiable, empirical reality of our world, our bodies, and our emotions. The Indian view further asserts that belonging to a community is the fundamental need of the human. Only if the human truly belongs to such a community, naturally and unselfconsciously, can he or she enter the river of life and lead a full, creative, and spontaneous life. And, of course, Hindu-Indian myths are very different from Greek myths or the Christian and Jewish legends that have irrigated the *terroir* of psychoanalysis for the last one hundred years.

At the beginning of my practice in India, I was acutely aware of the struggle within myself between my inherited Hindu-Indian culture and the Freudian psychoanalytic culture that I had recently acquired and in which I was professionally socialized. My romantic Indian vision of reality could not be easily reconciled with the ironic psychoanalytic vision, nor could the Indian view of the person and the sources of human strengths be reconciled with the Freudian view—now also mine—on the nature of the individual and his or her world. With Goethe's Faust, I could only say to a Western colleague:

> Your spirit only seeks a single quest
> so never learns to know its brother
> Two souls, alas, dwell in my breast
> And one would gladly sunder from the other.

Some Indian colleagues try to sunder the two souls by unreservedly identifying with their professional socialization, radically rejecting their Indian cultural heritage. Many of them have migrated to Western countries to work as therapists, to all apparent purposes indistinguishable from their Western colleagues. Some who stay back in India struggle to hold onto their professional identity by clinging to each psychoanalytic orthodoxy. Loath to be critical of received wisdom and exiled from Rome, they become more conservative than the Pope. Others enthusiastically embrace the latest fashions and analytic gurus from the metropolises of psychoanalysis. A few, like myself, live with the oppositions, taking comfort from the Hindu view that every contradiction does not need a resolution, that contradictions can co-exist in the mind like substances in water that are in suspension without necessarily becoming a solution.

And yet my experience with traditional Indian patients teaches me that psychoanalysis is still possible, if (as the Indian astrologer said on being asked how he cast horoscopes when new planets have been discovered which are absent in his ancient system) "one makes the required adjustments." In other words, if the translation of psychoanalysis gives equal value to both the languages, of psychoanalysis and of the culture in which psychoanalysis is being received.

Some of the adjustments are theoretical. The Indian analyst needs to recognize that many psychoanalytic propositions on what constitutes psychological maturity, gender-appropriate behaviors, "positive" or "negative" resolutions of developmental conflicts and complexes, that often appear in the garb of universal truths, are actually the incorporation of Western middle-class experience and values into psychoanalytic theory. But the most important adjustment one needs to make is to recognize that culture, as a fundamental way of viewing ourselves and the world we live in, is not a later substrate in the formation of the psyche but is present from the beginning of life. Alfred Margulies (2014), in a discussion of an earlier version of this chapter pointed out, at deep levels of the psyche culture and unconscious co-create each other, that their relationship is not like that of archeological layers but yin-yang, each shaping the other and that we know this to be true neurobiologically. He illustrates this by taking the example of the Muller-Lyer illusion where lines of equal length give impressions of different length, an illusion, created by the orientation of the arrow caps placed on their ends. This illusion is a consequence of our depth perspective shaped by the rectangular cues of buildings we live in. Children who grow up in round huts rarely experience the Muller-Lyer arrows as an illusion.

In other words, Marguiles goes on to say, "our cultural environment in its everyday structures, practices and aesthetics shapes the way our brains process visual information. And, if this is true for neurobiological non-conscious visual processing, it seems almost certain it would be true for psychoanalytically relevant unconscious processes and the impact of culture." (p.5)

To adapt the late anthropologist Clifford Geertz's quip about the Javanese, "To be human is to be Argentinian"; "To be human is to be Indian."

Why does the cultural unconscious which, too, is decisive in the formation of individual psyche, which flows into the same river that also receives the stream of the dynamic unconscious, receive such little attention in clinical case histories reported in the analytic literature across the world?

It is easy to see why narratives of cultural unconscious would be absent in cases when both the analyst and the patient share the same culture. As has been said, if a fish was a scientist, the last discovery it would make would be of water. In the analytic dyads from the same culture, both the analyst and the patient are two fish in the same water. Mostly, of course, it is the professional identity of the analyst—Freudian, Kleinian, Kohutian, Lacanian, or whatever, which almost completely overlays or trumps the analyst's cultural identity. As Fancher (1993) remarked some years ago: "By the questions we ask, the things we empathize with, the themes we pick for our comment, the ways we conduct ourselves toward the patient, the language we use—by all these and a host of other ways, we communicate to the patient our notions {Freudian, Jungian, Kleinian, Lacanian, etc.} of what is 'normal' and normative. Our interpretations {Freudian, Jungian, Kleinian, Lacanian, etc.} of the origins of a patient's issues reveal in pure form our assumptions of what causes what, what is problematic about life, where the patient did not get what s/he needed, what should have been otherwise" (pp.89-90).

The patient, of course, contributes her share to this tacit pact with the analyst. In the throes of transference love and quick to pick up cues that unconsciously shape his reactions and responses accordingly, the patient's intense need to be "understood" by the analyst gives birth to an unconscious force that makes her underplay those cultural parts of her self which she believes would be foreign to the analyst's experience.

My own project of "translation" in the last forty years of work with Indian and Western patients has been guided by a view of the psyche wherein the individual, dynamic unconscious and the cultural unconscious are inextricably intertwined, each enriching, constraining, and shaping the other as they jointly evolve through life.

REFERENCES

Fancher, R.T. "Psychoanalysis as culture." *Issues in Psychoanalytic Psychology* 15(1993): 81–93.

Freud, S. "Letter to Romain Rolland, 19 January 1930." In *The Letters of Sigmund Freud,* edited by E. Freud. New York: Basic Books, 1980 [1930].

Margulies, A. "Imagining the real: Discussion of Sudhir Kakar's 'Culture and Psychoanalysis,'" Boston, April 19, 2014.

Chapter Thirteen

Genealogies of Aboriginalization

Psychoanalysis and Sexuation in Cultural Crucible

Anup Dhar

This reflection sees psychoanalysis not just as a "philosophy of the unconscious," but also as a "philosophy of sexuation"; and it is on the question of "sexuation"—"the [il]logical development of the *cause* of gender"—that psychoanalysis is most creative; and it is also where it slips most. Jacques Lacan in *Seminar XI* (1998 [1977]) foregrounds *four* fundamental concepts of psychoanalysis: "the unconscious, repetition, the transference and the drive." This reflection argues for a fifth fundamental concept: sexuation. What however is sexuation? How has the concept of sexuation taken shape in Freud and Lacan? How has it been reshaped by feminist psychoanalytic and psychoanalytic feminist work? What form did it take in the works of the first non-western psychoanalyst—Girindrasekhar Bose (1886–1953)? Ragland (2004) shows how

> Lacan discovered the link Freud sought—but never found—between the pleasure principle and the reality principles. Having desexualized the reality principle, Freud could never place libido in it any more than he could locate the signifier in *Es* or Id. . . .
>
> Lacan's theory of sexuation argues that men and women are sexuated *psychically*, and not biologically. That is, there is a psychic asymmetric logic[1] at work in differentiating biological woman from biological man [hence "there is no such thing as a sexual relationship"]. . . . Lacan's rethinking of sexuation concerns the conditions of jouissance that rotate between pleasure and pain. He argues that the masculine and feminine are psychic identifications. The masculine identifies predominantly with the *symbolic* order of language and social conventions, while the feminine identifies with the *real* of affect, loss, and trauma. Whether one identifies as masculine or feminine does not concern

> one's biological sex, but the position one occupies in reference to the masculine *all* of knowledge, or the feminine *not all* of knowledge. (Ragland 2004: 29, 179)

What however is sexuation? Is sexuation— as in Freud's work—about *having* and *not having*, a culturally privileged part object, the penis? Is sexuation—as in Lacan's work—about *having* or *being* an Imaginary object, the "phallus"? Is it about the "position one occupies in reference to the masculine *all* of knowledge, or the feminine *not all* of knowledge" (Ragland 2004: 179)? Is sexuation—as in Luce Irigaray's (1985b) work—about an ethics of "sexual difference"? Or is sexuation—as in Bose's (1949) work—about the Moebius of "sexual ambivalence"? This reflection is premised on a dialogue between perspectives to sexuation; perspectives born in both the west and in the colonized east; perspectives that are at times in dialogue; perspectives that are at other times alien to each other; including questions of translation as Kakar suggests in this volume (in the chapter "As Psychoanalysis Travels"). It is also about how one can make sense of oneself as a sexuated subject in cultural context.

The reflection is also about feminism and woman. Not *who* is woman or who the woman *is*. But *what* is "woman." Not what is woman, in general, but in psychoanalysis; in both its original (i.e., Freudian), ab-original (i.e., Lacanian and feminist) and aboriginal (i.e., Bose-ian) forms; and what is its relation to the question of what is woman in feminism, in especially the Indian context? The reflection thus takes feminist enquiries beyond the standard sex-gender system to questions of sexuation, sexual difference, and sexual ambivalence.

Taking off from (i) Freud's own work on eros, pleasure principle, sexed subjectivity, and female/feminine sexuality, to (ii) "internal corrections" initiated by Jacques Lacan's "return to Freud," to (iii) "internal critiques" by French feminist philosopher Irigaray (in the feminist turn to psychoanalysis as also the psychoanalytic turn in feminism), this reflection would suggest how Bose (Ashis Nandy calls him "*Savage* Freud" [1995]); I don't; he is Girindrasekhar Bose; he is not a version of Freud, sage or savage) and his "aboriginal theory of mental life" (Bose called it "A *New* Theory of Mental Life"; why new? What is new about his theory? One will have to explore.) offers a different and distinctive understanding of mental life, sexuation, and sexual difference. What does such a "new" theory of mental life, sexuation, and sexual difference do to erstwhile understandings in psychoanalysis? What happens when Freudian psychoanalysis and sexed subject constitution with Oedipality, phallicism, and castration as central tenets are put in a cultural crucible?[2] What happens when a culture (here India) is put in the psychoanalytic crucible marked by its own and distinctive focus on and history of sexuation and sexual difference (Kakar [1982, 1989, 2011] has explored this "cultural crucible" and this "history" in *tales of love, sex and danger,* in re-readings of the *Kamasutra,* in the story of the *ascetic of desire*: Vatsayana, and in the relationship between Mira and Mahatma Gandhi . . . ; Foucault has explored it in *History of Sexuality* [1978]; also see Davidson, 2001 and Laqueur, 1990)?

In that sense, this reflection works its way through (i) Freudian psychoanalysis (which marks its own difference with medicine, psychiatry, and psychology), and (ii) Lacan's notion of sexuation and feminist philosophies of sexual difference (initiated by Irigaray, Julia Kristeva, Bracha Ettinger, Helene Cixous, Monique Wittig, and Sarah Kofman which marks its own difference with "feminisms of equality" and generates its own kind of *apposite* positionality with respect to psychoanalysis) to arrive at (iii) Bose's "new" theory of sexual life (marked by Bose's *aboriginalization* of Freudian psychoanalysis through the invocation of gendered "ambivalence," "double-wish," "psychic see-saw," "identification," and "Oedipus Point" [as against Oedipus Complex] as fundamental concepts). Bose is seen as rendering redundant the importance of the phallus (as part object or as signifier) that has been paradigmatic of much of psychoanalysis. In other words, Bose moves from having or not-having an (part) object to be*ing* or not-be*ing* (like) a subject; he is moving from *possession* (and hence the consequent pride, [penis] envy, and [castration] anxiety) to *identification* with a momentous Other; he is moving from the notion of a cannibalistic or devouring self to an image of self where the self extends itself outwards toward Others through identification, where Others are mirrors and not objects; Bose calls it "irradiation of identification." It is not just an argument for cultural relativism. It is not that Indian and European patients are different in psychic disposition. It is that, in the "Indian" outline of psychoanalysis, the phallus is not considered the fundamental object or signifier of sexed subjectivity. Here "India" is not an analysand who offers different case experiences to phallocentric psychoanalysis. Instead, India is an analyst of the European obsession with the phallus (and the Oedipal) as the structuring principle of psychic constitution.

GENEALOGIES OF ABORIGINALIZATION

This reflection is also about three possible, perhaps related, genealogies of aboriginalization. The first is about the now-known history of the "aboriginalization of non-western cultures" during the colonial era. The first is about the characterization of non-western cultures as aboriginal and the consequent degradation, devaluing. The first is about Orientalism (both white and brown). It is about representing the Other as the "lacking/lagging other."

The second is to "render the origin genealogical" (as in Michel Foucault) or to "put under erasure the origin-al" (as in Jacques Derrida).[3] The second—designated as ab-originalization in this reflection—is to render the "western originals" ab-original.

The third is about a possible post-Orientalist episteme. While the first was about how knowledge of cultures was made and unmade, the third is about what cultures of knowledge (as against the Orientalist knowledge of cultures) can be produced. The third is about creating cultures of aboriginalization as against an extant aboriginalization of cultures. The third is not just about making micro-changes in western theories, keeping its architechtonics intact; but about aboriginalizing its very archi-texture (see Dhar and Siddiqui, 2013).

Through a close reading of the long correspondence (1921–1933) between Freud and Bose one could argue for a possible culture of the aboriginalization of western knowledge systems put in place by Bose through conceptual resources drawn from the Bhagvad Gita, the Puranas, and the Yoga Sutra; as also through the invocation of a theory of mental life not circumscribed or limited by what Foucault in *History of Sexuality* calls "The Repressive Hypothesis" (see Dhar, 2017).

Was Bose-ian psychoanalysis, then, stemming from the realization that India cannot perform conventions laid down according to Hebraic-Hellenic-Christian stories? Is the parricide story the beginning of human history? Does not Freud foreclose possibilities of looking at a different (rather than deviant) language game by relegating matrilineal polytheisms and pagan polymorphisms to the pre-history of humankind or by making Islam an "abbreviated repetition of the Jewish religion" (see Spivak, 1994; also see Siddiqui and Davar's chapter in this volume)? This chapter therefore asks: what happens when psychoanalysis and India come close? Does India become the analysand? Does India provide to western psychoanalysis case material about the aboriginal world? Or can India emerge as the analyst in this exchange? Can India give back to the west interpretation about the west? What was the nature of aboriginal psychoanalysis? Was it *Indian* psychology? In which sense was it Indian? Was it the Indian logic of the psyche? Or was it the logic of the "Indian psyche"? In that sense, this reflection problematizes the space that has now come to be known as "Indian Psychology"; all the more because India is not an undivided perspective; it is a perspective that is deeply marked, or perhaps, scarred by relations of caste, gender, and class as also experiences of aboriginality.

AT THE EDGE OF PSYCHOANALYSIS

The urge and inspiration for this reflection flows from *our* ("our" includes Ranjita Biswas, Asha Achuthan, and the author of this chapter) experiences in and around science, experiences that have to it the history of the last 30 years. 1987 was when it began. Medicine was interesting. But I had no time for it. First three years I was more interested in (left) theater—writing scripts, acting, directing plays; it was a kind of group work: working in groups, under groups, as groups; forging contingent collectives around a script where each acted, and acted out; much later I understood why it is important to understand *groups* and not just *individuals*, as also why it is important to understand groups psychoanalytically and not just politically, through the works of Bion (see *Experiences in Groups,* 1961) and Guattari (see *Transversality* 2015). The next three years I had joined radical left student politics; our student organization, Medical College Democratic Students' Association (MCDSA) had terminated its affiliation to Maoist Communist Parties; it had begun to call itself an *independent* student organization; I felt student organizations should not be part of or under Communist Parties; students formed a heterogeneous mass and were not marked by *only* the class question. Once again the attention was elsewhere. Medicine was now to be put to the service of the "third world nation" if not exclusively to the working class or the poor peasant. We were doctors sensitized to "*human* society, or socialized humanity" (see Marx, 2016); the writing on the wall was, doctors have only diagnosed, in various ways; the point, however, is to take treatment, cure, relief, and healing to the malnourished and suffering masses. For two years in a distant village in Murshidabad district we tried to take health to the villagers. We tried to build a model of public health through people's participation; a model not sponsored by the state or by international funding agencies; a model put in place by individuals who had come together (a kind of nascent *being-in-common* [see Luc-Nancy, 1991]) to economically and intellectually contribute to people's health. We ran free clinics in working-class colonies of jute factories along the river Ganges. We also read dialectical materialism with working-class youth. However, free clinics were not enough. "The Condition of the Working Class in Bengal" could be understood only through a close reading of Marx (as also questions of sexual and cultural difference). It could not be a question of setting up a human relation with the worker only. It had to be a question of *knowledge*: one had to understand "work," "working class," and the question of "class."

On the one hand was a *clinical* experience tuned to public health concerns; this experience took me later to community mental health and to some work with *Anjali* and *Iswar Sankalpa* in Kolkatta and *Banyan* in Chennai; and has now taken me to a deep doubt: How does one practice psychoanalysis *in* India, in *adivasi* contexts, in say the Kalahandi district of South Odisha? Does psychoanalysis become critical developmental or transformative *social praxis* by the time it reaches Kalahand? The MPhil program in Development Practice at AUD is an attempt to think psychoanalysis in Kalahandi-like contexts. In that sense, Development Practice *is* psychoanalysis. It is psychoanalysis is poor contexts. It is psychoanalysis amongst adivasi forms of life, forms of life not attuned to the kind of psychological interiority and the confessional attitude classical Freudian psychoanalysis requires or demands. It is psychoanalysis of groups; it is informed and driven by the psychoanalytic work with groups (a la Bion and Guattari). It is psychoanalysis with community and not with individuals. It is perhaps, as Sudhir Kakar suggests, *psychoanalysis under a tree*. Most people think Development Practice is *only* about development. It is not. That word "development" sometimes serves as a distraction. Development Practice is about a relationship between the MPhil student and the community/group; a relationship that cannot be described as just transferential (which is dyadic); but is understood in terms of also transversality (a la Guattari, which is within groups); a relationship that leads to both an arrival at the *truth* of the community and *transformation*: both self and social. It is, like psychoanalysis, an exercise where new knowledge is generated from and through practice. Does Bion and Guattari's work on groups become more important than Freud's case histories, in Kalahandi? Or do we need to rethink the standard practice, idioms, language, ethos, and logic of psychoanalysis when we work in India; all the more when we work in Kalahandi? Do we need to arrive and create a new theory of mental life, or a new theory of the psyche? Do we then need to move to *how* we do psychoanalysis *from* India, rather than just doing (Freudian or post-Freudian) psychoanalysis *in* India? Kakar had asked this question a little differently in Pondichery some years back: how does one do psychoanalysis *under a tree*? Was he asserting in the process the need to do psychoanalysis under a tree and not on a couch or in what could be called a strict psychoanalytic *setting*, which is also and usually an *urban* setting, which is also and usually a *square* and *rectangular room* with *four brick and mortar walls*? It is important to remind ourselves in this context what the shape of the rooms does to us (see Kakar's paper in this volume for how the difference of the *habitat* of square/rectangular cottages and round cottages has an effect on how we experience the world thereafter; it is, as if, our being-in-a-square/round-world determines our being).

On the other, was *critical-political* experience tuned to Marx; and later feminism and the postcolonial?

How to connect the two, if at all (this question of the connection between the clinical marked by psychoanalysis and the political marked by sexual-cultural difference haunts this reflection).

More particularly, this reflection flows from my discomfort with the workings of medicine in general and psychiatry in particular. It takes off from the question of the patient/client/survivor/user in the psychiatric clinic; what the patient feels; what is her position in the clinic? Does she at all secure a position for herself in the clinic? How does the institution of mental health treat her? How does the mental health professional treat her? How does the professional relate to her? What are the relations between the professional and the patient/client/survivor/user? How does one set up a relation with someone who is purportedly "mad"/abnormal? Further, how do we do mental health *today*? What are the new questions? Neurobiology is one new question; community mental health is another; rights of the mentally dis-eased is yet another. Are we beginning to see and sense our bodies differently? What is it doing to our subjectivities? What is our consciousness of such emergent conditions of corporeality? While in the world of the economic there are corporate realities in their boom and their depressions/recessions, there are in Other worlds, corpo-realities. How does one relate to these corpo-realities? How does one relate to the contemporary? Does the past (the distant precolonial past, and the not so distant, colonial past) offer us a few interesting insights? Does the fashionable present (Lacan and the Lacanese) offer us some other insights?

Further, where do we place mental health today? On the one end of the spectrum we have neurobiology; on the other, we have socio-political processes; both are in turn immersed in culture. While we would not like to collapse the space of mental health or of the psyche into either the neurobiological or the discursive—into either the materialist (which at times lapses into mechanical materialism) or the culturalist (which at times becomes ruthlessly constructivist), we would still like to ask what is it that is *psychic* and how does one attend to the psychic *in* India, *from* India? For cure (we have in mind the hegemony of the cure model, though medicine hardly cures!)? For healing? For care of the Other? For the arrival at (self) truth? Davar (2002: 20) is right when she says that in epistemological, methodological, and ontological terms, somatic experiences are different from psychic experiences.

This reflection is thus about the connection between clinical and critical perspectives, between depth psychology and critical psychology, between Freud and Foucault (see Butler, 1997). It is also about a theory of the *outside*. Critical psychology relies on a notion of the outside. Can this be revisited, in the context of two outsides: sexual difference, which has remained the outside of Indian psychology and cultural difference, which has remained the outside of critical psychology. Critical psychology, born out of the womb of the west, is an *internal critique* of the west's intimate principles. Critical psychology, drawing upon a critical version of psychoanalysis and an equally critical version of discourse analysis and setting to dialogue in the process the *dissenting children* of the west, has tried to carve out a space for a re-formed (not merely reformed) psychology in the west. What can India offer to this field? India can offer "Savage Freud" Girindrasekhar Bose's re-reading of one of the resources of critical psychology: psychoanalysis. Will this add value to the "critique" that critical psychology embodies? Perhaps; but we will also have to demonstrate how and where it adds value. In this chapter, I would like to suggest that the tradition of critical psychology in India cannot just rely on a critique of psychiatry or mainstream psychology. It has to be, simultaneously, a critique of Orientalism. Critical psychology in India is thus premised on a *dual critique.* It is critique of both the hegemonic Occident and the Occident's hegemonic description of the Orient. It is critique of both the West's hegemonic principles and principles (emanating from either the West or from the East) that hegemonize the East (see Dhar and Siddiqui, 2013). Premised on such a dual critique, this reflection becomes a search for a "new theory of mental life" and a new epistemo-ontology and an ethico-politics of engaging with "madness" in historico-cultural context.

SEXUATION

This reflection engages with the question of sexual difference and cultural difference within the space of psychoanalysis. This engagement with the *two-ness* of sexual and cultural difference is indeed a task because phallocentrism does skew the narrative of gendering; one needs to be appreciative of the text of sexuation beyond a phallocentric cloud; just like one needs to be appreciative of *culturing* beyond a Eurocentric blur.

It asks: would the question of woman (as also of sexuation) remain central in this rethinking of psychoanalysis? Why would woman figure as central? While in psychiatry the pervert and the (masturbating) child has figured as the trope around which psychiatry was organized, in psychoanalysis it was perhaps woman (and the hysteric). Is the woman-question also built into the crisis of Indian modernity; the woman, the machine, the ethnic Other, nature as Other, are all edges of this reconstitution/reconfiguration (of Otherness in modernity) within which we are still moving and trying to find our way. It is not as if woman is alone; one is not over-emphasizing sexual difference to the detriment of other differences, especially caste in the Indian context. But in any case, the centrality of the feminine Other and the organization of our entire modern way of thinking around the feminine Other is not altogether negligible.

Taking off from my own experiences as a medical doctor and from my unease with(in) the psychiatry clinic, this reflection turns instead to an "ab-original" form of psychoanalysis—a psychoanalysis marked also by a postcolonial feminist mindset. To think a postcolonial feminist form of psychoanalysis as also a psychoanalytic form of postcolonial feminism this reflection looks at three figures who are all *at the edge of psychoanalysis*: Bose. Lacan,

Irigaray. This reflection builds on a turn first to western psychoanalysis (i.e., the works of Freud and Lacan) and then to *native psychoanalysis* (i.e., the works of Girindrasekhar Bose); a turn, marked albeit by questions of sexual difference (i.e., the works of French feminists).

Lacan takes us to the "incommensurate *two* of sexual difference." This understanding of the incommensurate *two* of sexual difference is important for both psychoanalysis and feminism. Both psychoanalysis and feminism have in their own ways inaugurated the question of sexual difference; both have tried to think the incommensurate *two* of sexual difference; both in their own ways have tried to think "woman"; both have tried to think through unreason and affect; both in their own ways have tried to set up a dialogue with unreason and affect. Yet there is a fundamental difference between the ways psychoanalysis approaches the question of "unreason-affect-sexual difference-woman" and feminism approaches the question of "woman-sexual difference-affect-unreason." While both could possibly think of crucial convergences over the question of unreason, affect, and sexual difference, both for their respective perspectives-standpoints produce radically different renditions of the question of woman. Respective renditions of woman produce a fundamental torsion in their relationship; the relationship remains forever skewed. A possible relationship could be forged through a more commensurate rendition of the question of woman, a rendition that could possibly make possible a feminist (form of) psychoanalysis as also a psychoanalytic (form of) feminism. To think, to arrive at a more commensurate rendition of woman, we first have to move through a number of moments in the conceptual history of psychoanalysis—moments that mark a rupture, a discontinuity with the existing paradigm. Our voyage through uncertain seas passes first through the notion of sexuation; through the invocation of the question of sexuation, through a moving away, through a turning away of psychoanalysis from the logic of the One, and an arrival, albeit tentative, at a logic of the two, at the incommensurate two of sexual difference. From *One*, from the possible absence of a relationship, from the absence of a possible relationship to *two – to* an impossible "relationship between "them-two" (*la relation d'eux*) . . . them-two sexes" (Lacan 1998: 6). In its strange flirtations with the *two* psychoanalysis comes face to face with man-woman and masculine-feminine; in its strange flirtations with man-masculine and woman-feminine psychoanalysis comes face to face with the phallic *jouissance* and the Other *jouissance*. Irigaray however remains critical of the Freudian-Lacanian engagement. Irigaray returns once again to the question of sexual difference (1985a, 1985b) within Western Philosophy, or for that matter, to the question of woman within Freud's return to unreason as also Freud's inauguration of the question of sexual difference (see Dhar, 2009).

CULTURES OF AB-ORIGINALIZATION

Jean and John Comaroff (2012) has argued that "Western enlightenment thought has, from the first, posited itself as the wellspring of universal learning" as also of science and philosophy. It has, in turn, "regarded the non-West—variously known as the Ancient World, the Orient, the Primitive World, the Third World, the Underdeveloped World, the Developing World, and now the Global South—primarily as a place of parochial wisdom, of antiquarian traditions, of exotic ways and means." It has also regarded the non-West as largely a repository of "unprocessed data." The non-West was as if offering unprocessed data to Western thories or to theories from the West, including psychoanalytic/Freudian theories. The non-West is thus "treated less as sources of refined knowledge than as reservoirs of raw fact: of the minutiae from which Euromodernity might fashion its testable theories and transcendent truths"; which would then get transported to the non-West (through colonialism) as Universals. Freud wanted to capitalize on non-Western patient/analysand data or case/raw material Bose was offering by "ostensibly adding value and refinement to them" ("this continues to be the case," even today!). It looked like Bose was to offer an archive of Indian experiences to Freud and Freud would in turn analyze, and generate theories out of the data. Bose was however not offering Freud *Indian* case material. He was offering Freud "a new theory of mental life." Bose was thus inverting the *Order of Things*. It was as if the so-called Global South or India was offering "privileged insight" or "refined knowledge" into the workings of the psyche—Western and non-Western.

This section of the chapter is premised on the layered life-history[4] of the first "savage" psychoanalyst, Girindrasekhar Bose, who also practiced psychiatry in a mental hospital, taught psychology and psychoanalysis in the University, and wrote (psychoanalytically singed) commentaries on the Bhagvad Gita (1931), the Yoga Sutras (1966), the Puranas (1934), and proposed in lieu of Freudian psychoanalysis, *A New Theory of Mental Life*.[5] This section of the chapter however remains menaced by a somewhat primal doubt, doubt marked by the question: is the history of psychoanalysis in India *indeed* the history of psychoanalysis? Is it psychoanalysis *turned upside down*? Or is it the *Other side* of psychoanalysis? Is it the history of a new theory of mental life and of sexuation, different from the one offered by Freudian psychoanalysis? It is possible that taking off from an extant logic of the Indian psyche (exemplified by epic manuscripts like the Mahabharata as against Greek Tragedy[6]) it offers to the west the *Indian logic of the psyche* (and not just the logic of the *Indian psyche*). We are thus left with *two* possibilities. It is possible that Bose was re-conceptualizing the given contours of (western) psychoanalysis and of sexuation in the Indian context. In the process, he was giving birth to an ab-Original form of psychoanalysis, a form different from the western Original. It is also possible that Bose was giving birth to an aboriginal form of psychology, where aboriginal psychology was not about an isolated insight or data but about questioning the basic paradigm, architectonics, and culture of western psychology; this could possibly grant alternative/aboriginal psychologies the right to integrate within what they see as the best of modern psychology and to reject the bad; and inaugurate in the process a new theory of mental life and of sexuation marked, in this case, by the interminable see-saw of the eroticized *double wish* (Bose 1948, p. 108–205; 1949, p. 54–75; 1951, p. 203–214; 1952a, p.1–11; 1952b, p. 53–69; 1952c, p. 191–200).

Let us examine both possibilities. One would be to read Bose from the perspective of Freud; that would be akin to (Freudian) Psychoanalysis *in* Indian Terroir. The other would be to read Freud from the perspective of Bose; and that would be akin to Psychoanalysis *from* Indian Terroir; which in other words, is psychoanalysis from Bose's vantage point; where Bose is not a *savage* version of Freud; there are *two* psychoanalytic thinkers: Bose *and* Freud, standing face to face in their exchange of letters and their respective understandings of the psyche.

This is, of course, not to clinch the exchange between Bose and Freud in favor of the one or the other; this is not to declare a winner, but to see what possibilities emerge out of the table-turning. One would be to see Bose's psycho-logic as a *version of (western) psychoanalysis*; one then uses Freudian psychoanalysis as the paradigm or at least, benchmark, for understanding Bose's psycho-logic. Here one wishes to see whether Bose was concurring with the principles of Freudian psychoanalysis. Or whether in his engagement—in his immersion/submersion in psychoanalysis—he was moving far from being psychoanalytic in his psycho-logic. He was in the process inaugurating a different psychoanalysis—an ab-Original psychoanalysis. Was then Bose a *savage* Freud, or a savage Klein, or a savage Lacan or at best/worst a savage Jung? Or was he in the process inaugurating an altogether *different* or a radically different psycho-logic—different from psychoanalysis, so different that his version is *not* a version of psychoanalysis; his version is not a version at all; it is original; it is *aboriginal*. In the process, he was giving back Freud *another* psycho-logic—or an Other psycho-logic (which was also not merely about the psycho-logic of the cultural or colonial Other)—a psycho-logic that could be the ground for rethinking mental health (and such rethinking is the inspiration and mandate of this reflection) not just in India but *even in the West*. Bose's psycho-logic is then not a displaced Oriental/Indian version of the western Universal. It is not what could then be represented as an Indian version of the Universal—or an Indian version of the Western Modern—it is not what our modernity was all about. We were actually giving back to the west an *aboriginal* insight—an insight that would need to be adopted by the West as well; and this insight was not about *who we were*; it was not just about the Indian psyche; it was not about the possibility that Indian males don't have the castration complex; it was about questioning the very deployment of the castration complex as a constitutive node/anchor of psychic life. It was not about saying that we are or were different. It was to build on this difference and give to the west *and* to ourselves a *different* psychology. It was psychoanalysis *from* India. Not just *in* India; and not just about or on India(s).

It was about asking: what kind of a psychoanalysis is born from a psychological culture not determined/dominated, by what Thomas Laqueur calls the "two-sex model" (1990), where men and women are not seen as the *opposite* sex, but as a *dynamic appositeness*—an unconscious "see-saw" between gender(ed) identifications? Kakar develops this line of thought through Boss's case histories—

> reading early Indian case histories, one is struck by the fluidity of the patients' cross-sexual and generational identifications. In the Indian patient, the fantasy of taking on the sexual attributes of both the parents seems to have a relatively easier access to awareness. Bose . . . tells us of a middle-aged lawyer who 'took up an active male sexual role treating both of them as females in his unconscious and sometimes a female attitude, especially towards the father, craving for a child from him. In the male role sometimes he identified himself with his father, and felt a sexual craving for the mother, on the other occasions his unconscious mind built up a composite of both parents towards which male sexual needs were directed; it is in this attitude that he made his father give birth to a child like a woman in his dream . . . Another young Bengali, whenever he thought of a particular man, felt with a hallucinatory intensity that his penis and testes vanished altogether and were replaced by female genitalia. While defecating he felt he heard the peremptory voice of his guru asking, "Have you given me a child yet?" In many of his dreams, he was a man whereas his father and brothers had become women. During intercourse with his wife he tied a handkerchief over his eyes as it gave him the feeling of being a veiled bride while he fantasized his own penis as that of his father and his wife's vagina as that of his mother (Kakar 2007, 111).

The reflection thus argues for a *pentagonal* critique. It argues for the need to begin with a critique of science—psychiatry and behavioral or quantitative psychology. What however is a critique of science? Critique of scientism? Critique of objectivity? Critique of instrumental rationality? Or critique of the hidden metaphysics or the hidden theology in modern science? Critique of science—either for its avowed anti-metaphysics or its hidden metaphysics

– made us arrive at psychoanalysis. But arrival at psychoanalysis meant both a turn to metaphysics and a critique of metaphysics/theology. Both critiques of science and psychoanalysis meant in turn a critique of Christianization. Critique of colonization or maybe, a more ambitious decolonization, meant a critique of Christianization, Theology, Metaphysics, and Science. While feminism of the post-metaphysical kind and feminist critiques of science do create conditions for decolonization, while deconstruction does create conditions for a critique of onto-theology and metaphysics, Bose's work remains a good example of and window to critiques of Christianization and a more thorough-going decolonization. One perhaps needs to work at the cusp of "ab-Originalization" (for example, deconstructive feminism or psychoanalytic feminism [Mitchell, 2000]) and aboriginalization (for example, Bose's "New Theory of Mental Life" [1948]).

FROM/IN

Psychoanalysis *in* India is premised on the idea of an *implant*. Why implant? It is, as if, a plant—called psychoanalysis—was born in western Europe from Judaic-Christian-Hellenic terroir. Later the plant was implanted in Indian terroir. The plant took a certain form as it grew in Indian terroir.

Psychoanalysis *from* India is premised on the idea of multiple plants, or an originary multiplicity. It is somewhat like psychoanalysis from Germany, from Britain, from India, from Japan; each a different plant; growing in a different terroir; having a different terroir-plant relation. Kakar's work, according to my understanding, has tried to discover-invent a psychoanalytic form *from* India delving deep into the inner world of the Indian child and of *Indians* and the graph/archaeology of eros-thanatos in India.

NOTES

1. While Lacan speaks of a logic of asymmetry, Irigaray speaks of a logic of *difference*, thus inaugurating the *two of sexual difference* ("this sex which is not one") in psychoanalysis in particular, and philosophy in general.

2. I owe the idea of "cultural crucible" to the psychoanalysis group in the School of Human Studies, Ambedkar University Delhi, and especially to my colleagues Ashok Nagpal and Honey Oberoi. How do we understand cultural crucible? How is culture a crucible? Is it one? Is it a "container"? Container of what: psychoanalysis? Is it *containing* it, keeping it *contained*? What is it made of? Resilient stuff that can withstand high temperatures/adversities? What is its use, ancient and modern? Crucibles historically were usually made from clay. They however can be made from

any material that withstands temperatures high enough to melt or otherwise alter its contents. Is the crucible then a form-altering apparatus? Or can the contents corrode, reform, deform, and alter the crucible itself?

3. Deconstruction is the ground or pre-text on which *aboriginalization* as an obstinate impulse works; in that sense, deconstruction is for aboriginalization the necessary foreplay that renders vulnerable the structure of the text or the text of structure. Thereafter aboriginalization sets up a particular relation with the Original text (here psychoanalysis). It is however not to look into the origin of psychoanalysis; it is not to see whether it originates from one of the two western approaches to the self: (i) the Greek pagan marked by the "know thyself"—"care of the self" continuum or (ii) the Roman Christian marked by the flesh-sin-guilt-confession continuum. I however take psychoanalysis as a determinant original to our colonial modernity. We want to see what our relation with this original was. Was it aboriginalization? However, how does aboriginalization qua cultural critique work? Does it work through the marking of (cultural) *difference*?

4. When graduate training in psychology was introduced at the University of Calcutta, Girindrasekhar Bose, already a medical professional, obtained a Master's degree in psychology (1917). He was awarded the first doctorate in psychology at an Indian university in 1921. His dissertation was titled "The Concept of Repression."

5. See Bose (1921; 1931; 1948; 1949; 1951; 1952a; 1952b; 1952c; 1966; 1980; 1999; 2001).

6. When one takes Oedipus Rex as the "text of the psychic" one ends up with a narrative of "acts committed in the context of non-knowledge/ignorance" (Oedipus did not know who his parents were), remorse/guilt at what one has done, self-chastisement or sacrifice to atone for one's deeds (Oedipus blinds himself). This guilt-ridden traumata sets off the "psychic teleology." Freud tries to make a case for such a psychic teleology in *Moses and Monotheism*. However, if one takes the Bhagvad Gita as the text of the psychic, as Bose does, one gets a different psychic teleology, a teleology sparked off by an affront to a menstruating woman in the blind king's court of justice now being avenged by the collective of husbands she has; however there is a deferral; one of the five husbands is haunted by a near-primal doubt that could be so characteristic of the conception of *dharma* (what should I do?) and why not the human (who am I?) as well; the doubt is premised on the question: can I kill? Not ordinary killing. Can I kill my relatives, my brothers, my teacher, my grandfather even if I am here to avenge the trauma inflicted on "my" woman? The answer was "yes, you have to" to forestall further harm and auxiliary destruction by a group of marauding men. While the premise is guilt (what have I done? The "should" and "should not" being known beforehand) in the Oedipal narrative, the premise is dharma (what should I do? Should I kill? The should and should not needs reflection) in the narrative of the Bhagvad Gita; even the call of dharma (the a-dharma woman has been subjected to) requires further reflections on dharma (avenge an originary a-dharma over woman); it is, as if, dharma sparking off further reflections on dharma. While in the Oedipal narrative the psychic teleology is sparked off by guilt *a posteriori* (guilt after the event), in the Bhagvad Gita the psychic teleology is sparked off by reflection on self and dharma *a priori*. The choice is thus not between Oedipus (a la Freud) and

anti-Oedipus (a la Deleuze-Foucault). The task is to look for perhaps non-Oedipal psychic economies (a la Bose). Does this then offer interesting insights for another or even a new theory of mental life; a theory relevant to both east and the west?

REFERENCES

Bion, W.R. *Experiences in Groups and Other Papers*. London: Tavistock, 1961, 139–189

Bose, G. *Concept of Repression*. Calcutta: Sri Gauranga Press and London: Kegan Paul, Trench, Troubner and Co, 1921.

Bose, G. "'Gita." In *Pravasi*. Part 2(1) (1931): 9–16.

Bose, G. *Purana Pravesa*, Calkutta: M. C. Sarkar, 1934.

Bose, G. "A New Theory of Mental Life." *Samiksha* 2(1948): 108–205.

Bose, G. "Ambivalence." *Samiksha* 3(1949): 55–75.

Bose, G. "The Nature of the Wish." *Samiksha* 5(1951): 203–214.

Bose, G. "Analysis of Wish." *Samiksha* 6(1952a): 1–11.

Bose, G. "Pleasure in Wish." *Samiksha*, 6(1952b): 53–69.

Bose, G. "Sex and Anxiety." *Samiksha*, 6(1952c): 191–200.

Bose, G. *The Yoga Sutras*. Calcutta: The Indian Psychoanalytic Society, 1966.

Bose, G. *Svapna*. Calcutta: Bangyia Sahitya Parishad, 1980.

Bose, G. *The Beginnings of Psychoanalysis in India: Bose-Freud Correspondence* Calcutta: Indian Psychoanalytic Society, 1999.

Bose, G. ed. *Agranthito Girindrasekhar: Girindrasekhar Boser Nirbachito Rachana*. Kolkata: Granthalay Pvt Ltd, 2001.

Butler, J. *The Psychic Life of Power: Theories in Subjection*, Stanford, California: Stanford University Press, 1997.

Davar, B. and Bhatt, P. *Psychoanalysis as a Human Science: Beyond Foundationalism*, New Delhi: Sage, 2002.

Davidson, A. I. *The Emergence of Sexuality: Historical Epistemology and the Formation of Concepts*. Cambridge, Massachusetts, London: Harvard University Press, 2001.

Dhar, A. "Sexual Difference: *Encore*, Yet Again," *Annual Review of Critical Psychology*, 7, 2009. 168–186. http://www.discourseunit.com/arcp/7.htm.

Dhar, A. "The Other Father: Oedipus, Anti-Oedipus and the An-Oedipal" in *Imperial Maladies: Literatures on Healthcare and Psychoanalysis in India*. Ed. D. Bandyopadhyay and P. Kundu. Nova Science Publishers: New York, 2017, 17–48.

Dhar, A. and Siddiqui, S. "At the Edge of Critical Psychology," *The Annual Review of Critical Psychology* (ARCP), 2013.

Foucault, M. *The History of Sexuality*.Vol. 1. An Introduction. Trans. Robert Hurley—New York: Pantheon Books. 1978.

Guattari, F. "Psychoanalysis and Transversality: Texts and Interviews 1955-1971." Semiotexte/Smart Art, 2015 (1972).

Irigaray, L. *Speculum of the Other Woman*, trans. Gillian Gill—Ithaca, NY: Cornell University Press, 1985a.

Irigaray, L. *This Sex Which is Not One*, trans. Catherine Porter—Ithaca, NY: Cornell University Press. 1985b.

Jean, Comaroff and John L. Comaroff. "Theory from the South: Or, How Euro-America is Evolving Toward Africa." *Anthropological Forum* 22(2012): 113–131.

Kakar, Sudhir & Kakar, Katharina. *The Indians: Portrait of a People*. New Delhi: Penguin-Viking, 2007.

Kakar, Sudhir. & Ross, John Munder. *Tales of Love, Sex and Danger*. New Delhi: Oxford University Press, 2011.

Kakar, Sudhir. *Shamans, Mystics and Doctors. A Psychological Inquiry into India and its Healing Traditions*. New Delhi: Oxford University Press, 1982.

Kakar, Sudhir. *Intimate Relations: Exploring Indian Sexuality. New Delhi:* Penguin India. 1989.

Kakar, Sudhir. "Intimate Relations" in *Indian Identity*, New Delhi: Penguin Books, 2007.

Kakar, Sudhir. *A Book of Memory: Confessions and Reflections*. New Delhi: Viking Penguin. 2011.

Lacan, J. *The Four Fundamental Concepts of Psychoanalysis*. New York: W. W. Norton and Co. 1977/1998.

Lacan, J. *The Seminar of Jacques Lacan. On feminine sexuality: The Limits of Love and Knowledge . . . Encore (1972–1973)*. Vol. 20 of *The Seminar of Jacques Lacan*, ed. J.-A. Miller, Trans. B. Fink. New York: W. W. Norton. 1998.

Lacan, J. 2006. *Ecrits*. Trans. B. Fink. New York: W. W. Norton.

Laqueur, Thomas. *Making Sex: Body and Gender from Greeks to Freud.* Cambridge, Massachusetts: Harvard University Press. 1990.

Luc-Nancy, J. *The Inoperative Community*. Minneapolis: University of Minnesota Press, 1991.

Marx, K. "Theses on Feuerbach." Trans. C. Smith (2002). Marxists Internet Archive. Accessed 7 September. https://www.marxists.org/archive/marx/works/1845/theses/, 2016.

Mitchell, J. *Psychoanalysis and Feminism: A Radical Reassessment of Freudian Psychoanalysis*, Basic Books. 2000.

Nandy, Ashis. *The Savage Freud and Other Essays on Possible and Retrievable Selves*. Delhi: Oxford University Press. 1995.

Ragland, Ellie. *The Logic of Sexuation: From Aristotle to Lacan.* Albany: State University of New York Press, 2004.

Spivak, Gayatri. "Psychoanalysis in the Left Field and Fieldworking: Examples to Fit the Title." In *Speculations after Freud: Psychoanalysis, Philosophy and Culture*. Edited by S. Shamdasani, & M. Munchow. London: Routledge, 1994.

Index

Page references for figures are italicized

About the Editors

Anup Dhar (PhD in Philosophy) is professor, School of Human Studies, and director, Centre for Development Practice, at Ambedkar University, Delhi, India. His co-authored books include *Dislocation and Resettlement in Development: From Third World to World of the Third* (2009), and *The Indian Economy in Transition: Globalization, Capitalism and Development* (2015). His co-edited books include *Breaking the Silo: Integrated Science Education in India* (2017), and *Clinic, Culture, Critique: Psychoanalysis and the Beyond* (forthcoming: 2018).

Anurag Mishra is a psychiatrist and psychoanalytical psychotherapist heading the Psychoanalytical Unit of the Department of Mental Health and Behavioral Sciences at Fortis Healthcare (India), Adjunct Faculty at the School of Human Studies, Ambedkar University–Delhi, and Visiting Faculty at Institute of Psychotherapy, Antarnad–Ahmedabad. He is the founder of Psychoanalysis India and Livonics Infotech, a psychobionics start-up. He has been the founder and organizer of the Annual International Psychoanalytical Conferences in Delhi.

Manasi Kumar is a senior lecturer at the Department of Psychiatry, University of Nairobi, Kenya and holds a dual appointment as a research fellow at University College London, UK and University of Cape Town, SA. She works on issues around psychological ramifications of poverty, trauma, and social adversities in different geopolitical "terroirs," and the seamless interrogation of the cultural and clinical in the Indian terrain provokes her work. This interrogation has paved way for more critical as well as implementation driven systems thinking in her mental health work. She holds a PhD in psychology from University of London.

About the Contributors

Amrita Narayanan is a psychologist in private practice in Goa, India. Amrita earned her doctorate in psychology at the Pacific-Stanford University Psy.D. consortium in 2007. She completed her pre-doctoral training at the National Center for Asian-American Psychology, a psychoanalytic internship site in San Francisco, California, and her post-doctoral training and license hours at the California State Mental Hospital in Napa Valley. Amrita moved back to India in 2010 and has had a private practice since then. Outside of her private practice she has provided psychotherapy services at the Indian Institute of Technology, Gandhinagar, and taught at the Antarnad Foundation, Ahmedabad. She has written and published essays in peer-reviewed journals such as *Psychodynamic Practice* and *Psychoanalytic Review* and in magazines such as *India Today*.

Sabah Siddiqui is currently completing her PhD at the University of Manchester on Faith Healing practices in India that situate the subject between discourses of Science, Religion, and the State. She has received training in cultural studies and psychoanalytic psychotherapy. She has worked on research projects connected to gendered violence as well as the philosophy of science and higher education. Her book *Religion and Psychoanalysis in India: Critical Clinical Practice* was published in April 2016 (Routledge, London).

Bhargavi Davar works as a "human rights activist" and a "survivor" in the mental health sector, due to her childhood experiences of trauma which carried forward intensely, and well into adult years. She started Bapu Trust in 1999, to place her experiences within social services, informed by research and advocacy. Bhargavi finished her Ph.D. in philosophy and psychology, from the Indian Institute of Technology, Mumbai; and also post-doctoral studies at the University of Hyderabad. Her orientation has been in existential, person-centered practice. She has published in areas linking gender, culture, disability, human rights, and mental health. Her books include, *Psychoanalysis as a human science: Beyond Foundationalism* (with PR Bhat, Sage, 1995); *Mental Health of Indian Women* (Sage, 1999); *Gender and mental health* (Sage, 2001); and more recently, *Gendering mental health: Knowledges, identities, institutions* (OUP, 2015). Having always been interested in the connection between madness, creativity, and spirituality, and following intense engagement in the field with spiritual places of healing, she trained as an Arts-Based Therapist, and started supporting the use of ABT in Bapu Trust Services from 2006.

Urvashi Agarwal is a trained psychoanalytic psychotherapist from Ambedkar University Delhi. Together with her four friends, she has set up a clinic in New Delhi where they offer psychotherapy services to individuals, couples, adolescents, and children. Her practice includes work with borderline and psychotic states and she has been interested in understanding the "negative" as a way to understand clinical states where self-destruction becomes the predominant way of relating and living, where losses are unrecognizable, and particularly the psycho-somatic state. Of special interest to her is exploring the mother-daughter relationship in India and maternal depression, engaging with the woman in the mother and what happens to a woman's identity when all that she can be is a mother.

Nilofer Kaul, Ph.D., is a Delhi-based training analyst. She is also an associate professor of English at Hansraj College in Delhi University. Her doctorate was on "Masks and Mirrors: Configurations of Narcissism in Women's Short Stories" (2012). She has since then written on bisexuality (presented at Istanbul 2013), child sexuality "Afterwords" in *Dark Room* (ed. Pankaj Butalia), on "Three degrees of Separation" (at the Second International Psychoanalytic Conference in Fortis, Delhi)," on homosexuality ("Morphology of the Closet" in the *Psychoanalytic Review* 2015, ed. Salman Akhtar), and on "The Rehearsed Language of Psychonanalysis" (a paper presented at the International Conference in Mumbai 2016), and has written "On Strangerness" (forthcoming in *Div/Review*. She is also a part of a supervision group of the Delhi Chapter of psychoanalysis.

Shifa Haq, Ph.D., is an Assistant Professor at School of Human Studies, Ambedkar University Delhi. She is also associated with Centre of Psychotherapy and Clinical Research, Ambedkar University Delhi. Trained as a psychoanalytic psychotherapist, she is interested in studying mourning, social suffering, and psychoanalysis. Her doctoral research is a study on mourning in the lives of survivors of the "missing" persons in Kashmir. She practices in Ehsaas, a low-fee clinic, housed in Ambedkar University Delhi.

Shalini Masih was trained in Psychodynamic Psychotherapy from Centre for Psychoanalytic Studies, Delhi, and at present she is Convenor and Psychoanalytic Psychotherapist at Ehsaas Psychotherapy and Counseling Clinic, Centre of Psychotherapy and Clinical Research, Ambedkar University Delhi. She has been working in the field of counseling and psychotherapy for approximately a decade and has experience working psychoanalytically with traumatized children, adolescents, and with borderline and psychotic young adults. She is also involved in supervision of Psychoanalytic Psychotherapists training in MPhil Psychoanalytic Psychotherapy program of School of Human Studies, Ambedkar University Delhi. Her doctoral thesis was a Psychoanalytic Study on Beauty in Ugliness in Spirit Possession and Exorcism. She has a particular interest in states that do not render themselves easily to representability, body in psychoanalysis, cultural processes, and the kind of psychoanalysis feasible to a given cultural soil. She is also a member of Division of Psychoanalysis (Division 39).

Zehra Mehdi is a graduate student at the Department of Religion at Columbia University pursuing her doctoral research on religious-political violence in India and the question of Muslim Identity in relation to Unconscious. She was named the Dean's Scholar for the academic year 2016–2017. She has an M.Phil in Psychotherapy and Clinical Thinking from Ambedkar University, Delhi, and has worked as a psychoanalytic psychotherapist since 2010. She has written on the trans-generational trauma of Partition, religious and political identity within the clinic, psychotherapy as a means for social justice as well as on cultural reading of India cinema around themes of stammering, memory as history, political violence, and popular representations. In her papers as well as her clinical work her impetus remains to explore the relationship between psyche and religion in its political and social constructions. She has published papers in Karanc and Palgrave McMillian and has forthcoming essays in Routledge and Harvard University Press.

Atreyee Sen is Associate Professor in the Department of Anthropology at the University of Copenhagen. She is a political anthropologist of urban South Asia. She completed her PhD in Social Anthropology from the School of Oriental and African Studies (2003), University of London. Between 2004–2015, she held academic positions at the University of Sussex and the University of Manchester. Her research and publications trajectory focuses on militant political movements in the city that create micro-cultures of violence in confined urban spaces. She has carried out multidisciplinary projects on right-wing activism, communal conflict, resistance and guerrilla movements (Mumbai, Hyderabad, Calcutta, and Dharamsala), and explored the impact of these movements on slums, refugee colonies, and prisons. She is author of *Shiv Sena Women: Violence and Communalism in a Bombay Slum* (2007) and co-editor (with Dr David Pratten) of *Global Vigilantes: New Perspectives on Justice and Violence* (2008).

Ajeet N. Mathur (Ph.D., IISc. Bangalore) is a Professor at IIM Ahmedabad, Affiliate Life Member of the Indian Psycho-analytic Society, "Yoga Shikshak" of the Bihar School of Yoga, and member of the International Society for the Psychoanalytic Study of Organisations.. He was elected to the Fellowship of Sumedhas Academy of Human Context, is a Founding Member of Harmoninen Laulu Yhdistys Ry, (Harmonic Music Foundation) and an Invitee to the Finnish Chapter of the Club of Rome. His publications include 27 books and over 150 papers in scientific journals and anthologies. He is the recipient of the Prestige Award as "Professor of the Year 2014." He has held visiting academic appointments at K.U. Leuven, Belgium, Cornell University, University of California at Berkeley, University of Bielefeld, Germany, Helsinki School of Economics, Aalto University, Turku School of Economics, Royal University of Bhutan, and Fresenius University, Cologne. He has been a Fulbright Scholar and a Friedrich Ebert Stiftung Scholar. He has been a member of the Board of Directors with Corporates in India and Europe and is consulted by businesses, governments, international organizations, and the policy research community. He served a term as the Director and CEO, Institute of Applied Manpower Research with the rank of Secretary to the Government of India. He is Chairperson, Centre for Gender Equity, Diversity and Inclusivity, IIM Ahmedabad. He has directed IIM Ahmedabad's Group Relations Conferences since 2009.

Sudhir Kakar is a psychoanalyst, novelist, and a scholar in the fields of cultural psychology and the psychology of religion. He has been Lecturer at Harvard University, Senior Fellow at the Center for Study of World Religions at Harvard (2001–02), and Visiting Professor at the universities of Chicago, (1989–92), McGill, Melbourne, Hawaii, and Vienna.

Kakar has been a Fellow at the Institute of Advanced Study, Princeton, Wissenschaftskolleg, Berlin, and the Centre for Advanced Study of Humanities, Cologne. His many honors include the Kardiner Award of Columbia University, Boyer Prize for Psychological Anthropology of the American

Anthropological Association, Germany's Goethe Medal, Rockefeller Residency, McArthur Research Fellowship, and the Order of Merit of the Federal Republic of Germany. He is also on the board of Freud Archives, Library of Congress, Washington.

Kakar is the author of eighteen books of non-fiction and five of fiction. His latest books are *Young Tagore: The Makings of a Genius* (Penguin-Viking, 2013), and the novel *The Devil Take Love* (2015). His books have been translated into twenty-two languages around the world.

Alfred Margulies, M.D., is a Training and Supervising Analyst, The Boston Psychoanalytic Society and Institute, and Associate Professor of Psychiatry, Harvard Medical School, at The Cambridge Health Alliance. Dr. Margulies co-founded the Program for Psychotherapy, directed Out Patient Services in Psychiatry, and for many years served as Director of Medical Student Education in Psychiatry at the Cambridge Health Alliance. He is the recipient of the Harvard Medical School Faculty of Medicine Prize for Excellence in Teaching; the Cynthia Kettyle Award for Excellence in Teaching of the Department of Psychiatry, Harvard Medical School; the Havens Faculty Award for Excellence in Teaching at Cambridge; 2013 Outstanding Psychiatrist Award for Clinical Psychiatry, Massachusetts Psychiatric Society; Plenary Speaker, American Psychoanalytic Association, June 2014. He is the author of The Empathic Imagination, a study of the complex nature of attempting to feel into another's experience, and his scholarly interests have continued at the nexus of psychoanalysis, existential studies, and postmodern critique, with a particular interest in the nature of the construction of time, self, and memory.

Erica Burman is Professor of Education, and a United Kingdom Council of Psychotherapists-registered Group Analyst. She trained as a developmental psychologist, and well known as a critical developmental psychologist and methodologist specializing in innovative and activist qualitative research. She is author of *Deconstructing Developmental Psychology* (Routledge, 3rd edition, 2017), *Developments: Child, Image, Nation* (Routledge, 2008), and is co-editor (with Dan Cook) of the *SAGE Encyclopaedia of Childhood and Childhood Studies* (forthcoming). Erica co-founded the Discourse Unit (www.discourseunit.com) a transinstitutional, transdisciplinary network researching the reproduction and transformation of language and subjectivity. Erica's research has focused on critical developmental and educational psychology, feminist and postcolonial theory, childhood studies, and on critical mental health practice (particularly around gender and cultural issues). She has co-led funded research projects on conceptualizing and challenging state and interpersonal violence in relation to minoritized women and children, and on educational and mental health impacts of poverty and "austerity." She currently leads the Knowledge, Power, and Identity research strand of SEAN at MIE (see http://www.seed.manchester.ac.uk/education/research/research-themes-and-projects/sean/projects/knowledge-power-identity/. For further information see http://www.manchester.ac.uk/research/Erica.burman/ and www.ericaburman.com). She is a past Chair of the Psychology of Women Section of the British Psychological Society, and in 2016 she was awarded an Honorary Lifetime Fellowship of the British Psychological Society in recognition of her contribution to psychology.

www.ingramcontent.com/pod-product-compliance
Ingram Content Group UK Ltd.
Pitfield, Milton Keynes, MK11 3LW, UK
UKHW021906150926
475560UK00003B/204